Introduction to Information Security and Cyber Laws

Surya Prakash Tripathi
Ritendra Goel
Praveen Kumar Shukla
&
DT Editorial Services

Published by:
dreamtech PRESS

ISBN: 978-93-5119-473-6

Reprint: 2025

Printed at: **Srk Graphics**

About the Authors

Dr. Surya Prakash Tripathi has been gracing the academic field for almost three decades starting as a lecturer in the Computer Science and Engineering (CSE) department of the Institute of Engineering and Technology (IET), Lucknow. Dr. Tripathi completed his Masters of Science (M. Sc.) in Mathematics from Allahabad University and his Masters of Technology (M. Tech.) in Computer Science from Indian Institute of Technology (IIT), Delhi. He received his Ph. D. in CSE from the Lucknow University. Dr. Tripathi has keen interest in research and development and has published numerous research papers in various international conferences and journals, including IEEEXplore and Springer. Prior to Joining IET, Dr. Tripathi served as a Programmer Analyst with Prime Consultant Pvt. Ltd., Lucknow for six months between June 1985 and January 1986. Presently, Dr. Tripathi is a professor and the head of the department of CSE, IET, Lucknow, coming through the ranks of a lecturer, senior lecturer, assistant professor, and associate professor.

Ritendra Goel is currently working in the department of Computer Science and Engineering in Institute of Engineering and Technology, Lucknow. He possesses more than 21 years of experience in the field of Information Technology. He has been associated with several industrial projects relating to MIS, Web and E-commerce in India and abroad.

Praveen K. Shukla is working with the department of Information Technology at Babu Banarasi Das Northern India Institute of Technology in the capacity of Head of Department. He is B. Tech. in Information Technology and M. Tech. in Computer Science & Engineering. Presently he is also a Ph. D. scholar at department of Computer Science & Engineering, Uttar Pradesh Technical University, Lucknow. He has published 11 papers in reputed International Journals and 12 papers in reputed International Conferences. He is working in the area of fuzzy systems, genetic algorithms and evolutionary multiobjective optimization. He is also the member of IEEE, International Association of Computer Science & Information Technology (IACSIT), International Association of Engineers (IAENG) and Society of Digital Information and Wireless Communications (SDIWC).

DT Editorial Services has seized the market of engineering textbooks, bringing excellent content in engineering and technical education to the fore. The team is committed to providing excellence in quality of content by judiciously analyzing the needs of its readers and ensuring dedication of its authors and editors in catering.

Table of Contents

Introduction

The book contains comprehensive content on the various concepts of information security and cyber laws. Broadly, the book provides an introduction to information systems, their development methodology, and threats to them. In addition, it outlines the need for information systems' security and explains information assurance and cyber security. The chapters in the book also cover some concepts regarding data and application security, the physical security of information assets, security related to the Internet transactions, and the use of cryptography and digital signatures. In this book, topics related to the development of secure information systems and applications, risk management and governance, and security of backups are also discussed. Moreover, the book also includes a thorough study of policies, standards, laws, and other specifications.

We hope that your learning experience with this book will prove as enjoyable as it has proved for us while authoring and editing it.

About this Book

Introduction to Information Security and Cyber Laws describes at length about security issues faced by information systems today. The book explores information system's vulnerabilities and threats and discusses the ways to reduce and overcome them. Unlike other books, *Introduction to Information Security and Cyber Laws* provides a proper explanation of the security policy, governing laws, and IT Act, 2000. The range of topics and coverage offered by this book are a superior mix of description about the various aspects of security, its architecture, vulnerabilities, threat countermeasures, patents, copyright, security standards, patent and copyright laws, and software licenses.

Beginners, who intend to be familiar with the basics of information system's security and policies that govern information system's security aspects, will find this book ideal.

This book mainly covers the following:

- Introduction to information systems, their types, and their development approaches
- Introduction to information security and its requirements
- Discussion about threats to information systems, information assurance, cyber security, and security risk analysis
- Introduction to the security of applications and data security considerations
- Description of various security technologies and threats to E-commerce security
- Discussion on frauds in E-cash, electronic payment system, and credit/debit/smart cards
- Explanation of digital signature and cryptography
- Discussion on the development of secure information systems and applications

- Explanation of security architecture; various types of security issues with hardware, data storage, and peripheral devices; and measures taken for the physical security of IT assets
- Description of information security policy, ISO security standards, security review process, and policy for publishing and notification
- Introduction to Indian cyber laws, IPR issues, IT Act, 2000, software license, copyright laws, and patent laws

This is just an indicative list—there is a lot more inside. Our sole intent has been to provide a book with in-depth and sufficient information so that you enjoy reading and learning from it. Happy reading!

How to Use This Book

Each chapter of the book provides an in-depth knowledge on a particular topic. First of all, read the chapter and then test your learning by going through the Multiple-Choice Questions and Subjective-Type Questions provided at the end of the chapter.

The objectives achieved in each chapter are mentioned on the first page of the chapter.

Conventions

There are a few conventions followed in this book that need to be taken care of. For example, every figure contains a descriptive caption to enhance its clarity:

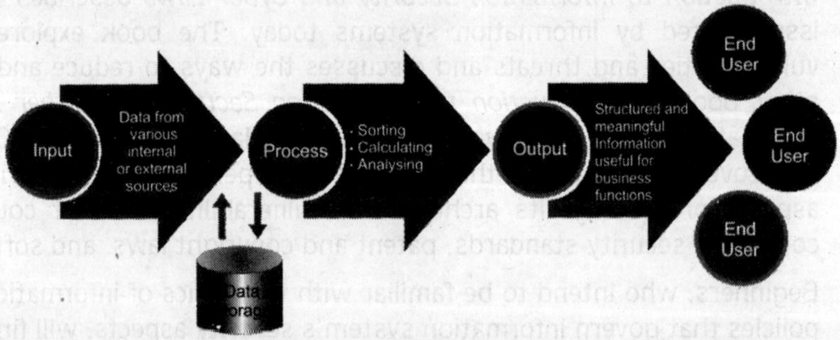

Figure 1: Displaying the IS Model

In this book, tables are placed immediately after their first references. An example of this is as follows:

Table 1 provides a list of major trends that occurred at the gap of one decade in the field of IS:

Table 1: Trends in IS

Trends (in ascending order)	Data Processing 1950s–1960s	Management Reporting 1960s–1970s	Decision Support 1970s–1980s	Strategic Support 1980s–1990s	E-Business 1990s onward
Major contributions	Electronic data processing systems	Management IS	Decision support systems	End-user support, executive support systems, expert systems, strategic IS	Internet-based e-business and e-commerce

01 Introduction to Information Systems and Security

OBJECTIVES

- Information Systems
- Types of IS
- Development of IS
- Introduction to Information Security
- Need for Information Security
- Threats to Information Systems
- Information Assurance
- Cyber Security
- Security Risk Analysis

The use of Information Technology (IT) has helped businesses around the world to grow immensely, but its misuse has created equally threatening circumstances for organizational security.

The data and information stored in computers can be accessed for use with both positive and negative intentions. Some network users may use network traps to harm the status and reputation of an individual and the business. One of the most misused accesses in the computer world is violation of rights. Information systems are used in business for storing data and information about various products, services, employees, and customers. Rights are assigned to individuals who are responsible for protecting the information. However, due to a number of vulnerabilities and a few flaws in the information system may provide ways for the unauthorized access and violation of rights, which need to be prevented in order to maintain system and information security.

In this chapter, you will learn about information systems, their types, and the ways in which these systems are developed. The chapter explains security of information in organizations and its requirements. Further, it familiarizes with the threats to information systems and how we can provide information assurance. Later, the chapter discusses about cyber security and analyses the risks related to the security of information in an organization.

1.1 Information Systems

Information System (IS) was derived from IT, but it is not just a part of IT anymore. Today, IS has provided highly productive results, thus becoming more efficient. Essentially, it provides the necessary information for business operations. It has been designed to support all business functions. Currently, complex business functions get help from various types of IS to sustain and grow in the ever-changing business environment.

IS is made up of two terms, namely, information and system. Information can be defined as a well-structured data with a specific meaning, and a system is an arrangement that takes input and provides output after completing the required process. Thus we can define IS, in other words, as an arrangement that processes data and provides meaningful information. Essentially, it is a set of several components that process data to derive information. So, It can also be defined as a set of interrelated components that collect, store, process, generate, and disseminate information for effective business functioning. This information supports decision making and helps in controlling various organizational departments and their functions. IS can be useful for both individual departments and for all departments collectively. Figure 1 shows the interrelationship between the components of an IS:

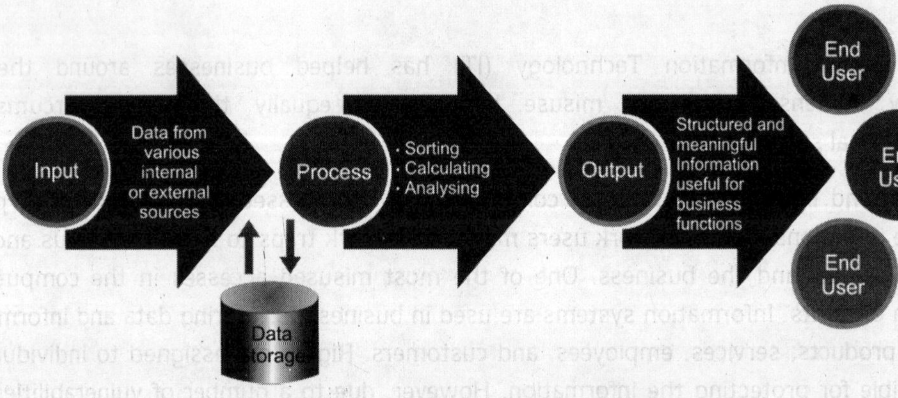

▲ **Figure 1: Displaying the IS Model**

The data for an IS can be collected from various inter-organization and intra-organization sources such as employees' personal details and competitors' performance. This data can be stored in both paper and electronic format. The processing of this data includes calculations, logical analysis, and other statistical methods, depending upon the information to be derived. After the data is processed, it is transformed into information. This information is disseminated to various end users to support their decision making, problem solving, strategy forming, and controlling functions in an organization.

For example, the data about individual sales by each sales associate in a month, the general sales target for each associate, and market sales trends for that month can be put to use. This data can be sorted, classified, calculated, and analyzed to produce information. This will provide information about the sales trends for that time period, gaps between the target and actual sales for individual associates, and the aggregate sales based on teams. The same data can be utilized to predict the next month's sales, target setting for the next month, strategy building for future sales, and the expected production level.

■ Computer Literacy and IS Literacy

Literacy means having the basic knowledge on any subject matter. IS literacy refers to having the knowledge about accessing, organizing, evaluating, and using data from various resources. However, computer literacy refers to having the knowledge about various computer peripherals, computer software, and usage of a computer.

Let us now understand the differences in the scope of computer and IS literacy. IS cannot become part of a computer system although Computer Science (CS) helped in updating IS with more user friendly and quick systems. The scope of CS is quite different from the scope of IS. CS is a discipline, while IS is an application. An IS might not be always computer-based. The scope of IS is wider than that of CS.

Nonetheless, it is an undeniable fact that the use of CS increases the efficiency of IS. Any IS can be installed on a computer system. The accuracy of calculation and time-saving technology of computer systems help in increasing the efficiency of a computer. File maintenance and data storage are also easy with a computer system.

Therefore, both the subjects have their own scope, and their integration will provide you an efficient system through which you can handle your business functions better.

Table 1 presents a comparison between computer literacy and IS literacy:

S. No.	Basis for Comparison	Computer Literacy	IS Literacy
	Coverage	Knowledge about various components of a computer system	Knowledge about data organization, use, and evaluation
	Scope	Computer literacy involves computer science discipline	IS literacy involves the IS application
	Relation with each other	Computer literacy improves IS efficiency	IS literacy helps to utilize computer systems better

■ IS Components

An IS has various components, which are mainly grouped under two heads. The first head is system resources and the other is system activities, as shown in Figure 2:

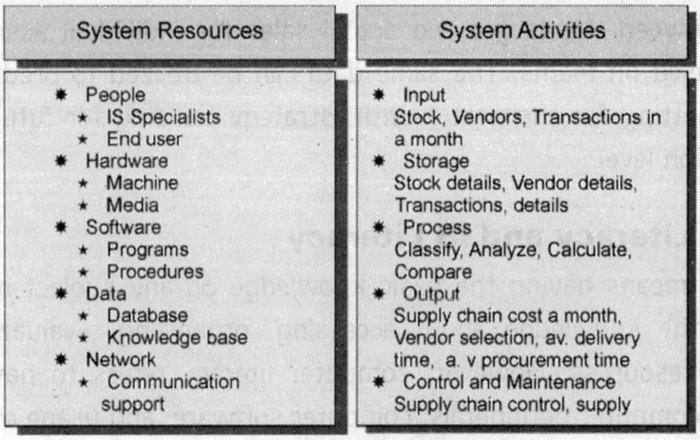

▲ **Figure 2: Showing the IS Components**

Let us discuss the components of IS (Figure 2) in detail.

IS Resources

System resources are those resources that comprise a system. An IS consists of five major resources, which are discussed as follows:

- **People:** Refers to the humans associated with an IS. This resource can be divided into two categories. The first category includes IS specialists such as system analysts, software developers, and system operators. The second category includes the end users of information, that is, anybody who uses the information derived from an IS.
- **Hardware:** Refers to the machine and media components of an IS. The machine components include computers, monitors, printers, and scanners, while the media components include floppy disks, magnetic tapes, and pen drives.
- **Software:** Refers to a set of programs and procedures of an IS. The programs include operating system and application software such as Microsoft Office. The procedures include data-entry procedures and information-distribution procedures.
- **Data:** Refers to various observations and facts derived from external or internal organizational sources. The internal sources are product descriptions, customer records, employee records, etc. The external sources are supplier details, market conditions, and competitors' information.
- **Network:** Refers to the communication and media components of an IS; for example, network access and control software.

- **Information:** Refers to the reports and results derived after data processing. For example, management reports and business documents including text, graphics, audio, and paper reports.

IS Activities

IS activities involve a set of components that belong to a particular system activity. These components are as follows:

- **Input:** Involves data entry activities such as recording and editing. Generally, data is entered into a computer system or reordered in a paper form.
- **Data storage:** Involves maintaining and organizing records such as details related to customers, employees, and various other parties. Data is generally stored in file folders and hard disk.
- **Processing:** Involves those activities that are performed to process the data to produce information. For example, calculating, classifying, and summarizing.
- **Output:** Involves communicating the processed information to the end users. For example, presenting sales performance of an organization in the form of videos and reports is an output activity.
- **Control and system maintenance:** Refers to the feedback at each activity level to maintain the standard of performance and ensure the flexibility of a system.

Trends in IS

Over the years, there has been continuous expansion in the applications of IS. The roles that it has taken up in business functioning are also upgraded along with the updates in the systems and system applications. Table 2 provides a list of the major trends that occurred at the gap of one decade in the field of IS:

Table 2: Trends in IS

Trends (in ascending order)	Data Processing 1950s-1960s	Management Reporting 1960s-1970s	Decision Support 1970s-1980s	Strategic Support 1980s-1990s	E-Business 1990s onward
Major contributions	Electronic data processing systems	Management IS	Decision support systems	End user support, executive support systems, expert systems, strategic IS	Internet-based e-business and e-commerce

Table 2: Trends in IS

Trends (in ascending order)	Data Processing 1950s-1960s	Management Reporting 1960s-1970s	Decision Support 1970s-1980s	Strategic Support 1980s-1990s	E-Business 1990s onward
Functional contributions	Transaction processing: record keeping and traditional accounting applications	MIS: management reports of pre-specified information to support decision making	Decision support: interactive ad-hoc support of the managerial decision-making process	End-user computing: direct computing support for user, executive support: critical information for top management expert system: knowledge-based expert advice for users, strategic support: strategic product, and services for competitive advantage	Internet-based electronic- business and electronic-commerce; Web-enabled enterprise and global e-business structure, operations, e-commerce with Internet, Intranet, and other network
Forming concept	Era of efficiency	Era of effectiveness	Era of effectiveness	Era of competitiveness	Era of e-business

It can be seen in Table 2 that the major trends became evident from 1950s till 1960s—the first decade of IS, as Electronic Data Processing (EDP) was popular. This trend brought transaction processing systems that performed record-keeping and traditional accounting-functions electronically.

Until the 1970s, management support systems assumed managers as the end users. This provided managers with pre-specified reports and supported their decision making. However, the pre-specified information did not prove to be effective for decision making, resulting in the emergence of decision support systems. It was an interactive ad-hoc support system for decision making in business functions.

By the end of 1990s, several new contributions popularized. The updates in technology provided microprocessors, new software packages, and end-user support concepts. All these provided end users with their own computing systems to support their functions instead of centralized services. As a second contribution in the same decade, executive support systems emerged; this enabled the top managements to access critical information in their preferred format. Yet another contribution was of expert systems—artificial intelligence. With the introduction of artificial intelligence, the business functions became more user friendly. A number of functions developed as expert systems and replaced human efforts. They were knowledge-based systems that could advice the end-user on limited subjects.

Simultaneously, the concept of strategic support for competitive advantage was developed. Systems based on this concept were called Strategic Support Systems. At this point, information technology had become a global business concept. A significant trend of this decade was the Enterprise Resource Planning (ERP) system.

Since 1990s, there has been astounding growth in the field of Internet and other networks for business information sharing and business promotion. Electronic business and Web-enabled enterprises emerged in a big way. Simultaneously, there has been growth in the IS field. They have become not only effective but also an essential part of business functions. If IS continues to grow and develop faster, it can play an immensely important role in organizational success.

■ IS and Business Organization

IS has become an integral part of business organizations. For example, those organizations involved in share trading are highly dependent on IS. Figure 3 shows how IS integrates various functions and users of an organization:

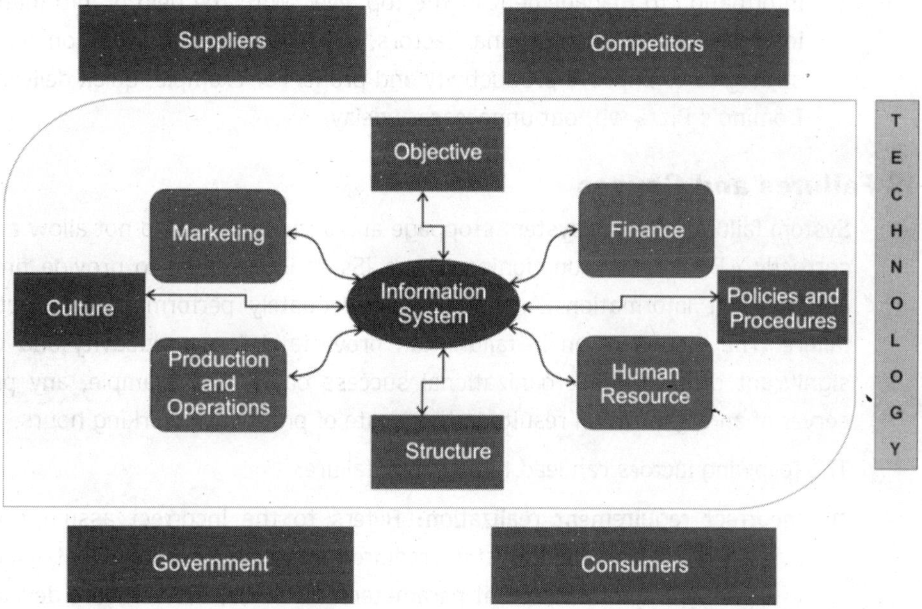

▲ **Figure 3: IS and Business Organization**

It can be seen in Figure 3 that IS has become a core component of a business organization. It plays a vital role in providing coordination between internal and external organizational factors. The internal organizational factors include various departments and organizational behavioral factors such as culture, objectives, structure, policies, and procedures. The external organizational factors include suppliers, competitors, consumers, and legal system.

IS supports the following business processes:

- **Operations support process:** Use of IS in various business processes at the operational level. For example, running of plant and machinery for production and purchase of material. Organizations certainly depend on IS for productive business processes.
- **Decision support process:** Use of IS for business decision making. IS provides useful and relevant information after processing data from various inter and intra-organizational sources. This information helps in effective decision making and logical functioning of a business.
- **Strategic support process:** Gaining competitive advantage by providing critical information to management at the top level. With the help of information on various inter and intra-organizational factors, management can work on various business strategies to improve productivity and profit. For example, quick delivery of orders by Domino's Pizza without unnecessary delay.

IS Failures and Causes

System failure refers to system stoppage and accidents that do not allow a system to run correctly. For correct functioning of the ISs, it is essential to provide timely, accurate, and relevant information. Any failure in adequately performing its functions is an IS failure. The results of an IS failure can prove fatal for productivity and may lead to a significant drop in the organizational success curve. For example, any problem in the server of an organization results in the waste of productive working hours.

The following factors can lead to a system failure:

- **Incorrect requirement realization:** Refers to the incorrect assumptions about the system requirements. A system required for quality management should be able to evaluate quality on all the set parameters. At times, the software developed does not match the requirements and results in a system failure.
- **Insufficient system development practice:** Refers to the inefficiency of system developers. At times, system development lifecycle fails to perform a proper system testing, which results in failures such as system stoppage or slow processing.
- **Untrained or poor system usage:** Refers to an improper user interface. Any untrained user can harm or produce undesirable results using an IS. Poor usage may cause internal or external system damage.

- **System damage:** Refers to harming the system physically or with the help of software. This can be intentional or unintentional that can result in unproductive functioning or non-function of the IS. For example, a mouse may cut the wiring in the local area connection, causing system damage.
- **Other causes:** Refers to any unforeseen situations such as network failure or network congestion. Improper electricity support and inefficient backup of the system can also result in system failure.

Thus, it can be concluded that besides avoiding the obvious causes of system failure, proper back-up and maintenance are required even with an IS.

1.2 Types of IS

IS supports all the different business operations in an organization. For an IS to be able to fully support each business process, we divide it into different categories on the basis of its application. There are three basic categories, namely, operation support system, knowledge-based system, and management support system.

Figure 4 shows the primary categorization of an IS:

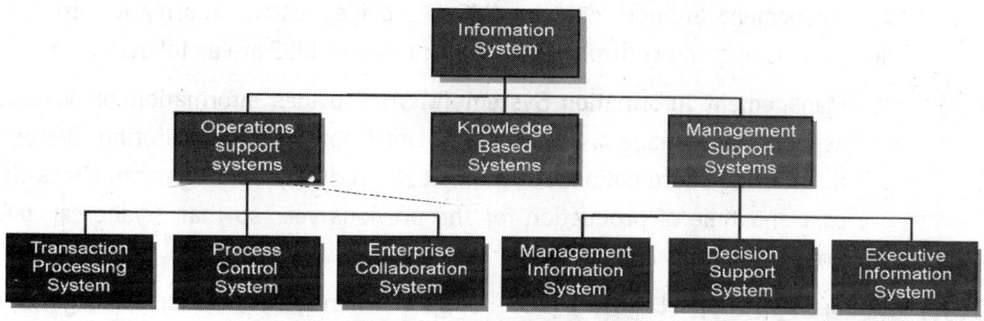

▲ **Figure 4: Displaying the Classification of IS**

In the next few sections, let us learn about the different categories of IS.

■ Operations Support Systems

IS has been supporting various business operations such as accounting and production. Those systems that support some business operations are grouped under Operations Support Systems (OSS). There are three main divisions of OSS, which are as follows:

- **Transaction processing system:** Helps in processing various business transactions and retrieving information from them. Processing a transaction can be done in two ways, namely, batch processing and online or real-time processing.

In batch processing, transactions are stored over a period of time and then processed, while in real-time processing, transactions are processed during their occurrences. For example, at retail stores, the cash receipts or card payments are registered and processed simultaneously.

- **Process control system:** Helps in monitoring and controlling physical processes in an organization. This system helps in making day-to-day decisions and controlling operational processes. This system automates the adjustment of a production process. For example, in an underground mining plant, electronic sensors can monitor the pressure and send automated warnings if the pressure is about to reach the danger level. It can also identify water sources in a particular range in the mining field.
- **Enterprise collaboration system**: Helps in sharing information among employees. A proper flow of information helps in increasing the productivity of an organization. For example, use of electronic mail to share information by one team member to the other and a team leader addressing a meeting with the team through video conferencing.

Management Support Systems

A Management Support System (MSS) provides useful information to managers for decision making and control. The different types of MSS are as follows:

- **Management Information System (MIS)**: Provides information on various business aspects to managers. It generates information for monitoring performance and maintaining coordination. For example, a production manager can check the report of cost and time of production for the previous year so that he/she can take effective production decisions for the current year.
- **Decision Support System (DSS)**: Supports managerial decision making. For example, a sales manager can set sales targets for the coming year by considering the existing market conditions.
- **Executive Information System (EIS)**: Provides critical information to the executive and top-level managers for making strategic decisions. It provides statistical representation of information. For example, an executive can check for a brand image by looking at the graphs representing customers' preferences and the sales of competitive brands in the last five years.

■ Knowledge-Based Systems

A knowledge-based system provides information to users in different business areas when required. The following are the two types of knowledge-based systems:

- **Expert system:** Provides adequate knowledge and expert advice for making various managerial decisions. An expert system is composed of two main components, namely, knowledgebase and software modules. It not only helps in management decision-making but also enables non-management employees in taking job-related decisions.
- **Knowledge Management System (KMS):** Provides knowledge and expertise for making various management-level decisions. For sharing knowledge, KMS uses a group of collaboration systems, such as the Intranet. It provides two types of knowledge, namely, explicit knowledge and tacit knowledge. Information that is documented, stored, and coded with the help of an IS is known as explicit knowledge. Information based on processes and procedures stored in the human mind falls under tacit knowledge. The major benefits of using KMS are as follows:
  - Allows free flow of ideas in an organization through innovation and creativity
  - Improves the productivity and performance of an organization
  - Achieves high level of customer satisfaction

1.3 Development of IS

Development of IS, similar to the application development procedure, has various approaches. The suitability of an approach depends upon the specific input conditions, preference of approach, and development objective. You can follow any of the different approaches, based on your requirements, for an effective IS development. The main approaches are listed as follows:

- Waterfall model
- Prototyping model
- Evolutionary model
- Spiral model
- Incremental model

In the following sections, let us discuss these approaches in detail.

■ Waterfall Model

Waterfall model is the basic model of system development. This model follows a flow of steps beginning from feasibility check upto system maintenance in a sequence. This method is also called linear sequential model. The steps in the waterfall methods are shown in Figure 5:

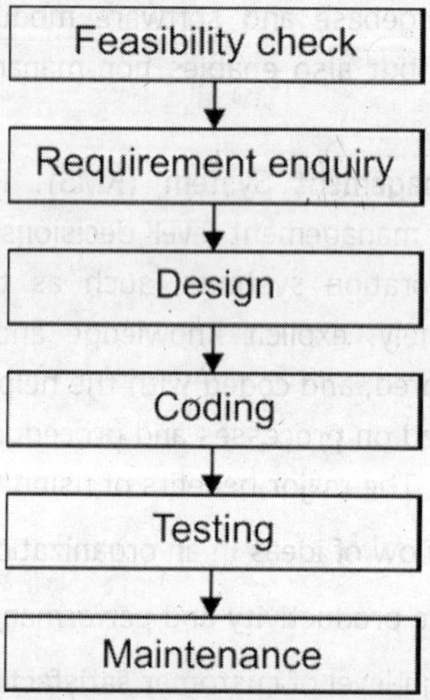

▲ **Figure 5: Showing Waterfall Approach in System Development**

The various steps shown in the preceding figure are explained as follows:

- **Feasibility check:** Technical and financial feasibility check about system development.
- **Requirement and specifications:** Gathering knowledge about the required system and developing the specifications needed.
- **Design:** Converting the requirements and specifications into a system model.
- **Coding:** This is a very important step in system development. Coding is the process of designing a bridge between the understanding of the user and the system. This is also called programming.
- **Testing:** Ensuring that the system performance is according to the user requirements. This is done after a system is set for use.
- **Maintenance:** Changes in the system after testing or use to correct the shortcomings or further requirements.

The waterfall method is a simple and an easy to understand model. However, it suffers from the following drawbacks:

- It approaches feasibility analysis before requirement analysis, which is not practical.

- It tests the system after implementing and designing; therefore, any change required after testing can be hard to be introduced.
- Any feedback to the previous process has not been approached.

The error of providing feedback has been corrected in the model and the corrected model has been named as iterative waterfall method.

■ Prototyping Model

Prototyping approach is an effort to improve the drawbacks of the waterfall model. A prototype is similar to the model or blueprint of a system before the actual development is done. This model first performs requirement analysis and develops a prototype or draft of the whole development process. This approach helps in understanding the shortcomings before the actual design is built and implemented.

This understanding of the shortcomings helps in system evaluation. Hence, any specification or further improvement can be done easily at a much lesser cost with the support of prototype software and physical design modeling. After finalizing the prototype, the actual system building is done similar to that in the waterfall method. Figure 6 illustrates the prototype approach to system development:

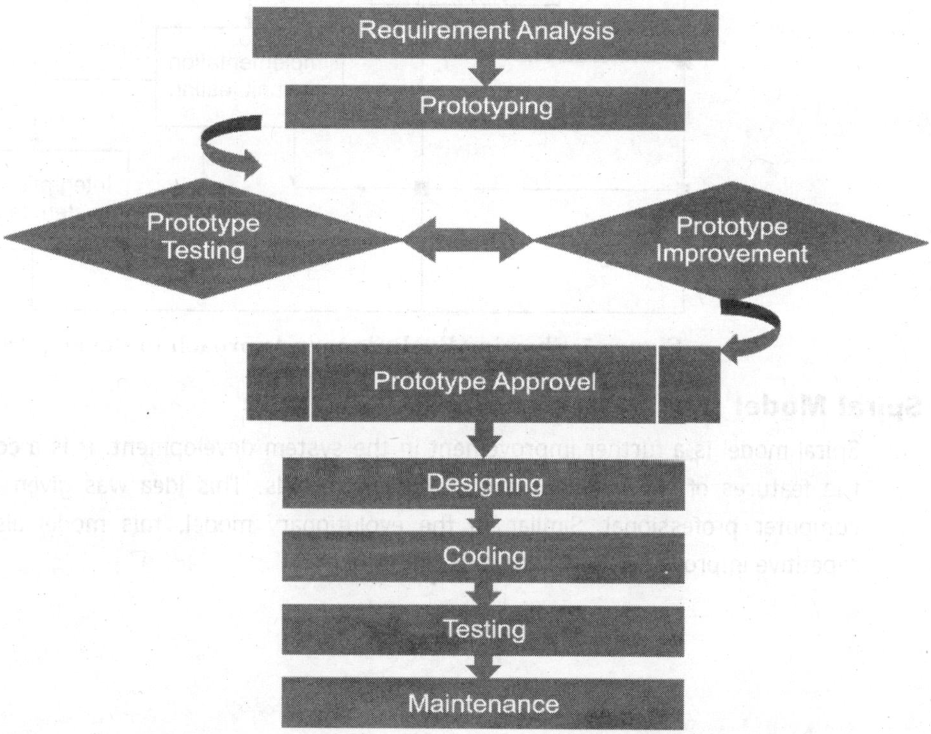

▲ **Figure 6: Showing the Prototype Approach to System Development**

This model helps in matching the client requirements for system development, as any suggestion can be easily incorporated in the prototype. Also, any constraint in the system development process can also be identified and improved.

■ Evolutionary Model

Evolutionary model approaches to improve the classic waterfall model by providing scope of feedback and improvement at every stage of the system development. This model tries to develop a realistic view that clients can change the requirements in the system at any stage of the system development. Therefore, every stage should be taken as a separate evolutionary phase.

There is scope of improvement in design and software. Figure 7 shows the typical structure of evolutionary model:

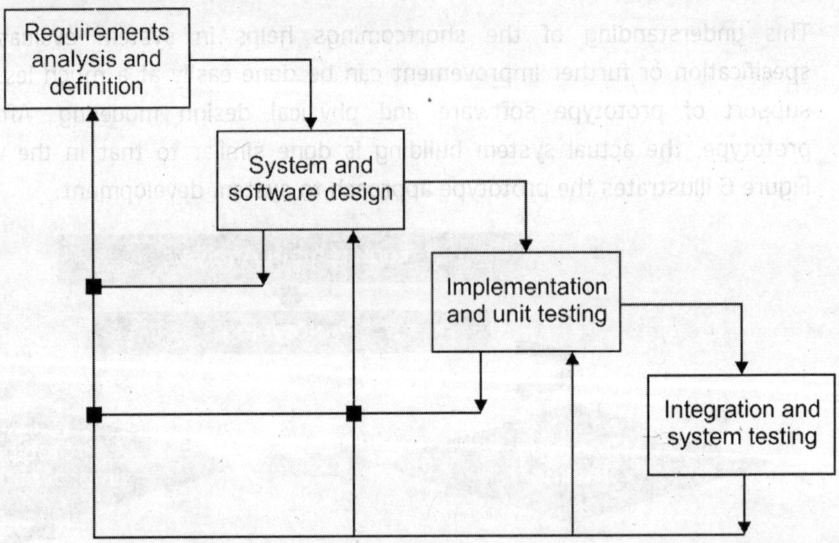

▲ **Figure 7: Showing Evolutionary Approach to Develop IS**

■ Spiral Model

Spiral model is a further improvement in the system development. It is a combination of the features of the waterfall and prototype models. This idea was given by Boehm, a computer professional. Similar to the evolutionary model, this model also adapts to repetitive improvement, as shown in Figure 8:

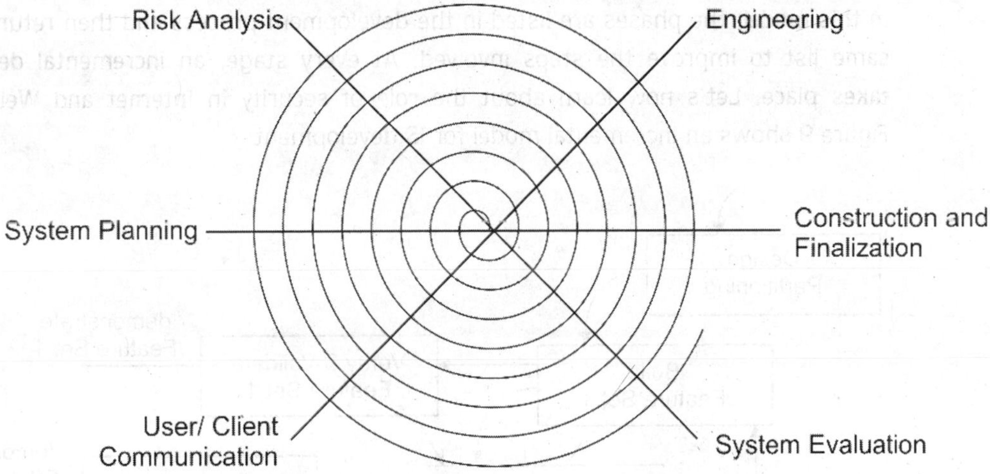

▲ **Figure 8: Showing the Spiral Model**

The following phases are included in the spiral model of system development:

- **User/client communication:** Interaction with the client or users of the system to identify the requirements and specifications in the system
- **System planning:** Planning the system to be developed and preparing a rough draft and schedule of the development process
- **Risk analysis:** Identifying the problems in the plan and developing solutions to check them
- **Engineering:** Involves system hardware and software design, coding, and testing the system
- **Construction and finalization:** Involves system building and testing to release it for use
- **System evaluation:** Evaluation by user or client to use the system

All these phases are repeated in the process of system development until users approve the system.

Incremental Model

Incremental model approaches system development through various incremental steps, where every step tries to add more functions in the system development process. Each step of system development is a separate group of activities. This model can also be called continuous improvement model.

In this model, the phases are listed in the development process and then returned to the same list to improve the steps involved. At every stage, an incremental development takes place. Let's now learn about the role of security in Internet and Web services. Figure 9 shows an incremental model for IS development:

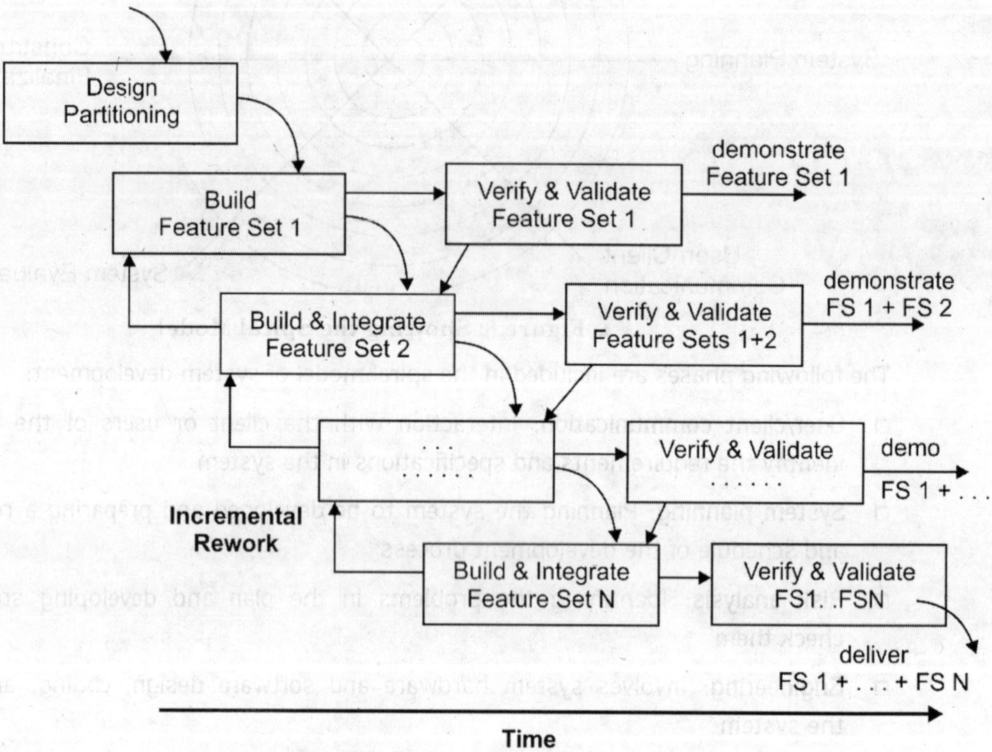

▲ **Figure 9: Showing the Incremental Model**

1.4 Introduction to Information Security

Information security refers to the protection of information. In other words, it is the process of securing, protecting, and safeguarding the information from an unauthorized access, use, and modification. Information is an important part of an organization or a business that requires more attention to preserve its integrity, privacy, and availability. There are several methods to provide security to information in an organization. The password protection method is the basic level of security that can be used for securing information. In this competitive world, there are several programs, such as viruses and bugs, which are used to hack the password of a computer system or network to access and misuse the information. The main goals of information security are integrity, confidentiality, and availability.

The relationship between goals of information security is shown in Figure 10:

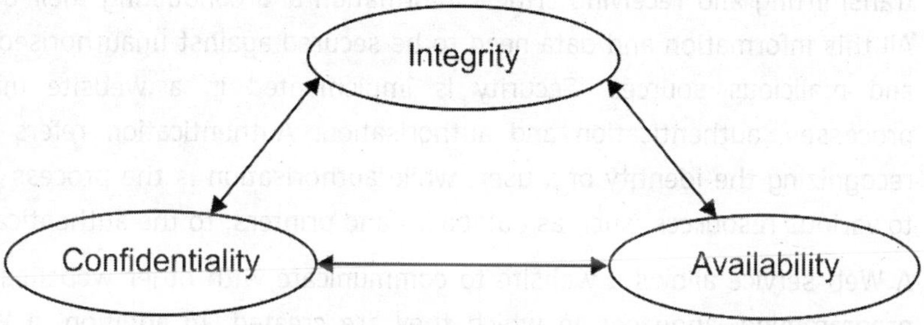

▲ **Figure 10: Displaying the Relationship between Goals of Information Security**

The goals of information security are explained as follows:

- **Confidentiality:** Refers to the process of securing information from unauthorized access. Confidentiality ensures that only an authorized person can access the network resources to get the valuable information provided on the network. A good example where confidentiality of information plays an important role is the credit card transaction. When we use a credit card to pay our dues through a computer system, the credit card number is transmitted over the network in encrypted form so that other persons cannot read the information.
- **Integrity:** Refers to the accuracy of information or data. In other words, integrity means securing the information from unauthorized modification. Data integrity and data accuracy are related to each other, but this is not always possible that both of these co-exist. For example, you may have entered incorrect data in the network, but it is possible to have data integrity in such a scenario. The data can only be modified by an authorized user.
- **Availability:** States that information must be available when it is needed. The information is said to be available if the following conditions are satisfied:
  - It is provided on time
  - The fault tolerance exists in the computer system or network
  - There is a fair allocation of resources over the network
  - There is a concurrency control management in database
  - There is a deadlock management in database

Role of Security in Internet and Web Services

In the present scenario, the Internet is emerging as the most widely used medium for performing various tasks such as exchanging data and information as well as conducting online shopping and bank transactions. Apart from the common people, most of the governmental organizations and big business houses entirely depend on this medium for transmitting and receiving critical information and conducting their day-to-day business. All this information and data need to be secured against unauthorised access from illegal and malicious sources. Security is implemented in a website mainly through two processes, authentication and authorisation. Authentication refers to the process of recognizing the identity of a user, while authorisation is the process of providing access to various resources, such as databases and printers, to the authenticated users.

A Web service allows a website to communicate with other websites irrespective of the programming languages in which they are created. In addition, a Web service can be accessed by any application, regardless of the software and hardware platforms on which the application is running because the Web service complies with common industry standards such as Simple Object Access Protocol (SOAP) and Web Services Description Language (WSDL). A Web service does not have any user interface; it only contains the logic for providing specific services to its consumers. A Web service provides an abstraction between the consumer (client) and the provider of the Web service. The Web service only needs information about input, output and location of the client and the Web service provider. Before the introduction of Web services, developers employed technologies, such as Component Object Model (COM) and Distributed Component Object Model (DCOM), to use the functionality of one application in another. These technologies allowed a developer to create code components once and then bundle them so that they could be shared across multiple applications by multiple developers. However, there were some fundamental difficulties in using these components. One such difficulty was that these components needed to be physically distributed and explicitly registered on each client machine. Web services overcome these difficulties as they can be shared among multiple websites without the need to install them on each individual client machine.

Web services have become popular because of the added functionalities they provide over component-based technologies. The advantages of Web services over COM and DCOM are as follows:

- Web services are simple to use; and consequently, they can be implemented on varied platforms
- Web services are loosely coupled; as a result, their interfaces and methods can be extended
- Web services do not carry any state information with them, thus enabling multiple requests to be processed simultaneously

Web services are most appropriate while communicating across platforms or enforcing trusted connections between the server and the client.

Securing Web Services

If you want to create a Web service and host it over the Internet, you need to be able to control and regulate access to the Web service. Web service requests and responses are sent as XML documents, which are in text format. Therefore, you need to secure the Web service from unauthorized access during such transmission.

You can prevent a Web service from being accessed by unauthorised access in the following two ways:

- Using encryption and message-based security
- Using authentication and access controls for the Web service

Now, let's learn about these methods in detail.

Encryption and Message-Based Security

Encryption is the process of scrambling the text that your Web service contains so that only the intended user is able to decrypt (convert encrypted data back into its original form) it with the help of a key.

Message-based security allows you to send encrypted messages to anyone without worrying about the decryption of the messages by a malicious user. You can detect any modification made by someone in the message straightaway because the signature (private key) attached to the message becomes invalid, and you can then safely discard the message. This type of security works by encrypting the message at both the request and the response levels.

Authentication and Access Controls for the Web Service

Authentication is the process of validating a user against the user credentials provided by the user. One way to secure a Web service is to make it mandatory for the users, who want to use the Web service, to provide their credentials in the form of a user ID and password. If they fail to do that, they are refused access to the Web service.

1.5 Need for Information Security

To maintain proper security of information in an organization, we need to apply certain measures, policies, and procedures so that no harm is caused to the confidentiality, integrity, and availability of organizational information. These policies, procedures, and standards are included in a system called Information Security Management System (ISMS), whose main goal is to remove any possible loss or destruction of information. It ensures information security over the network or multiple computer systems.

The idea behind ISMS is that an organization should design, implement, and maintain a logical set of processes for managing threats to information security in an organization. In addition, ISMS ensures satisfactory levels of information security that helps in maintaining the integrity, confidentiality, and availability of information. The concept of ISMS is that an organization has to focus on maintaining and improving the integrity, confidentiality, and availability of information.

Let's learn about benefits of ISMS.

■ Benefits of ISMS

Information security protects information or data against unauthorized access and modification. The benefits of ISMS are as follows:

- ❒ Helps to protect and secure information in an organization because information is its vital resource.
- ❒ Maintains the security of the data and information.
- ❒ Protects and maintains integrity, confidentiality, and availability of information. ISMS is a standard of the International Organization for Standardization (ISO), which is compatible with other standards prevailing in the market.
- ❒ Provides effective organizational management.
- ❒ Encourages clients, including individuals and other organizations, to invest in an organization. The organization having a sound information security system would attract more organizations for investment purposes.
- ❒ Utilizes information and data more effectively and efficiently.
- ❒ Provides high-level information security. ISMS cultivates a sense of responsibility and accountability in the employees of the organization.

■ Security Implication for Organizations

Security can be defined as the process of ensuring the integrity, availability, and confidentiality of computer data and resources against threats, viruses, bugs, and vulnerability. The main components of a computer where an attacker attacks are software, hardware, and data. Therefore, you should give more focus on these components and try to protect them from the attackers. Security is divided into two categories, computer security and network security. Computer security refers to the protection of a single or standalone computer, while network security refers to the protection of computers in the network. Security is the major concern in an enterprise as the data and resources of the enterprise are distributed over the network. Therefore, the network administrator needs to ensure the security of the network resources or information by configuring various security settings such as password protection and firewall settings. Security is required to reduce or remove impact of an unauthorized access as well as usage and modification of information and resources. You can use various methods, such as identification and authentication, to secure your network. Identification means identifying the user with the user's credentials, such as password, pin number, or any other ID proof. Authentication is the process of verifying whether or not the user who enters into the network is authorized to access the resources or information.

Intrusion Detection (ID) is a system that is implemented by organizations to protect their crucial and confidential data from unauthorized access. ID monitors network traffic and alerts the system or network administrator of any malicious activity that may be taking place, such as tampering or unauthorized access of data. If any such activity is detected, the ID system blocks the user or source IP address of the user from accessing the network. The main purpose of an ID system is to provide security to a system from various external or internal intrusions. The ID system works by scanning all the information present on the system or the network to which it is connected to identify certain security breaches, such as unauthorized accesses and virus attacks.

■ Monitoring the Network

Network monitoring refers to the process of tracking the activities that are being performed in the network. This task of monitoring the activities of a network can be assigned to a specific computer or a set of computers. The computer that acts as a network monitoring system must always be kept on and consists of strong power lines and backup generators.

The system performing the task of monitoring the network sends a ping command to all the computers that are available on the network. If other systems on the network do not respond to the ping command or this command takes a long time to execute on any of the systems connected to the network, then notifications about the same are sent to the network administrator. These notifications informs the administrator about problems in the network such as overloaded systems, crashed servers, lost network connections, virus infections, and power outages. These notifications are then sent in the form of e-mail messages, pager alerts, or phone calls. The network activities can also be tracked by regularly taking virtual snapshots of the network's workflow.

The ID system can also be used to track the user's activities such as websites they are visiting, time of visit, number of pages on the site visited, and entry and exit Uniform Resource Locators (URLs). This kind of network monitoring is generally not done for reporting problems, but for analyzing activities.

Understanding Intrusion Detection Systems

Intrusion Detection System (IDS) is one of the main components of the present-day security systems. It is used for monitoring the network traffic for performance problems, illegal or malicious activities, and attempts of unauthorized accesses. If any of these kinds of activities are detected, the IDS system sends alerts to the network administrator.

Figure 11 shows the sequence in which the IDS activities are performed:

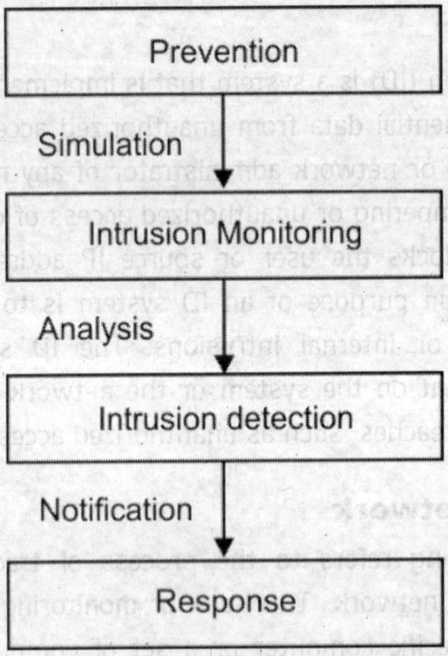

▲ **Figure 11: Showing the Sequence of the IDSActivities**

Figure 12 shows the diagrammatic representation of the tasks performed by an IDS:

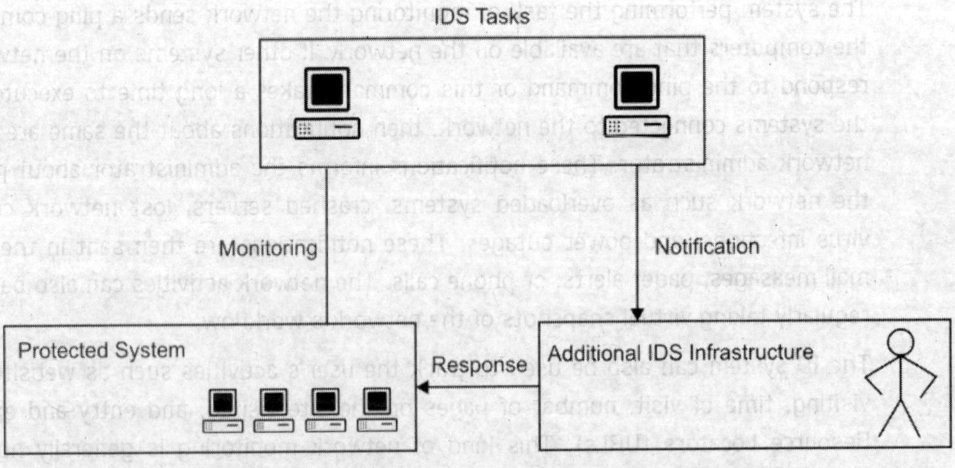

▲ **Figure 12: Showing the Activities of an IDS**

The IDS system also allows you to install patches to detect any future attempts of attack. However, there are also instances when an IDS can raise false alarms such as sending description of an attack or signatures through e-mails.

1.6 Threats to Information Systems

The hardware and software components of a computer system are highly vulnerable to many threats. In IT, a threat is an illegal activity that can cause damages such as loss of information and data corruption to the network of an organization. There are two basic types of threats—accidental threat and intentional threat. Accidental threat is an activity that occurs accidentally and its occurrence is not dependent on any entity. It can occur due to exposure of confidential information and unauthorized modification in information. On the other hand, intentional threat is an activity that is performed by an entity to violate security of the computer system and network.

Attacks on the network can breach the security of data and resources over the network. There are two types of attacks over the network, which are as follows:

- **Passive attack:** Refers to the type of attack in which the attacker does not intend to cause any harm to the network. He/she just monitors, analyzes, or observes the information available over the network. For example, the aim of the attacker is not to alter the message; however, he/she just reads the message. In passive attack, the attacker observes the information for which he/she does not have access rights. Passive attacks are of the following three types:
  - **Brute force attack:** Breaks the encryption of data by finding the appropriate key.
  - **Algebraic attack:** Refers to the type of attack in which you can write a cipher as a system equation. After writing a cipher, you can read it by using an appropriate key.
  - **Code book attack:** Refers to a technique for cryptanalysis. The attacker tries to build a code book in which he/she describes the cipher text and its corresponding plaintext.
- **Active attack:** Refers to the attack in which the attacker is aware of the attack. In active attack, the attacker tries to steal information from the network. In addition, he/she can create, delete, alter, modify, and replace a message.

1.7 Information Assurance

Information Assurance (IA) is the term related to the management of risks associated with the information system of an organization. IA is defined as the set of measures applied to protect information systems and the information of an organization. It ensures availability, integrity, authentication, confidentiality, and non-repudiation of an organization's information and IS. IA ensures these critical security functions by providing the restoration capability to IS with the measures that include protecting the system from potential risks, detecting possible risks, and reacting to the vulnerable situations.

IA is, in fact, the management of risks in relation of processing, transmitting, or storing data or information. Most of the people are unable to differentiate between IA and information security, which means to protect information and information systems from accessing, misusing, disclosing, disrupting, destructing, and modifying in an unlawful manner. Information security has a limited scope as compared to IA, which is wide and covers all the measures for protecting information. The differences between IA and information security are presented in Table 3:

Table 3: Difference between Information Security and IA

IA	Information Security
Focuses mainly on strategy	Focuses primarily on tools and tactics
Covers information management and protection in a larger domain	Gives importance and priority to technology and operations
Keeps focus on the overall risk management for the security of an organization	Concentrates on applications and infrastructure developed to provide security

IA, on one hand, includes the measures to ensure that the overall security of an organization is maintained. On the other hand, information security includes use of tools and techniques so that the infrastructure and applications of an organization are secured from potential threats. It has three goals that are established for maintaining the security in an organization. These goals are called CIA, abbreviated from Confidentiality-Integrity-Availability.

IA comprises a number of disciplines that also include information security. IA provides ways for organizations to mitigate the potential risks for information security. All the risks cannot be exposed and mitigated at a time. Hence, organizations must explore, examine, and assess the risks for their information and information systems on a continuous basis to provide IA. Systems and devices used for data processing, governing principles, and privacy and regulatory norms are part of IA. IA also defines and sustains the rules and policies for recovery from any kind of disaster and for continuity of business in relation with information systems. To provide IA, you need to provide ways in which we can assess, mitigate, and transfer the risks and threats to the security of an organization.

IA, as per the definition given by the Information Systems Security Committee (NSTISSC), includes:

- "Information operations (IO) that protect and defend information and information systems by ensuring their availability, integrity, authentication, confidentiality, and non-repudiation. This includes providing for restoration of information systems by incorporating protection, detection, and reaction capabilities."

IA is not limited to protection only, but it expands to the point of taking offensive measures also in order to secure the information systems and the information. The scope of IA is very widespread, as shown Figure 13:

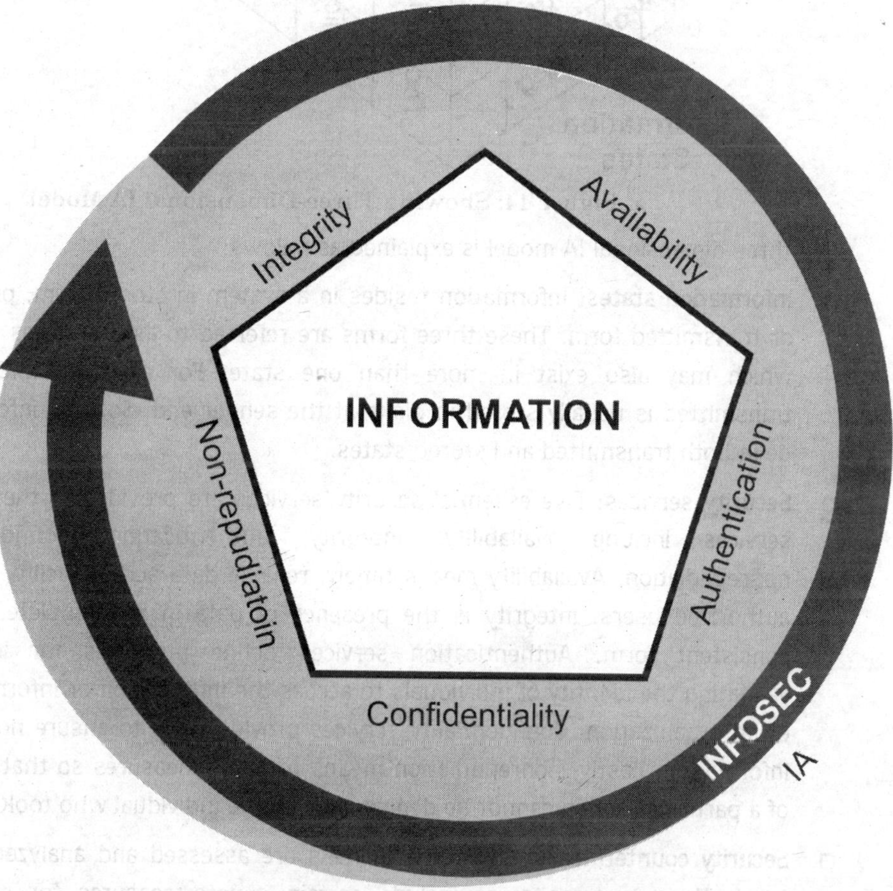

▲ **Figure 13: Displaying the Scope of IA**

IA is not a single discipline, as stated earlier. It also covers multiple dimensions. The three-dimensional IA model covers information states, security services, and security countermeasures that are established over time. This model can be represented as shown in Figure 14:

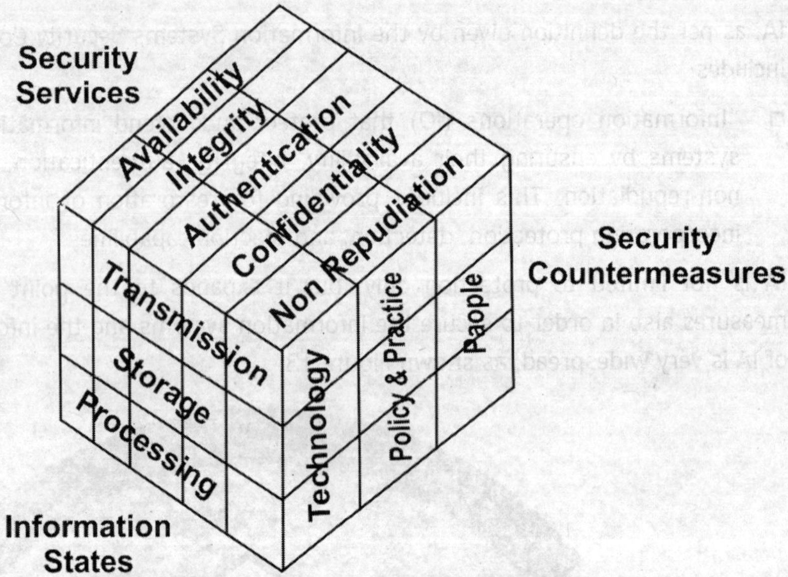

▲ **Figure 14: Showing Three-Dimensional IA Model**

The three-dimensional IA model is explained as follows:

- **Information states:** Information resides in a system in stored form, processed form, or transmitted form. These three forms are referred to as the states of information, which may also exist in more than one state. For example, information being transmitted is usually stored in disks at the sender end. So, this information would be in both transmitted and stored states.
- **Security services:** Five essential security services are provided in the IA model. The services include availability, integrity, authentication, confidentiality, and nonrepudiation. Availability means timely, reliable data access facility is available for authorized users. Integrity is the presence of data in its complete, accurate, and consistent form. Authentication services define measures for identifying and validating the identity of individuals to access the information or information systems of an organization. Confidentiality services provide ways to ensure non-disclosure of information. Lastly, nonrepudiation means to apply measures so that the ownership of a particular action cannot be denied later by the individual who took the action.
- **Security countermeasures:** After the risks are assessed and analyzed, it is time to react. Your systems must include certain countermeasures for maintaining the security and IA. These security countermeasures are applied against vulnerabilities through technology, people, and operations. In terms of technology, you can use cryptography, firewalls, routers, intrusion detection systems, and a number of other components for the maintenance of IA.

Operations that you can apply as countermeasures are policies, procedures, and configurations implemented by users and administrators of the system. In the operations paradigm, we can also include software-defined conventions while the system operates. Operational and personnel security domains are also included in the operations-related countermeasures for security. In the people paradigm, we require awareness, training, and education.

If the people concerned with a system have no knowledge of security risks and countermeasures for those risks, the system can never be totally secure. IA, as we have already studied, is related to the management of risks associated with information and information systems of an organization, and people must be aware of the risks and trained to take effective countermeasures. The people paradigm is actually the most significant part of IA. Figure 15 describes the importance of people as a part of information systems of an organization:

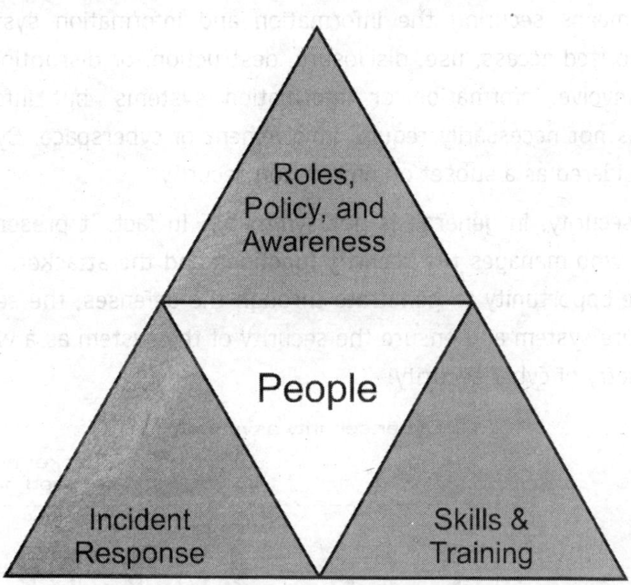

▲ **Figure 15: Showing the Importance of People in IA**

It can be seen in Figure 15 that people, who are given various kinds of roles and responsibilities in organizations, will define the policies about which they need awareness. These people also need to respond whenever specific incidents take place. Organizations provide training to impart different skills into the individuals so that they can decide about the countermeasures that need to be taken in particular circumstances.

1.8 Cyber Security

Cyber security is the protection of information and information systems against the potential threats on the Internet. Today, almost every person uses the Internet for various purposes that include learning, exploring, searching, sharing information, entertaining and getting entertained, connecting with people, etc. All these involve pleasure and value, but the potential vulnerabilities cannot be overlooked. The Internet can be very valuable if used responsibly. However, it may be extremely harmful in case some unlawful, indecent actions are taken by using the Internet. Cyber security is the ability to protect yourself and your cyberspace (or the Internet) from the attacks caused through the Internet.

Cyber security should not be confused with information security. Cyber security means securing information related to the use of the Internet. Information security, on the other hand, means securing the information and information systems against all kinds of unauthorized access, use, disclosure, destruction, or disruption. Security on the Internet must involve information or information systems, but information and information systems not necessarily require involvement of cyberspace. Cyber security can therefore be considered as a subset of information security.

Cyber security, in general, is not symmetry. In fact, it presents a skewed view for the person who manages the security functions and the attacker. Where attacker needs only a single opportunity to penetrate through the defenses, the security manager must view the entire system and ensure the security of the system as a whole. Figure 16 shows the asymmetry of cyber security:

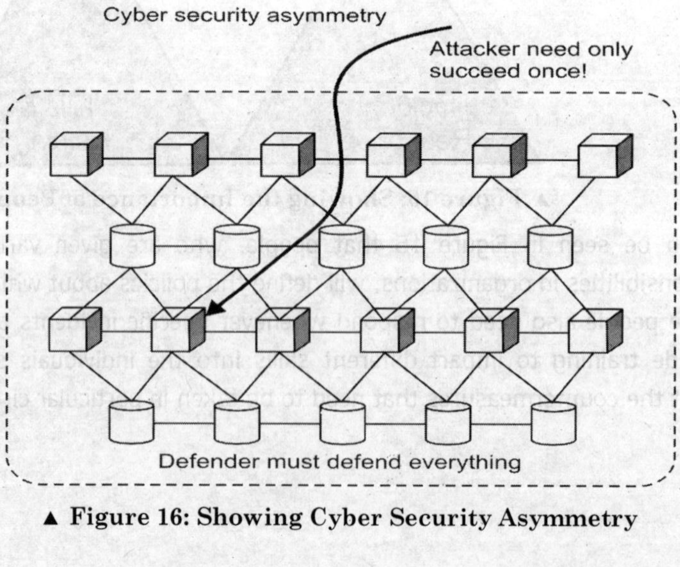

▲ **Figure 16: Showing Cyber Security Asymmetry**

Protecting against attacks on the Internet involves phishing and malware protection, security from identity theft, safety of applications and individuals, prevention of online predators and cyberbullies, etc.

In the next section, let's learn about these specific measures taken to maintain cyber security.

■ Viruses, Phishing, and Identity Theft

People on the Internet do not know everything about security. Considering this as a weapon, one can attack another person (who has limited knowledge about the use of the Internet) through viruses (a program written to cause harms to a system) and can steal their identity through phishing (an act of convincing people to provide confidential details such as passwords and PINs) or spyware (a program that is created to read the personal information of a person from their accounts or systems). You must protect yourself from such kind of attacks. People may launch viruses through e-mails or blog posts. For example, if you like a specific game and you shared this information on your social networks, someone who wants to access your personal data may send you an e-mail with a link to download the new version of the game and advertising himself/herself as a person from the company that developed the game. After you have downloaded the software from the given link, the software starts forwarding your personal information to the individual who sent you the link. There can also be other methods to launch such kinds of attacks that are known as phishing.

In order to protect yourself from such types of attacks, you must be aware of the ways in which the attacks may harm you. Also, you need to be careful about what kind of data you are sharing on the Internet, what kinds of people are connected to you through the Internet, and what types of people may use the information shared by you. Confidential information should never be shared on the Internet. Your likes, dislikes, and the preference for particular things should be known only to the people you trust. Protecting from viruses and phishing is one of the most difficult things when it comes to the harms caused by the Internet.

People steal identity for criminal purposes that may prove harmful for victims of the identity theft. The financial crime is one of the most noted consequences of identity theft. Consider someone who knows the PIN of your ATM card and the ATM card number. He/she might use this information for online purposes and funds transfer for his/her benefits. Therefore, no secret and confidential information should be shared with anyone on the Internet however dear they are.

To protect yourself from viruses and spyware, you need to have your firewalls and antivirus software up to date. Antivirus software and firewalls are very effective ways to keep yourself protected from cyber attacks, but installing too many security software programs harms your system's performance. The privacy and the security settings in your Web browser must not expose your system to any potential threats on the Internet.

■ Protection for Applications and Individual Privacy

Today, online advertising has become a way to go for business. Catchy phrases and various offers are used to drag people into the business domains. However, the activities have their potential misgivings. People who are not well aware of cyber attacks may get trapped by some malicious people. Advertisements might contain a spyware or a software application that can be run on computer systems. Such software can damage another application already running on the system or can send information from the system to the person who advertises with these programs. This may harm individual privacy and application security. One must protect oneself from all such kinds of advertisements or attacks.

If you are sharing important information about yourself, that information may be taken by advertisers who want to know the maximum they can about you. This information can be crucial for their purpose. Advertises can send cookies on the Web browsers so that they could record the online behavior of user, and advertisement on the basis of behaviors might be sent. These could be harmful for your individual security and the security of your applications. You must therefore check all new e-mails independently and ignore advertisements that you have no concerns with. You must keep privacy and security settings of your browser that asks you to run or ignore cookies from sites. This can help you avoid tracking of activities on the Internet and Web.

Some applications and mobile phones are designed to store user information. You, as users, are not allowed to deny storage of the information, such as the unique ID of your device. These information may be used by advertisers to send user-specific advertisements, which may cause harm for individuals and applications.

Development and prominence of social networking sites in the Internet era has been one of the most noted developments. People use social networks to connect with people, share thoughts and preferences, stay in touch, and for various other purposes. You must note that the Internet has nothing private. Whatever you share on the Internet can be used globally. Therefore, you must be careful while projecting your views and giving details about yourself through the Internet.

■ Protection from Online Predators and Cyberbullies

Cyberbullying has been seen as one of the most common offenses online. A lot of people use the Internet to stalk other people, harass them, and assault and extort sexually. People may hide real identities easily on the Internet. Some people use this trick to exploit children and girls. A number of complaints all around the world about sexual offenses, sending of texts to arouse sexual feelings, calling on cell phone to disturb the peace of mind, etc. are some of the actions of cyberbullies. Cyberbullying is considered as a crime all over the world because these activities may cost victims their life. Irreparable damages can be resulted from all such incidents. Some other ways to chat with strange people are also included under cyberbullying. These activities include chatting through mobile applications (WhatsApp and Hike, for example), consoles of video games, and anonymous chat rooms.

As a solution from being bullied online, people can use information sharing and empowerment of the family members, guide children of the family, apply a set of rules for children to use the Internet safely, and giving tips on texting and cyberbullying. Teenage girls or boys are the most vulnerable to cyberbullying. They can be easily misguided. Also, children may trust people easily, leading to sexual exploitation, harassment, and stalking. In the process of tolerating such kinds of incidents, the victims may have to lose their lives. So, protection against online predation and cyberbullying is a must these days when it comes to cyber security.

1.9 Security Risk Analysis

When it comes to security information and information systems in an organization, analyzing potential risks is very crucial. Your system can be secure only at the depth of your risk analyzes. If you can properly analyze the risk of possible threats to your organization's information and information system security, you can well take the measures to maintain the security of your organization. Therefore, risk analysis has a lot to do with matters related to organizations' information system security. Measures taken by an organization are never enough to counter all the security threats to the organization's information and information systems. So, it becomes very important to assess the vulnerabilities and possible risks for the system. Also, it is necessary to analyze the risks involved in leaving some of the vulnerabilities without countermeasures. If some of the risks are not affecting the security of information systems, then strict countermeasures will not be required.

There are certain cases where the risks associated with a threat have meet consequences, whereas countering the threat requires too much cost. In such conditions, the vulnerability can be left with little protection. Analysis of risks is a process that involves identification of threats and measuring their effect on the security of the organization. The entire process of maintaining organizational security involves assessment, analysis, and management of risks. Where the assessment is identification of any potential risks for a system, analysis means measuring the effects that may be caused to the system and providing details to the management team for taking steps that will counter the most concerning issues. Management of risks is to take appropriate steps for removing system vulnerabilities.

Risks analysis process acts as a link between both risk assessment and risk management processes. So, the process of defining the consequences on the system due to vulnerabilities needs special care. Risk analysis is a continuous process that requires you to constantly monitor the measures employed to maintain security of your systems at present. In addition, you must keep calculating threats evaluating their further effects. Generally, the objective of security analysis is to keep the economy of a system and the security measures established to keep it safe and secure in balance. Risk analysis activities also assess the importance of data or information that has risk of potential losses and then it accounts effective steps to counter them. On one hand, it keeps the economy in check, that is, the cost of applied security measures never exceed the possible losses. On the other hand, if the data that runs the possibility of being lost is not much important, then the security measures do not need to be much strict. The analysis of risks requires analysts to consider intersection of multiple remedial actions to counter a security issue in an organization, whereas a sum of multiple risks that can be reduced with a single remedial action may also need consideration. So, the analyst must be open to accepting both. Sometimes, remedial actions can improve or degrade the effects of other actions.

With these considerations in mind, an analyst gets some idea about the appropriateness of certain steps to protect the system from security threats. The protective measures to be taken must be compared so that their cost effectiveness and security implications can be appropriately calculated. Some cost indicators on which you can base your comparison between the effectiveness of security steps are as follows:

- The time duration required for the recovery of costs employed in taking steps for maintaining security
- The amount of cost that you can avoid annually if you apply a specific protective measure

- The amount of loss that you can avoid by applying certain measures for security

In this manner, you can protect your system cost effectively by assessing the implications of security threats and measures on your organization's information and information systems.

The common terminology that comes out from the process of security risk analysis is described as follows:

- **Assets**: Assets for an organization means everything that has some value and needs to be safeguarded.
- **Threats**: Threats are defined as potential actions or actual actions having the possibility of damaging the assets of an organization.
- **Vulnerabilities**: Vulnerabilities refer to some weaknesses or loopholes in securing assets. Vulnerability exposes the assets of an organization to some probable damage from threats.
- **Countermeasures**: Countermeasures are the devices or actions with an intent and capability to reduce system vulnerabilities.
- **Expected losses**: Expected losses are expected impacts of threats on an organization's assets.
- **Impact**: The loss of assets resulted from a threat activity. It is usually categorized into four areas, namely, destruction, disclosure, modification, and Denial of Service (DoS).

The process of risk analysis involves the following three key elements:

1. **Impact statement**: The impact statement describes the damages that may be caused by threats.
2. **Effectiveness measure**: The effectiveness measure presents the calculated effectiveness of individual actions taken to counter the impact of threats.
3. **Recommended countermeasures**: The recommended countermeasures involve possible actions that are cost effective and maintain security of assets in a proper manner.

Summary

In this chapter, you have studied about the basics of information systems that included discussion about structure of information systems, their components, and types. Nowadays, it can be noted that organizations are putting a lot of emphasis on securing the information and information systems they have. This need for security has given rise to a number of disciplines, including some interdisciplinary areas also. The center of focus for all these areas is information, which is probably the most valuable asset for organizations. Next, the chapter has explained the approaches that are followed in developing information systems for various organizations. It has also discussed the needs for maintaining the security of information and information systems and threats. The areas that take particular care for information and information system security are information assurance, information security, and cyber security. All of these areas include security risk assessment, analysis, and management. Then you have learned about information assurance and cyber security. Finally, the chapter is concluded with a brief discussion on risks for the security of assets in an organization.

Exercises

■ Multiple Choice Questions

Q1. Information system supports:

a. Implementation of security in an organization

b. All the business functions of an organization

c. Only database functions of an organization

d. All of the above

Ans. The correct option is b.

Q2. Which of the following is not a type of information system?

a. Operations support systems

b. Knowledge-based systems

c. Employment systems

d. Management support systems

Ans. The correct option is c.

Q3. Operations support system involves:

a. Transaction processing system

b. Process control system

c. Enterprise collaboration system

d. All of the above

Ans. The correct option is d.

Q4. Which of the following is not a type of attack on the network?

a. Active attack

b. Passive attack

c. Neutral attack

d. All of the above

Ans. The correct option is c.

Q5. Information assurance is best described as:

a. Management of risks associated with infrastructure security of an organization

b. Management of risks associated with the security of an organization's information systems and information through measures to ensure availability, integrity, authentication, confidentiality, and non-repudiation

c. Management of risks associated with the employees and hardware systems of an organization

d. All of the above

Ans. The correct option is b.

Q6 The primary focus of information assurance is:

a. Strategy

b. Tools

c. Infrastructure security

d. None of the above

Ans. The correct option is a.

Q7 Cyber security is a term related to:

a. Security of individuals from frauds related to the use of the Internet

b. Security of individuals and organizations from frauds related to the use of the Internet

c. Security of information from computer hackers

d. None of the above

Ans. The correct option is b.

Q8 Cyber security is related to:

a. Viruses, phishing, and identity theft

b. Protection for applications and individual privacy

c. Protection from online predators and cyberbullies

d. All of the above

Ans. The correct option is d.

Q9. Security risk analysis acts as a link between:

a. Security risk assessment and security risk measurement

b. Security threats and their impacts

c. Risks and their assessment

d. None of the above

Ans. The correct option is a.

Q10. Security risk includes the following element(s):

a. Impact statement
b. Effectiveness measure
c. Recommended countermeasures
d. All of the above

Ans. The correct option is: d.

■ Subjective Type Questions

Q1. What do you mean by information system (IS)? What are its components?

Q2. How do you classify information systems in general? Explain in detail.

Q3. Explain in detail the different approaches followed to develop information systems.

Q4. What is information assurance and how is it provided?

Q5. Describe security risk analysis.

02 Introduction to Application Security and Counter Measures

OBJECTIVES

- Introduction to application security
- Data security considerations
- Security Threats
- Security threats to e-commerce
- E-cash and electronic payment system
- Credit/debit/smart cards
- Digital signature
- Cryptography and encryption

Security of information and information systems is, undoubtedly, the leading challenge for organizations. However, they cannot ignore the importance of third-party vendor applications such as Web browsers, and therefore, security measures must be applied to maintain the data and application security. There are various considerations for the security of applications and data associated with them. Any of these measures cannot be overlooked. In order to secure applications, we have various technologies such as firewall, Virtual Private Network (VPN), and access control systems. Since a lot of attackers keep pressing for any loopholes in the security measures applied by an organization to keep its applications secure, applications are always under threat. We all use the Internet for buying lots of products from various websites, including Flipkart and Amazon. Online purchase of products and services is considered to be one of the most vulnerable uses of the Internet as it involves exchange of finances and identity. Data transfer over the Internet has been common through e-mail and chat. All these applications run on the Internet, which is a highly vulnerable place. People all over the world use the Internet for a variety of purposes. Some people use to connect with friends, family members, and relatives; some of them purchase goods and avail services; and other may use the Internet for sending receiving mails. The Internet also allows people to take malicious actions. There are people who attack other Internet users by sending e-mails containing malicious software to steal identity or to obtain crucial information. Security of applications is therefore an imperative in today's era of the Internet.

In this chapter, you learn about application security, especially the security of applications provided by third-party vendors. You also learn about some data security considerations regarding data backup, data archival, and data disposal. Further, you learn about technologies to secure data and applications. In addition, the chapter discusses about security threats for applications and for E-commerce.

It explains electronic payment system and transactions using credit/debit cards. Later, the chapter introduces you to digital signature, cryptography, and encryption.

2.1 Introduction to Application Security

Information systems employed in an organization must have proper security measures applied so that the organization's operations are well supported. In addition to securing information systems, nowadays, it has become necessary to secure the applications developed or used by the organization. Attackers, in the last decade, not only targeted the servers and operating systems (OSs) but also attacked the client applications. Security professionals are aware that applications, especially client-side, third-party applications, must be properly secured. Organizations and individuals use various types of client-side applications that include browsers, multimedia programs, and document readers. These applications are used for Web interaction, gaming, social networking, and a number of other purposes. Browsers are also used to access critical applications, websites, and e-mails.

These applications have their own vulnerabilities that need to be removed in order to make them secure. Attackers mostly target client-side applications. The most common attacks on the client-side applications include phishing and social engineering. An attacker might send a malware through e-mail, and on downloading it, the user could instantly become a victim. The malware may send some confidential information from the computer system to the attacker who can take advantage of that information. Sometimes, attackers may also ask you to download a plug-in or a cookie to help you improve your search, but that may turn you into a victim of social engineering attack.

Application security is a huge challenge for organizations in today's context. Although OS vendors have improved their security metrics, yet attackers find new vulnerabilities in the system, which may be exploited to damage confidentiality, integrity, and availability of applications.

The Internet is a highly vulnerable place; any application interacting with the Web is always under threat. Attackers try to take advantage of any vulnerability through which they can affect the normal operations of a user. They wili continue to push, and whenever any weak point is found, the attack will be launched. Most of the OS vendors use patched systems to keep vulnerabilities to the minimum, but even the patched systems are not devoid of attacks. They are vulnerable to zero-day attacks that exploit the code of systems even before the notice to create patches for the systems is received by the vendors. Top vendors including Microsoft, Apple Computers, Adobe, and Mozilla are the targets of these kinds of attacks.

It has been established that the security of third-party, client-side applications is one of the hardest things to manage when it comes to securing all the processes of an organization. There are various challenges for vendors to prevent any malicious activity and for users to keep their system secure. One of the topmost challenges for vendors is to develop secure applications for different varieties and versions of platforms, whereas user challenges include keeping compliance with the standards and managing patch cycles.

Vendor Challenges for Application Security

The biggest challenge for software vendors is the availability of various OS platforms and different versions of software applications. Developing secure applications for every platform is a daunting task for organizations. The other big challenge for vendors to provide secure applications is the compatibility issue. Different platforms and versions have their own security considerations and requirements, which need to be taken care of. This creates complexity and therefore presents a huge challenge for vendors in developing secure software. Figure 1 shows an example of complexity presented by different applications on different platforms:

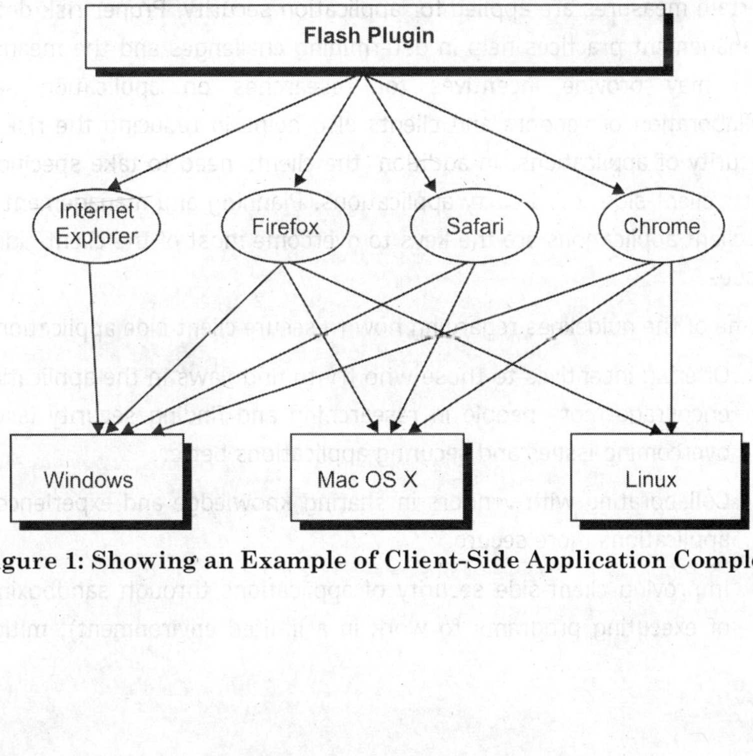

▲ **Figure 1: Showing an Example of Client-Side Application Complexity**

In Figure 1, it can be seen that the Flash Plug-in developed for different browsers is running on specific platforms. First, not all browsers are supported on every platform. Second, the vendors need to consider different versions of the application that runs on specific platform and browser. Third, the plug-in needs to be developed considering the specific requirements of both the browser and the OS. All these points create complexity. Due to these circumstances, it becomes very difficult for the vendors to develop secure applications.

■ User Challenges for Application Security

Software vendors bear the responsibility of managing development-related issues for secure applications. However, this is not the end of the road for application security. The client organizations and individuals face their own set of challenges in securing client-side applications to provide robustness and an all-round security to their systems. For example, if an organization fails to standardize its applications, it will not be able to utilize the hardened and the most recent security measures that are included in the upgrade.

In patch cycles also, organizations seem to ignore most client-side applications very often. Vendors release patches in cycles, but system administrators hardly care to download and upgrade systems in most cases. A lot of these patches do not notify administrators automatically. Moreover, different platforms may need different patches and updates, which may be time-consuming and might interrupt the usual operations. These are certain challenges that clients face while keeping their system updated and secure.

Certain measures are applied for application security. Proper risk detection, analysis, and management practices help in determining challenges and the means to overcome them. You may provide incentives for researches on application security issues. The collaboration of vendors and clients also helps in reducing the risk associated with the security of applications. In addition, the clients need to take specific measures to secure their client-side, third-party applications. Planning and management of threats and risks to client applications are the keys to overcome most of the client-side application security issues.

Some of the guidelines regarding how to secure client-side applications are as follows:

- Offering incentives to those who try to find flaws in the application security. This will encourage more people in researching and finding security issues that will help in overcoming issues and securing applications better.
- Collaborating with vendors in sharing knowledge and experience will help in making applications more secure.
- Improving client-side security of applications through sandboxing (restricting rights of executing programs to work in a limited environment), mitigation of attacks on

buffer overflow and memory manipulations, and exposing the internal code used for applying security help in making the client-side applications more safe and secure.

- Standardizing applications whenever possible is also a good way to secure applications better.
- Updating software to newer versions is considered as a measure to tighten the security of client-side applications.

In addition to the preceding points, you must keep in check the security settings on browsers and a various other software applications so that the applications could remain safe and secure.

2.2 Data Security Considerations

Security of data means maintaining its Confidentiality-Integrity-Availability (CIA) properties, which requires certain points to be considered. These data security considerations are related to data backup, archival, and disposal.

Let us start discussing each of these considerations in detail in the following sections.

Data Backup Security Considerations

To manage data properly, we must consider data backup, which is primarily used for the purpose of data security against any kind of accidents or loss of data due to some malicious activities. In case of casualties resulting into loss of data, you can restore the original data from your backup. Backup of data is nothing, but the storage of a snapshot of data at certain points. You can take regular backups of data so that it remains in the latest stages, and in case your data is lost due to some reason, you could restore the most recent form of data. Data backup is seen as an essential part of data management operations. Some reasons for data to be lost due to accidents or malicious activities are as follows:

- Failure of hardware or faults in the hardware system
- Fault in the media or software
- Hacking of data or infection of viruses causing loss of data
- Failure of power, resulting in data loss
- Erroneous human activities, such as changes in or deletion of files

The preceding are the primary reasons for an accidental or malicious loss of data. Therefore, your data backup strategy should be based mainly on the considerations such as current state and quality of your hardware and software, local situations regarding supply of power, the value of your data, and levels of risk that you think are appropriate given that the situation at your place remains the same. You can take steps to analyze risks and accordingly formulize the backup strategy. All the considerations of precise backup taken in view will translate into a few points explained as follows:

Should you consider backing up your entire system or only a specific set of files?

Firstly, it should be considered whether you will require restoring the entire system in case of data loss or restoring only certain files will do. If the responsibility of restoring the system, except data files being accessed by you, is taken by some other authority, you will need to backup only your data files. However, you will require backing up the entire system if it is not being backed up by anyone else. Portable devices and home-bound computers are some of the examples that mostly require full-system backup by the user.

In formulating the backup strategy, the criticality of data must be taken care. For example, data files that contain personal information should have least number of copies possible. Creating a master file and one backup copy for such kind of data files can be one solution.

Does the organization you are working for has a backup policy?

After you have decided whether the entire system or only certain files need to be backed up, you should consider whether there is an organization-wide policy for data backup. However, if you are less confident about the organizational policies to fulfill your purpose, you should define backup strategies according to your needs and criticality of data.

How frequently should your data be backed up?

Generally, data needs to be backed up after every change so that the risk of losing any critical changes is reduced to the minimum. However, it can be time-consuming and hectic at times. So, automated backup of some critical and frequently used files at a definite interval can be a good strategy.

Which storage media should you use for data backup?

While selecting the media for backup, you need to consider certain aspects, such as the amount and criticality of data being backed up and the backup method being used by you. Some of the storage media to store your backup files are Compact Disks (CDs), Digital Versatile Disks (DVDs), removable hard drive, and magnetic tape. Copying small data files regularly on a recordable CD is a good option, but a CD cannot be used to store large amounts of data. You will find removable hard drives and magnetic tapes more convenient for storing a large number of files than a CD. Figure 2 shows the different types of storage media for data backup:

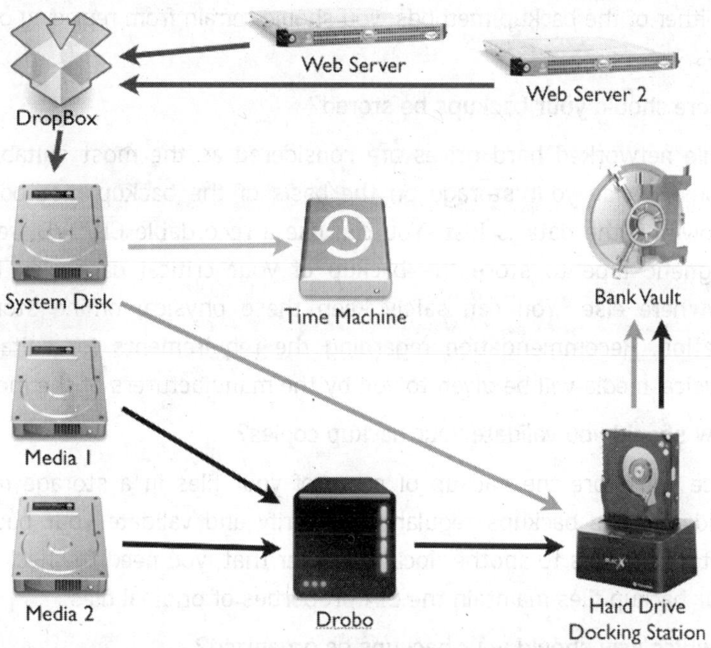

▲ **Figure 2: Showing Data Backup Options**

In which format should you store your backup files?

This question requires you to analyze the longevity of your storage needs. Master files should be backed up, ideally, in those file formats that can be digitally preserved for a long time. Most of the open file formats are more suitable for this purpose than the proprietary ones.

Should you back up your files incrementally or differentially?

Backup files are stored in two different ways, namely, incremental and differential. In incremental storage mode, you first create a backup of all the files of relevance. After that, you keep on backing up only those files in which some changes or modifications have occurred since the last backup. In this backup method, you should use removable storage media such as CDs/DVDs to store the backup files.

The other type of backup is known as differential backup. In this type of backup, you are required to first create a backup of the entire system (or the backup of relevant files). After that, every time changes are incorporated in the files or new files created, you will need to back up the files since the first full backup. The differential backup method does not allow you to back up your files only when some files after the most recent backup of some of your files were taken. In this backup method, you should use fixed media such as removable hard drives or networked hard drives for storing the backup files.

In either of the backup methods, you should refrain from replacing old backup files with new ones.

Where should your backups be stored?

While networked hard drives are considered as the most suitable backup storage, you should decide your storage on the basis of the backup method and the level of risks involved if the data is lost. You can use a recordable CD/DVD, removable hard drive, or magnetic tape to store the backup of your critical data files that are not contained anywhere else. You can safely keep these physical offline storage media in another location. Recommendation regarding the requirements for suitable conditions to keep physical media will be given to you by the manufacturers of the media.

How should you validate your backup copies?

Once you store the backup of some of your files in a storage media, you should keep validating the backups regularly. To verify and validate your backup, you first need to restore the files to another location. After that, you need to check with the original files if your backup files maintain the CIA properties of original files.

In which way should your backups be organized?

You need to provide proper labels and a well-organized structure to your backup files in the storage media that you are using to store your backups. A well-organized structure of backups makes it easy to restore data files later

Data Archival Security Considerations

Data, considerably the most valuable asset in an organization, may or may not be in active use. Some parts may be crucial for future references, but may not be actively used anymore. Therefore, most organizations move the currently inactive parts of data to a separate storage location in order to reduce complexity and keep active parts of data fresh. This process of separating older (or currently inactive) data from currently active, new, and fresh data is known as archival of data. The separated older data is moved to a different storage device so that the data can be retained for a long time and referenced whenever required. Figure 3 shows the typical data archival strategy used by most organizations (archive obsolete data):

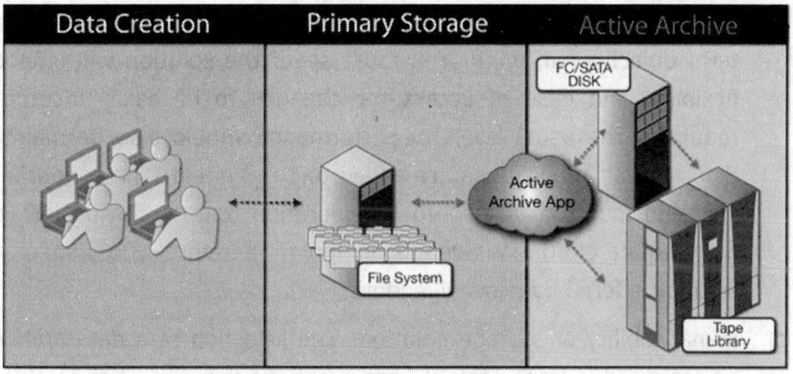

▲ **Figure 3: Showing the Typical Data Archival Strategy**

Archival of data is not the same as data backup, which is storage of data that can be used later to recover data lost due to disaster or malicious activities such as hacking. Data archiving requires retaining data that has become obsolete for current purposes but can be required, at a later stage, for reference. The process of data archival requires moving selected part of data to a different storage media in order to reduce cost, save storage space in the online system, reduce access complexity, and improve system performance. The information that should be preserved can be identified efficiently by most of the products that are used for the purpose of data archival. These products define various criteria for the identification of information to be retained as archive. The criteria can be defined by the user or the archiving products may take metadata for files and contexts of objects as defining criteria to select the information to be archived. Archived data is stored according to the object context and indexed so that finding them becomes easy whenever required in future.

Records being rarely changed or accessed and important but less accessed information are most suitable data for archival. Nowadays, organizations use data archival to preserve historical information for a long time duration, which helps them reduce the requirements to induct huge storage media in online systems and to backup large amounts of data. Archival of data ensures proper maintenance of records so that they can be produced as evidence when referenced later. An archiving storage system is reliable and supports current activities. These systems store records in a well-managed form so that we can use and understand the records in future. Archived data can be used in businesses or may be produced as evidence in matters having legal consequences. You can also use archived data for historical researches and for accountability to your business stakeholders, both internal and external.

Archiving solution should be selected on the basis of individual requirements. Selection of the best archival solutions for specific purposes involves the following points:

- **Longevity of storage solution**: Archiving solution should be selected keeping long-term objectives in mind. You must see if the solution will offer the required level of flexibility and ease of access for changes to be easily incorporated as and when required. The usual levels of performance should also be maintained even if users, data, and/or applications are added to the system. The vendor's sustainability in the long run must be taken into consideration. Data archiving is a complex matter that may require continuous vendor support. Therefore, you should select a data archival solution offered by proven vendors.
- **Manageability of storage solution**: The selection of a data archival solution that can be managed is imperative. IT organizations want to have a solution for data archival that provides security and role-based access control options. A good archival solution will also include granular provisioning and reporting. A data archival solution providing these manageability features helps in simplifying the archiving-service delivery. The IT staff is enabled by such archival solutions so that association of corporate policies with archiving requirements, retrieval of required information for every user, and distribution of management across functional teams are possible.
- **Amount of focus on intelligence of content**: The content intelligence quality of archival solutions helps organizations in identifying and defining the value of specific sections of data. All kind of data is not equally worth. So, the importance of certain data is a critical matter, which can be decided by an archiving solution that focuses on content intelligence. Data can be classified on the basis of relevance and categories can be formed by the archival solution so that information management becomes effective.
- **Optimization of total cost of ownership**: Cost is always an important point to consider. Archiving solutions should provide technical and administrative functionalities that help you in reducing costs in certain areas so that the ownership cost as a total can be cut down. Reducing the administrative time on Microsoft PST and Lotus NSF, reducing the amounts of data that requires backing up, and improving storage capabilities are some of the features of good archiving solutions that help in optimizing the cost of ownership in total.
- **Type of available solution**: After the preceding points are considered, the type of archiving solution you want should be selected among the best of the available lot. An archival solution should be capable of accommodating to the scaling needs, supporting third party product integration, and working with a large set of storage options. You should select archiving solutions that apply the best kinds of data security and retention measures.

■ Data Disposal Security Considerations

Data disposal is an act of permanently deleting or destroying the data stored in a media. Sometimes, we may require destroying the data permanently for some security or compliance reasons. Data, undoubtedly, is an asset of great value for organizations. However, at some point, its destruction is inevitable. Whenever legacy or obsolete systems and devices are replaced, removal of data stored in those systems and devices at present is a must. Also, your business must comply with the federal policy legislation, which requires you to destroy some of your data after a definite time period. You cannot destroy data just by sending items into the trash. Destruction of data requires you to take measures beyond this. Data sent to trash can be recovered easily.

Destruction of data means to completely wipe out the data from the storage media. This process of wiping out the data completely is known as data disposal. The National Institute of Standards and Technology (NIST) describes three primary ways in which data can be disposed. These methods are overwriting hard drive, degaussing the hard drive and backup tape, and destroying the storage media. The overwriting method means rewriting all the areas of hard drives, degaussing means demagnetizing all areas of storage on hard drives and backup tapes, and destroying storage media means demolishing the storage media itself. Data disposal methods are explained in detail as follows:

1. **Overwriting hard drives**: Hard drive overwriting is an exercise that can be carried out in the data disposal process. Hard drives are not overwritten just by selecting and deleting an item. Each area on your hard drive should be overwritten a number of times to erase previous records completely. According to the NIST recommendation, you should write your hard drives thrice to make sure no data remains to be deleted. You can use any of the various programs that are available to enable you to overwrite your hard drives. In the overwriting procedure, it is possible to reuse hard drives. However, your device becomes less secure when overwritten.

2. **Degaussing hard drives and backup tapes**: In degaussing method of data disposal, your magnetic storage devices, such as hard drives and backup tapes, are demagnetized so that all the stored data on these devices is completed destroyed. The magnetic media are unable to store any more data. As the storage media has served almost its entire usual life, demagnetizing the drives and tapes will cause no harm to the organization. Degaussing of storage media can be used as a rental service provided both onsite and offsite by service providers. However, you should choose a service provider that complies with the standards set by the authorized bodies, such as NIST.

3. **Destroying storage media**: Disposal of data is possible most securely through destruction of the storage media. You can use neither the data nor the media again after destroying the drives, tapes, and other such storage devices. The best way to destroy your device is to shred it in the same way as you shred a paper document. There are large shredding machines used in the industry that grind up the media into scrap metals, which cannot be even recognized. The shredding services can also be hired as a service. Service providers send shredding machines to your site for destroying your storage devices; so, you can watch the proceedings and ensure that the data currently stored on an undestroyed media is not accessed by any individual. Your focus should be kept on a destruction service that uses scrap metals for recycling purposes and complies with the standards set by authorized bodies.

You should be careful about certain things while disposing your data off. The first thing to consider is that deleting items to erase data is not reliable because you can recover deleted data from hard drives and other storage devices. This is a huge risk for the security of data. For example, if your media is thrown in a waste bin and someone else recovers some of the data stored in the device, he/she can use it for any malicious activity that can be harmful for you. Formatting your hard drives is not a secure option either. Data recovery software is available to retrieve data from formatted hard drives. Breaking your storage media is not a complete data disposal mechanism because few sectors on the disk may be used to recover some data that may cause harms to your security. But if your media have been converted into metal scrap, you can be sure that your data has been destroyed completely.

2.3 Security Technologies

Data and application security has become one of the most prominent issues; therefore, we must take care while applying security measures properly. We have a variety of technologies that enable security of application and data in an organization. Use of firewalls, VPN, Intrusion Detection System (IDS), and access control systems are among the few ways to keep data secure.

Let us discuss about these security technologies in detail in the following sections.

■ Firewalls

Firewall is a part of a computer system or network that is designed to inspect incoming and outgoing network traffic and alter the traffic flow by dropping or passing certain packets. It is designed to block unauthorized access while permitting authorized communications. Firewall is a device or a set of devices that is configured to permit or deny network transmissions on the basis of certain rules and criteria. A firewall inspects all the messages that enter or leave the company's Intranet and blocks those that do not meet the specified security criteria. It analyzes the incoming data to determine the IP address of the machine from which it is coming and the content that it contains. Next, the firewall checks if the content is compliant with the rules that you have already configured. It also analyzes the information at the application level and determines whether or not the application should send or receive data through the port with which you are connected.

A firewall also prevents computer hackers from accessing your computer through the Internet by blocking back doors or open ports that connect your computer with the Internet. This protects your system from being attacked by viruses from the Internet.

You can implement a firewall in your system in any form—hardware, software, or a combination of both.

Figure 4 shows a hardware firewall:

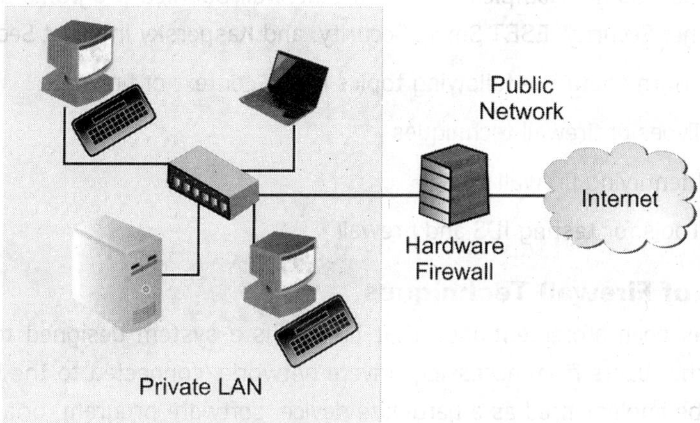

▲ **Figure 4: Showing a Hardware Firewall**

The hardware firewall is a physical piece of equipment that is kept between the Internet and your LAN network. An example of a hardware firewall is a broadband router. This kind of firewall can protect multiple computer systems that are connected to it simultaneously.

The software firewall is a software program that is installed on your computer. It also works in the same way as the hardware firewall by monitoring and blocking information that comes to your computer through the Internet.

Figure 5 shows a software firewall:

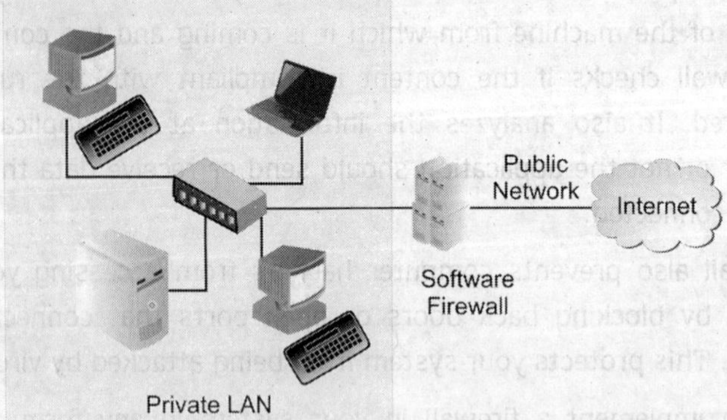

▲ **Figure 5: Showing a Software Firewall**

You can either install a software firewall from a computer disk or download it from the Internet. Some examples of software firewall bundled programs are Norton 360, Norton Internet Security, ESET Smart Security, and Kaspersky Internet Security.

Let's learn about the following topics in the context of firewalls:

- Types of firewall techniques
- Identifying firewall
- Tools for testing IDS and firewall

Types of Firewall Techniques

It has been aforementioned that firewall is a system designed to prevent unauthorized Internet users from accessing private networks connected to the Internet or Intranets. It can be implemented as a hardware device, software program, or a combination of both. A firewall can be based on a variety of techniques, which are as follows:

- **Packet filter:** Inspects the packets of data that are passed through the network and accepts or rejects the packets on the basis of the default or user-defined rules.
- **Application-level gateway:** Applies security mechanisms to specific applications such as File Transfer Protocol (FTP) and Telnet servers.
- **Circuit-level gateway:** Applies security mechanisms after establishing a TCP or an UDP connection.
- **Proxy server:** Checks all messages that enter or leave a network. It helps in hiding the real network addresses.

Let's learn each of these types in the following sections.

Packet Filters

Packet filter is also known as network layer firewall, which allows passing or blocking of the packets unless they are matched with the established rule set. A firewall administrator defines the rules or may use the default rules.

Network layer firewalls are of two types, stateful and stateless. Stateful firewalls maintain the state information of active sessions. An existing network connection is described by various properties, such as source and destination IP addresses, UDP or TCP ports, and the current stage of the connection's lifetime. If a packet does not match with any existing connection, it is evaluated against the rule set defined by the administrator for new connections. If a packet matches with an existing network connection, it is allowed to pass without further processing.

Stateless firewalls, on the other hand, require less memory and are faster than stateful firewalls. They require less time to filter the packets as they do not maintain the state information of sessions. Some common packet filters that are used on various versions of Unix are ipf, ipfw, pf, and iptables/ipchains.

Application Layer

Application layer firewalls are based on the application level of the TCP/IP stack. These firewalls intercept all packets that are sent or received from an application. Application layer firewalls help you in preventing unwanted outside traffic from reaching to protected machines. These firewalls can restrict or prevent spreading of computer worms and Trojans over a network.

Circuit-Level Gateway

The circuit-level gateway firewalls work at the session layer of the OSI model. They monitor TCP handshaking between the packets to determine whether or not the requested session is legitimate. The packets are passed through a circuit-level gateway to the Internet. In this firewall, a trusted client requests a service and the gateway accepts this request. Next, the gateway opens a connection to the requested untrusted host and then closely monitors the TCP handshaking.

Proxy Server

A proxy server is used to control and monitor the outbound traffic. It can be made to act as a firewall by assigning it the functionality and authority of blocking unauthorized packets. A proxy server hides the true network address and intercepts all messages entering and leaving the network. It also serves as an intermediary for requests sent by hackers seeking resources from other servers. A hacker connects to the proxy server, requesting for some service such as a file, connection, Web page, or other resource. Then the proxy server that acts as a firewall evaluates the request on the basis of some specified rules and guidelines.

How to Identify a Firewall

Prior to hacking a system or a network, a hacker tries to know what kind of firewall—hardware, software, or a combination of both—is implemented in it. Identifying a firewall helps a hacker to better plan how to break or bypass the firewall security to hack the system or network. A firewall can be identified on the basis of its type, version, or rule set. There are three basic methods to identify the firewalls, which are discussed as follows:

- **Port scanning**: Refers to the method in which firewalls are identified by using the port scanning technique. A port scanner checks a computer system running TCP/IP to determine which TCP and UDP ports are open and listening. Many firewalls have specific ports; for instance, CheckPoints Firewall-1listens on 256, 257, and 258. Some tools that use port scanning technique to identifying firewalls are Traceroute and Hping.

- **Firewalking:** Collects the information from a remote network that exists behind a firewall. It helps in identifying a firewall and mapping the routers of a network that exists behind a firewall. It is a method of disguising port scans.

- **Banner grabbing:** Helps you in detecting services run by firewalls. Banners are messages sent by hackers to a target system that is running and accepting the connection to check whether it is patched or not. The hacker can then grab the banners by using the telnet command with the specified service port number to see the output. An example of grabbing for the SMTP service, having the port 25, is as follows:

```
telnet mail.XYZcompany.org 25
```

Let's now learn about VPN.

■ VPN

VPN is a private communication network, which is the most secure, remote method of connecting a computer to a private network with the help of a public network, such as the Internet. It creates the virtual tunnel through which the data travels from one computer to the other over the network. Due to this, an attacker gets the way to use the remote client to relay attacks through the VPN tunnel. In this section, you will learn about the following vulnerabilities of VPN.

- Insecure storage of authentication credentials by VPN clients

- VPN fingerprinting
- Username enumeration vulnerabilities
- Offline password cracking
- Lack of account lockout
- Denial of Service (DoS) attacks
- Configuration vulnerabilities of VPN

Insecure Storage of Authentication Credentials by VPN Clients

VPN client programs store some or all of the authentication credentials, such as username and password, to identify and authenticate a user on the network. Although this setting makes the VPN easier to use, it also introduces security risks, especially if the credentials are not well protected. The common client issues that have been seen in VPN are as follows:

- Storing the username unencrypted in a file or registry
- Storing the password in a scrambled form
- Storing the plain-text password in memory
- Storing file permissions as credentials

VPN Fingerprinting

There are various methods, such as User Datagram Protocol (UDP) back-off fingerprinting and Vendor identity (ID) fingerprinting, through which VPN servers can be fingerprinted. This gives the useful information to potential attackers.

Username Enumeration Vulnerabilities

The most basic security requirement of a username/password authentication scheme is that the incorrect login information should not reveal the information about incorrect credentials (username or password) because this would allow an attacker to conclude whether a given username is valid or not. In VPN, if the user credentials are incorrect, it will inform the user (attacker) whether the entered username is valid or not.

The three common faults that are found in the way the VPN servers respond to the user are as follows:

- Some VPN servers only respond to the client which has the valid username
- Some VPN servers respond with a notification message, such as no-proposal chosen, if the username is incorrect

- Some VPN servers respond to both valid and invalid usernames, but in this situation, the invalid usernames hash payload is calculated using a null password, and it is difficult for the client to determine this.

In all the three faults, there is a difference between the response to an invalid username to that for a valid username, and this allows the client to determine if a given username is valid or not.

Offline Password Cracking

In VPN, an attacker can use the valid username with the Internet Key Exchange (IKE) aggressive mode to obtain a hash from the VPN server. After obtaining the hash, the attacker can use it to crack the associated password. This method of obtaining password is known as offline password cracking.

Lack of Account Lockout

When there are some instances of incorrect login attempts, an OS usually locks the accounts. However, several VPN implementations do not support this and allow an unlimited number of login attempts.

Denial of Service Attacks

DoS refers to the attacks in which an attacker prevents the intended user from accessing the resources. There are two types of DoS vulnerabilities that have been observed on VPN servers, which are as follows:

- **Malformed packet DoS:** Refers to vulnerability in which an IKE packet does not conform to the Request for Comments (RFC) specifications. In some implementations, this causes a buffer overflow condition that terminates the IKE process. Sometimes, this could be further exploited to run arbitrary code on the VPN server.
- **Resource exhaustion DoS:** Sends a large number of IKE packets on the VPN server due to which the VPN server runs out of negotiation slots. This makes the VPN server unable to process legitimate VPN connections. AsIKE uses the UDP transport, it is possible to spoof the source IP address of the DoS traffic, which makes both detecting the true source of the traffic and also blocking the DoS traffic difficult.

Benefits

A VPN can prove to be highly advantageous for a company if it is designed well. Some of the benefits it may provide are:

- A VPN can extend connectivity to different geographical locations

- It strengthens the organizational security and improves the performance of the network
- The operational cost in case of a VPN is much less when compared to traditional WAN
- It simplifies the n/w topology and provides telecommuter support

Overall productivity of an organizationincreases because of the aforementioned benefits it provides.The advantages offered by remote access are:

- The dial-up to the network is the responsibility of a third party.
- No additional cost needs to be incurred for adding new users.
- The expenses on WAN circuit and modem are not required.
- VPNs can be established from anywhere irrespective of geographical locations. This is done through the Internet.
- Cable modems are faster and more economical. Off-site users can easily access information in public places through the Internet.

Use of Tunnelling with VPN

As the name suggests, a tunnel is a logical path for transmitting VPN data from one node to the other. The VPN data which is thus transferred is called a payload. The payload is encrypted by the tunneling protocol so that it cannot be interpreted. The tunneling protocol which is used for transmitting payload is TCP/IP (Transport Control Protocol/ Internet Protocol). There are two types of tunneling, namely, voluntary tunneling and compulsory tunneling, which are explained as follows:

- **Voluntary tunneling**: In voluntary tunneling, the client directly sets up a connection with the server for the transfer of payload.
- **Compulsory tunneling**: In compulsory tunneling, a connection is established between two VPN servers and two VPN access devices, i.e., VPN routers. The client dials-in to the remote access server either through the local LAN or through an Internet connection. The remote access server then creates a tunnel for the transmission of a payload.

VPN tunnels can be established at one of the following two layers of the OSI reference model:

- **Data-link layer:** layer 2: VPN protocols that operate at this layer are Point-to-Point TunnelingProtocol (PPTP) and Layer 2 Tunneling Protocol (L2TP).
- **Network layer:** layer 3: The VPN protocol that operates at this layer is IPSec.

Authentication Mechanism

Authentication for VPN connections is done at the following three levels:

1. **User-level authentication by using PPP authentication:** When a VPN client attempts to establish a connection with a VPN Server, the server tries to authenticate the client. This authentication is done using Point-to-Point (PPP) protocol. In case mutual authentication is used, the VPN client also authenticates the VPN server to protect itself against computers that project themselves as VPN servers.
2. **Computer-level authentication by using IKE:** In order to establish tunnel using the IPSec protocol, the VPN client and the VPN server use the IKE protocol to exchange either their computer certificates or a pre-shared key. In this, the server and the client are authenticating each other at computer level, which is a much stronger authentication than the others. This authentication can only be done in case of L2TP or IPSec tunneling.
3. **Data origin authentication and data integrity:** This authentication is done to verify that the payload transmitted through a tunnel has originated at the other end of the tunnel and that the payload has not been modified on the way. The authentication is done with the help of a cryptographic checksum (based on an encryption key) that is transmitted along with the payload. This type of authentication can be done only for L2TP and IPSec protocols.
4. **Data encryption:** The data transmitted through VPN is encrypted so that it reaches the destination intact. The data is encrypted by the sender and decrypted by the receiver. This is done by using a common encryption key which is known only to the sender and the receiver. The length of the encryption key is very important. The larger is the size of the key, the better is the protection. In case the data is intercepted on the way, it is in an unintelligible form.

Types of VPN

There are several types of VPNs. Some of the common ones are discussed as follows:

1. **PPTP VPN(Dial-up VPN):** This is the most common and widely used VPN protocol. In this type of VPN, the authorized remote users can connect to the VPN server through the Internet and log on to the network with the help of its VPN password. This is often called dial-up VPN. It does not require additional cost on the part of the users as no extra hardware or software is required. One major disadvantage of these VPNs is that PPTP does not use encryption of data while transmission. Hence, they are less secure. Figure 6 shows PPTP VPN:

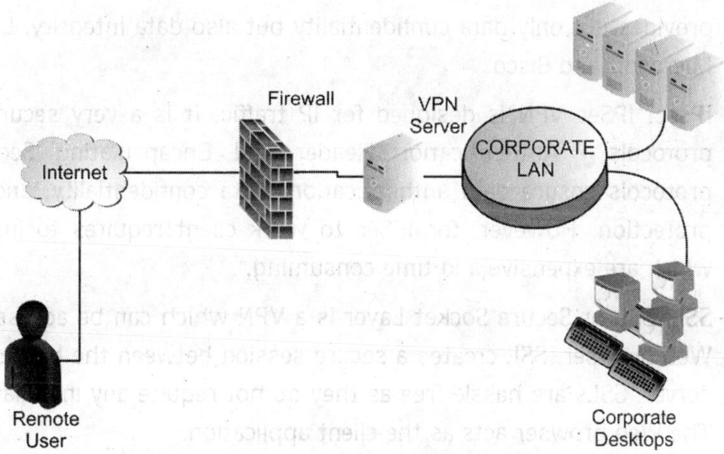

▲ **Figure 6: Showing PPTP VPN (Dial-up VPN)**

2. **Site-to-site VPN:** This is similar to PPTP, but there is no dedicated line for transmission in this. It allows different sites of the same organization, each having its own real network, to connect together to form a VPN. The routing, encryption and decryption, is done by the routers on both ends. These routers can be hardware based or software based. Site-to-site VPNs can work with hardware- or software-based firewall devices.

   Figure 7 shows the site-to-site VPN:

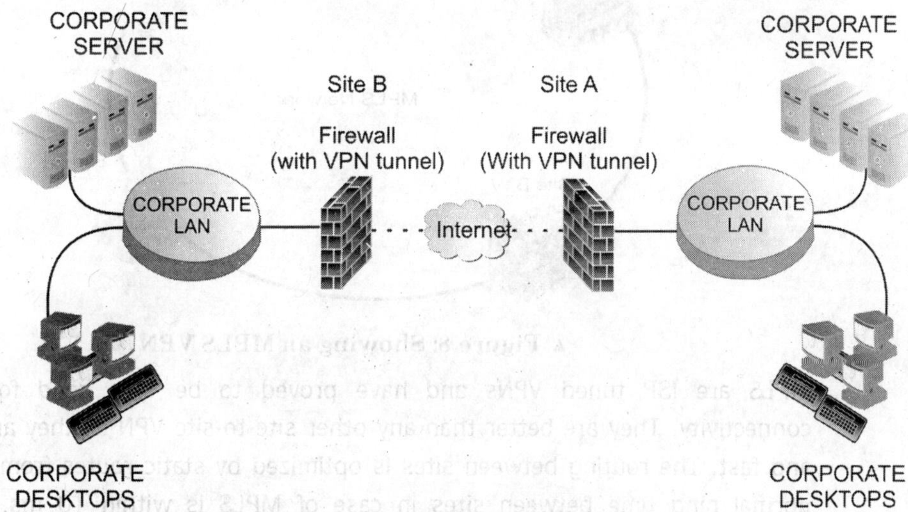

▲ **Figure 7: Showing the Site-to-Site VPN**

3. **L2TP VPN:** L2TP is similar to PPTP since it also doesn't provide encryption and relies on the PPP protocol to do this. The difference between PPTP and L2TP is that the latter

provides not only data confidentiality but also data integrity. L2TP was developed by Microsoft and Cisco.

4. **IPsec:** IPSec VPN is designed for IP traffic. It is a very secure VPN as it uses two protocols - Authentication Header and Encapsulating Security Payload. These protocols ensure data authentication, data confidentiality, and integrity, and replay protection. However, for IPSec to work client requires to install certain programs which are expensive and time consuming.
5. **SSL:** SSL or Secure Socket Layer is a VPN which can be accessed through https in a Web browser. SSL creates a secure session between the browser and the application server. SSLs are hassle free as they do not require any installation on the client side. The Web browser acts as the client application.
6. **MPLS VPN:** Multi-Protocol Label Switching (MPLS) was originally designed to improve the store-and-forward speed of the routers. MPLS was created by the combined efforts of Ipsilon, Cisco, IBM, and Toshiba.

Figure 8 shows an MPLS VPN:

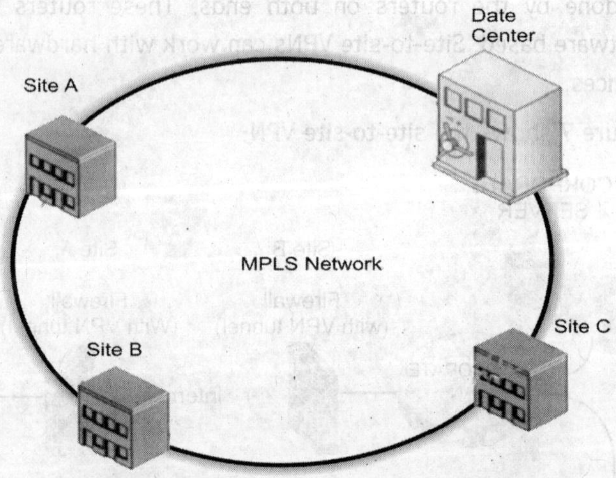

▲ **Figure 8: Showing an MPLS VPN**

MPLS are ISP tuned VPNs and have proved to be very good for site-to-site connectivity. They are better than any other site-to-site VPN as they are economical and fast. The routing between sites is optimized by static routes from the ISP. The normal ping time between sites in case of MPLS is within 10 ms, whereas for traditional site-to-site VPNs, it ranges from 30 ms to 100 ms.

7. **Hybrid VPN:** Hybrid VPNs combine the features of SSL, IPSec, and other types of VPNs. Thus, hybrid VPN servers can establish connections with multiple types of VPN clients. They are highly flexible at the client as well as server level and very expensive.

Security Concerns in VPN

There are two types of configuration vulnerabilities of VPN:

- **Poor default configuration:** Poor default configuration of a VPN server sets the level of usability rather than security. Usually, the IKE aggressive mode with Pre-Shared Keys (PSKs) is the default authentication method for remote access VPNs. The IKE aggressive mode with PSK authentication has some issues such as configuration issues. Normally, the users presume that the default configuration is secure. The poor default configuration supports many different ciphers and modes which weaken the VPN.
- **Poor guidance and documentation:** All VPN implementations do not provide appropriate direction and certifications to the end users to take decisions about which configuration to use. Some areas where guidance would be helpful but is very rarely given are as follows:
  - Using the weak ciphers, such as export grade or single Data Encryption Standard (DES) which can be cracked easily
  - Using weak authentication mechanisms such as PSK with IKE aggressive mode.
  - Selecting the Authentication Header (AH) protocol alone does not encrypt the VPN traffic at all

Intrusion Monitoring and Detection

Network monitoring refers to the process of tracking the activities that are being performed in the network. This task of monitoring the activities of a network can be assigned to a specific computer or a set of computers. The computer that acts as a network monitoring system must always be kept on and consists of strong power lines and backup generators.

The system performing the task of monitoring the network sends a ping command to all the computers that are available on the network. If other systems on the network do not respond to the ping command or this command takes a long time to execute on any of the systems connected to the network, then notifications about the same are sent to the network administrator. These notifications inform the administrator about problems in the network, such as overloaded systems, crashed servers, lost network connections, virus infections, and power outages, and are sent in the form of e-mail messages, pager alerts, or phone calls. The network activities can also be tracked by regularly taking virtual snapshots of the network's workflow.

The ID system can also be used to track the user's activities such as websites they are visiting, time of visit, number of pages on the site visited, and entry and exit Uniform

Resource Locators (URLs). This kind of network monitoring is generally not done to report problems but for analysis activities.

An intrusion detection system always has a sensor as its core element that is used to detect intrusions. The data received by these sensors is obtained from various sources such as IDS knowledge database, syslog, and audit trails.

Figure 9 shows a sample IDS system:

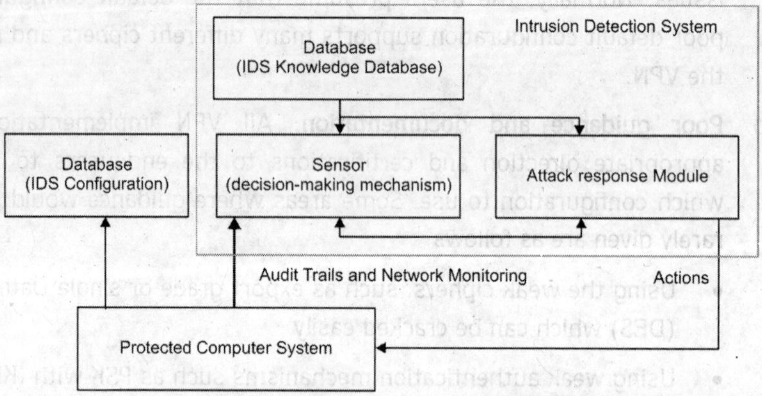

▲ **Figure 9: Showing a Sample IDS**

Figure 10 shows the integration of different components with the sensor:

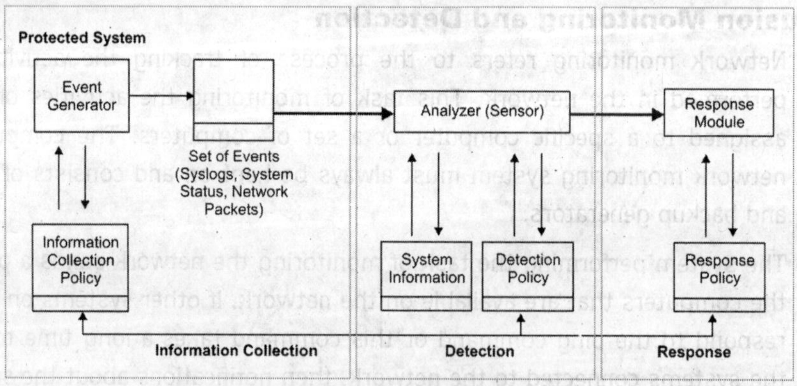

▲ **Figure 10: Showing the IDS Components**

Depending on the functionality and architecture, an IDS system can be of different types, such as NIDS or HIDS. In addition, there are IDSs that work similar to antivirus software, looking for specific signatures of known threats to protect the network even before an attack. Some IDSs detect malicious activities by comparing traffic patterns against a baseline and look for anomalies, whereas some IDSs come into action in response to a detected threat.

Now, let's discuss the two types of IDS—NIDS and HIDS—in detail.

Network-Based IDS

An NIDS captures network traffic to perform intrusion detection operations. These operations are performed at specific strategic points within the network in order to monitor network traffic to and from all the network devices. Scanning of the inbound and outbound traffics can create a bottleneck that results in impairing of the overall network speed.

An NIDS scans the network packets at the router or host-level, audits packet information, and logs any suspicious packets into a special log file with extended information. This type of IDS can also scan its own database for the attack signatures and then assign a severity level for each packet. If the assigned severity is of high level, the members of the security team are informed through e-mails or pager calls.

Figure 11 shows an NIDS:

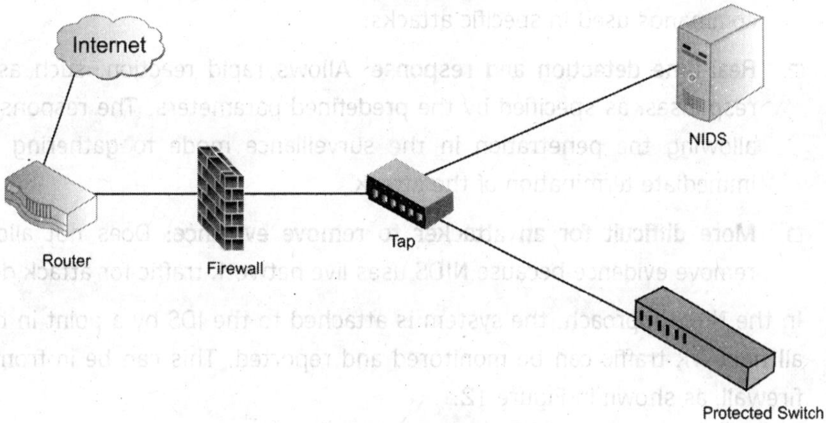

▲ **Figure 11: Showing a Typical NIDS**

The popularity of an NIDS has increased with the growth of the Internet. NIDSs, which are capable of scanning voluminous amounts of network activities, are in demand by industries that provide security measures in order to stop the security breaches; such industries also employ scanners, sniffers, and other network auditing and detection tools.

Some of the threats and activities that can be controlled by using an NIDS are as follows:

- IP spoofing
- Denial-of-service attacks
- DNS name corruption
- Man-in-the-middle attacks

The control mechanisms in an NIDS can be distributed or centralized. In a centralized control mechanism, the information present in the various IDSs is analyzed and processed by a central entity. However, in case of the distributed control mechanism, the logged information is distributed to every node present on the network.

Some of the advantages of using an NIDS are as follows:

- **Lowers cost of ownership:** Allows restricted access points for monitoring the network traffic. NIDSs do not require any additional software to be loaded and can be managed on different hosts. The low ownership cost of an NIDS is due to the small number of detections that it can make.
- **Detects attacks missed by the HIDS:** Examines all the packet headers for signs of malicious and suspicious activities. For example, the DoS attacks or the fragmented packets can be identified by looking at the packet headers that travel across a network.
- **Analyze the payload packet:** Examines the content of the payload, looking for commands used in specific attacks.
- **Real-time detection and response:** Allows rapid reaction, such as notifications and responses, as specified by the predefined parameters. The responses can range from allowing the penetration in the surveillance mode to gathering information or to immediate termination of the attack.
- **More difficult for an attacker to remove evidence:** Does not allow an attacker to remove evidence because NIDS uses live network traffic for attack detection.

In the NIDS approach, the system is attached to the IDS by a point in the network where all network traffic can be monitored and reported. This can be in front of or behind the firewall, as shown in Figure 12:

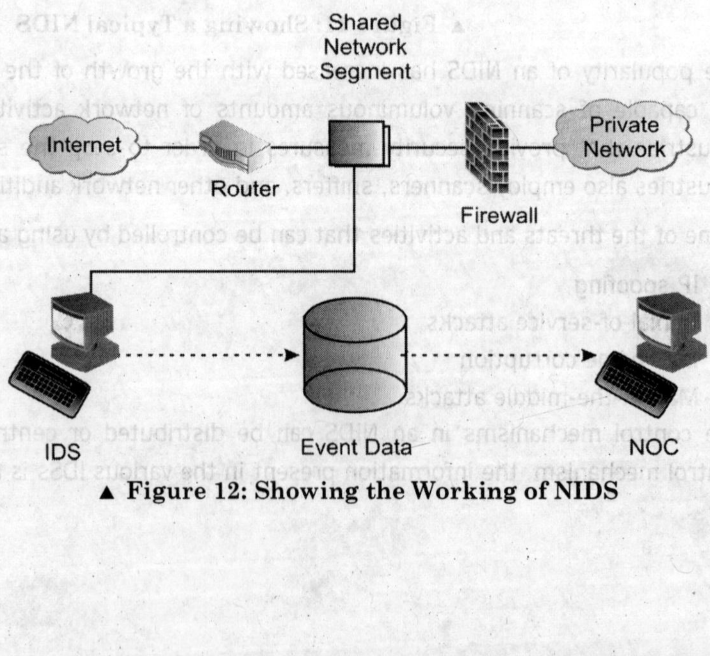

▲ **Figure 12: Showing the Working of NIDS**

When the NIDS is placed in front of a firewall, it monitors all the traffic going into the network, resulting in processing of large amount of data and allowing you to see all the traffic coming into the network. However, if the NIDS is placed behind the firewall, it only allows you to see the traffic that penetrates the firewall. The NIDS can be attached to a switch, a hub, or a tap. Many hubs or switches provide a monitoring port for troubleshooting and diagnostic purposes.

Figure 13 shows the connection to the network by using a hub:

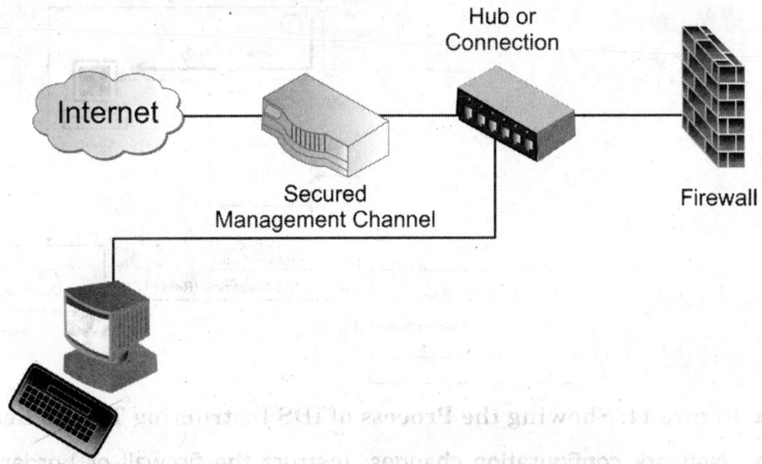

▲ **Figure 13: Showing a Connection to the Network Using a Hub**

The two basic types of responses that can be formulated at the network level are passive and active. When a system is threatened by some potential attack, the active response takes the immediate possible action required to decrease the impact of that attack, whereas the passive response notifies the administrator about the threat. A passive response is the most common type of response and is the easiest to develop and implement. Some of the common passive response strategies are as follows:

- **Logging:** Records an event and the circumstances of its occurrence. It should provide sufficient information about the nature of the attack. This information can then be used to devise methods to counter the threat.
- **Notification:** Communicates event-related information to the appropriate personnel when an event takes place.
- **Shunning:** Refers to the activity of avoiding the attack.

To implement an active type of response in a system, you first need to create definite plans and policies as to how the system should respond on being attacked. The active responses are set and implemented in the system according to these plans and policies.

Some examples of the active responses generated by a system in case of an attack are as follows:

- **Terminating processes or sessions:** Terminates all the unauthorized and unauthenticated processes and sessions that are trying to gain access to the system. In such cases, the IDS might need to reset all the network connections.

Figure 14 shows the process of resetting the connections by the IDS:

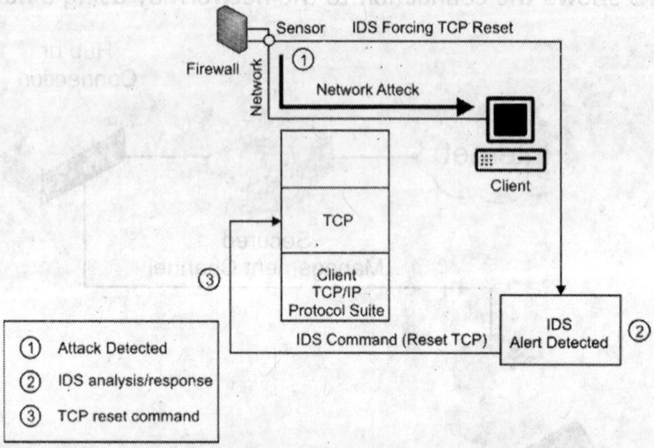

▲ **Figure 14: Showing the Process of IDS Instructing TCP to Reset All Connections**

- **Network configuration changes**: Instruct the firewall or border router to reject any request or traffic coming from a particular socket or port that is being attacked.

Figure 15 shows the IDS blocking a port from accessing a system:

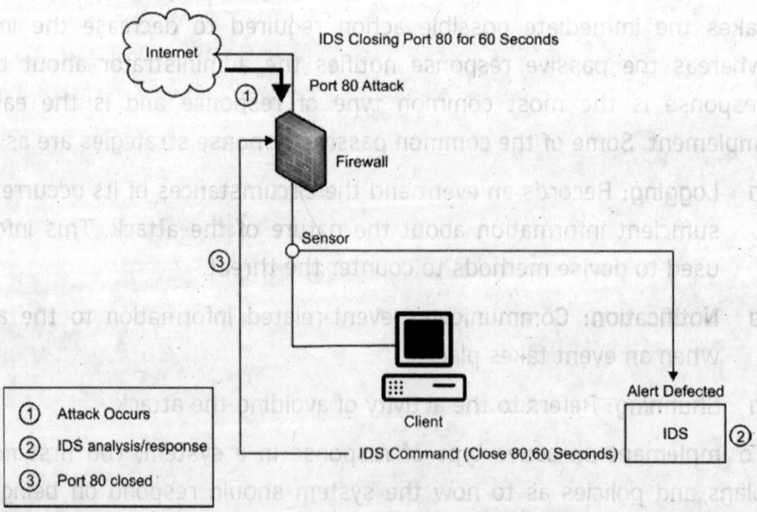

▲ **Figure 15: Showing the Process of IDS Instructing the Firewall to Close the Port**

- **Deception:** Fools the attackers and redirects them to a system that is designed to be broken. It helps in gathering data about how the attack is planned and what techniques are being used in the attack.

Figure 16 shows the process of how a honeypot deceives an attacker:

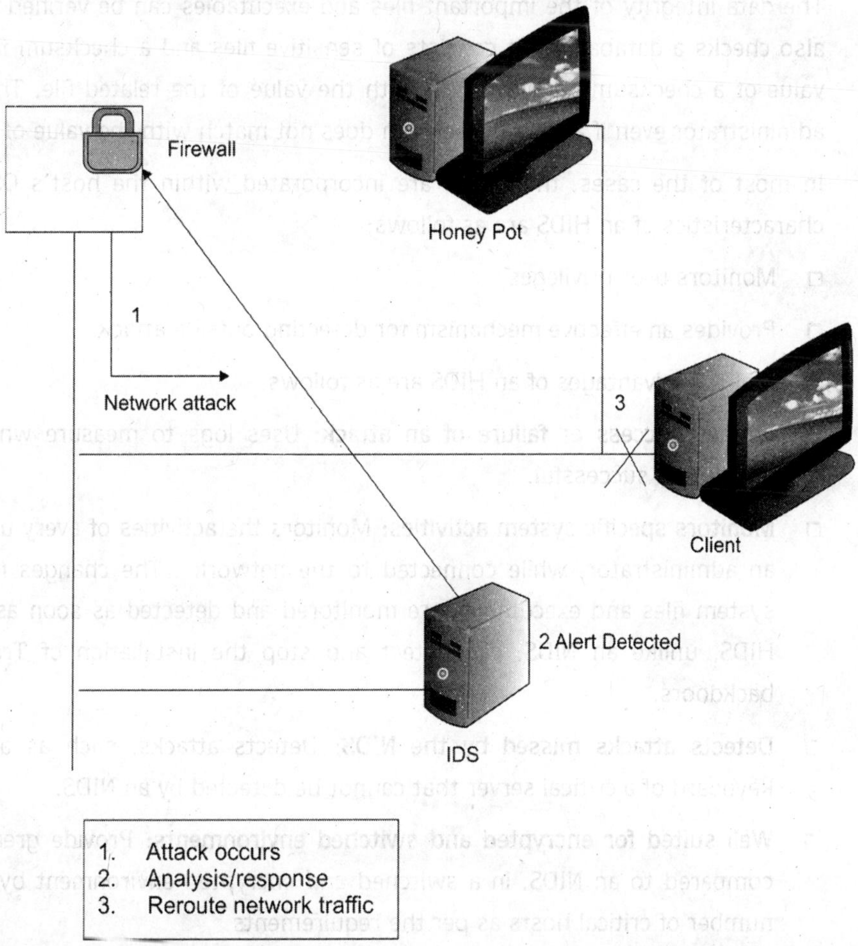

▲ **Figure 16: Showing the Process of a Network Honeypot Deceiving an Attacker**

Host-Based IDS

An HIDS is designed to monitor, detect, and respond to activities and attacks on a given host. In other words, it is used to monitor the packets, inbound as well as outbound, from the device and alerts the user or administrator of any suspicious activity. HIDSs are run on individual hosts or devices on the network.

Many different areas are analyzed to detect misuse or intrusion (breaches from the outside) by HIDS. It consults various log files, such as kernel, system, server, network and firewall, and compares these logs against an internal signature database for the attacks. Some of the HIDSs, such as UNIX and Linux HIDSs, use syslog. The logged events are separated depending on their severity level. An HIDS performs various functions such as filtering, analyzing logs, and re-tagging the anomalous messages.

The data integrity of the important files and executables can be verified by the HIDSs. It also checks a database that consists of sensitive files and a checksum for each file. The value of a checksum should match with the value of the related file. The IDS alerts the administrator even if a single checksum does not match with the value of the file.

In most of the cases, the HIDSs are incorporated within the host's OSs. Some of the characteristics of an HIDS are as follows:

- Monitors user privileges
- Provides an effective mechanism for detecting outside attacks

Some of the advantages of an HIDS are as follows:

- **Verifies success or failure of an attack:** Uses logs to measure whether or not an attack was successful.
- **Monitors specific system activities:** Monitors the activities of every user, even that of an administrator, while connected to the network. The changes made to the key system files and executables are monitored and detected as soon as they are made. HIDS, unlike an NIDS, can detect and stop the installation of Trojan horses and backdoors.
- **Detects attacks missed by the NIDS:** Detects attacks, such as attacks from the keyboard of a critical server that cannot be detected by an NIDS.
- **Well suited for encrypted and switched environments:** Provide greater visibility, as compared to an NIDS, in a switched and encrypted environment by residing on any number of critical hosts as per the requirements.
- **Near-real-time detection and response:** Offers real-time response if implemented correctly. Many current HIDSs receive a notification when there is a new log file entry. As soon as this entry is received, it gets processed immediately, thereby reducing the time between the attack recognition and response.

- **Requires no additional hardware:** Requires no additional hardware and can reside on an existing network infrastructure. Due to this feature, HIDSs are cost effective.

An HIDS runs as a service and examines the machine logs, system events and application interactions. It interacts with the logon audit and kernel audit files. The kernel audit files are used to process application interfaces.

Figure 17 shows how an HIDS interacts with an OS:

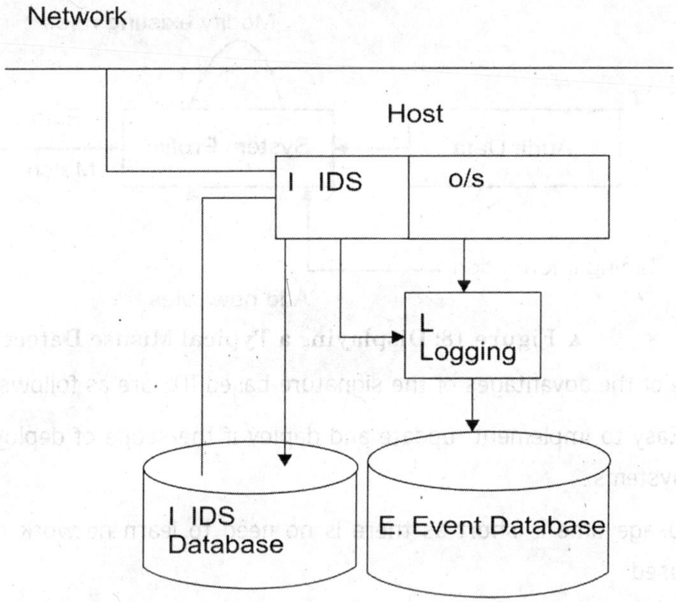

▲ **Figure 17: Showing the Interaction between an HIDS and an OS**

HIDSs also help in keeping checks on files, which inform system administrators about the status of the files that are altered by an attack. An HIDS detects an attack through either of the following mechanisms:

- Signature-based IDS
- Statistical anomaly based IDS

Let's now discuss both of these mechanisms in detail.

Signature-Based IDS

The signature-based IDS, also known as the knowledge-based IDS, compares the packets present on the network against a database of signatures or attributes from the known malicious threats. This process is similar to the process that is commonly used by antivirus software for detecting malware. There is always a short time period, known as lag, between a new threat and the signature for detecting that threat. During this lag, a new threat cannot be detected by IDS. Signature-based IDSs are characterized by low false alarm rates and are generally standardized and understandable by security personnel. An example of the signature-based IDS is the misuse-detection IDS. This IDS primarily focuses on evaluating attacks that are based on attack signatures and audit trails. It also helps in analyzing the system or network environment.

Figure 18 shows an example of misuse detection IDS:

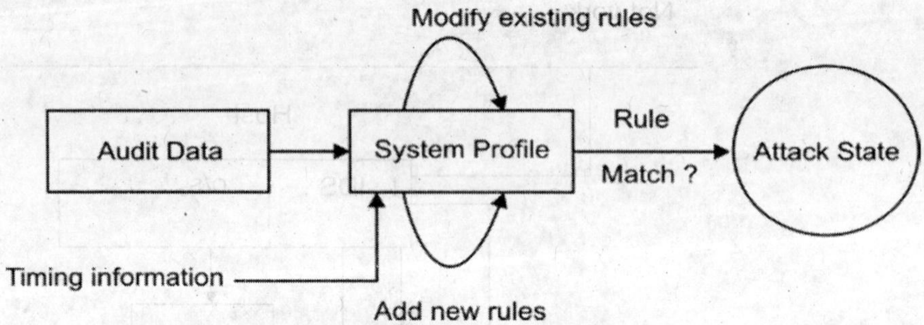

▲ **Figure 18: Displaying a Typical Misuse Detection System**

Some of the advantages of the signature-based IDS are as follows:

- Easy to implement, update and deploy if the scope of deployment is limited to small systems
- Usage time is short as there is no need to learn network behavior before it can be used
- The matching signature provides fewer false alarms as compared to other IDS methods
- Customized signatures of network administrators can be created according to the organization's security policy

Some of the disadvantages of the signature-based IDS are:

- It fails to characterize slow attacks that extend over a long period of time.
- It is unable to detect new threats. Only signatures that are stored in the database can be recognized.
- The IDS is resource-intensive. Continuous maintenance of knowledge database is required to keep the database accurate and protected from the vulnerabilities.

Statistical Anomaly Based IDS

Statistical anomaly based IDS is also known as behavior-based IDS. This IDS dynamically detects deviations arising from the behavior of the user and accordingly triggers an alarm. Using a statistical anomaly based IDS, network traffic can be monitored and compared against an established baseline. These baselines define commonly used bandwidth, types of protocols that are being used, and ports and devices that are used for inter-connection. The major concern with anomaly detection systems is that there should not be more than two threshold levels.

A block diagram of a typical anomaly detection system is shown in Figure 19:

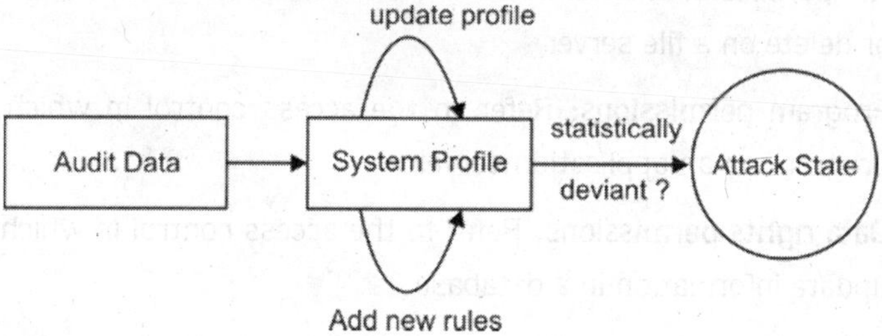

▲ **Figure 19: Showing a Typical Anomaly Detection System**

The blocks shown in Figure 19 represent the following different phases through which data passes in an anomaly detection system:

- **Audit data:** Refers to the phase during which an IDS collects data and defines the profile to be used by either the network or the host that is being monitored.
- **System profile:** Refers to the phase during which an IDS collects the samples of the system at a regular interval of time. The system samples include memory usage, network packet types, and CPU utilization.
- **Attack state:** Refers to the phase during which different attack types are detected.

Some of the advantages of statistical anomaly based IDSs are as follows:

- It is less dependent upon specific OSs as compared to signature-based IDS
- The system can dynamically adapt to new, unique, or original vulnerabilities

Some of the disadvantages of statistical anomaly-based IDSs are as follows:

- It will not detect an attack that does not significantly change the OS characteristics
- It might incorrectly detect a non-attack event that caused a momentary anomaly in the system
- It generates high false alarm rates

■ Understanding Access Control

Access control is a mechanism that defines and controls access rights for individuals who can use specific resources in the OS. In other words, you can say that access control is a security feature through which the system permits or revokes the right to access any data and resource in a system. The permission to access a resource is called authorization. Access control systems include:

- **File permissions:** Refer to the access control in which the user can create, read, edit, or delete on a file server
- **Program permissions:** Refer to the access control in which the user can execute a program on an application server
- **Data rights permissions:** Refer to the access control in which the user can retrieve or update information in a database

Let's learn about the identification and authentication.

Identification versus Authentication

Identification and authentication both are similar terms with a little difference, that is, identification refers to the process of labeling and recognizing a user, whereas authentication refers to the process of verifying whether the user is a valid user or not. These terms are used in access control, which means controlling the access of users over the network resources and information. In these processes, the user provides his/her credentials to a computer or a network, which identifies the user. If the user credentials are correct, the user gains access to the computers or network resources. However, if the user credentials are incorrect, the user's request to access the network resources is rejected. In this way, you can protect your network from unauthorized access and modification.

Authentication processes or methods are password based or PIN, smart card, token, or an identification device, and fingerprints or retinal pattern.

Let's discuss the single factor authentication (SFA) and authorization.

Authentication (Single Rule-Based Factor) and Authorization

SFA checks one set of values at a time; hence, it is the basic form of authentication. SFA implements authentication by using the combination of username and password. In the logon process, the usernames and passwords are used as a unique identifier. The username and password are unique identifiers for a logon process.

In the logon process, computer systems first identify the user by identification. Most of the systems identify the user by using the user ID and password. The information about user ID and password is passed to all the connections either as a plain text or in an encrypted form.

Then the logon process identifies the OS or the network.

The logon and password process is shown in Figure 20:

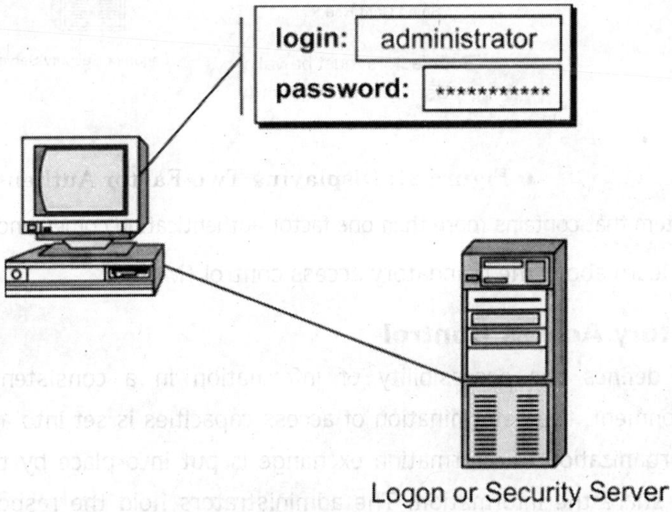

▲ **Figure 20: Displaying the Logon and Password Process**

In the logon process, the OS compares the username and password information to the stored information in the security server, and then accepts and denies the logon attempt.

The process in which more than one party authenticates each other is called mutual authentication. In mutual authentication, the client needs to prove its identity to a server, and the server needs to prove its identity to the client before any data communication on the client-to-server connection.

Let's discuss the multifactor authentication.

Multifactor Authentication

Authentication process that contains two or more access methods is called multifactor authentication. A system that uses smart card and password as authentication is called a two-factor authentication system. Figure 21 shows the two-factor authentication:

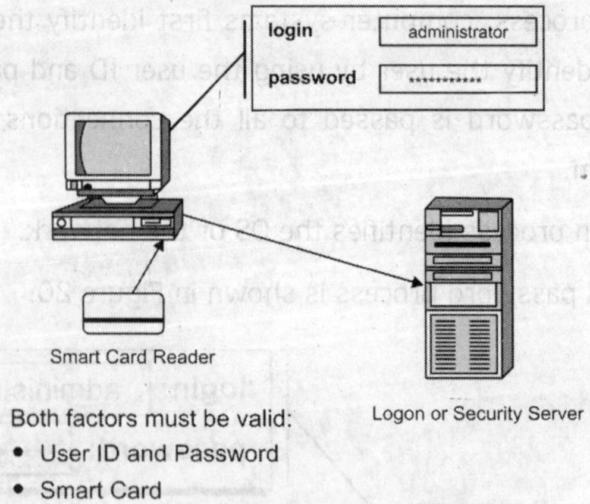

▲ **Figure 21: Displaying Two-Factor Authentication**

A system that contains more than one factor authentication comes under the multifactor system.

Let's learn about the mandatory access control (MAC).

Mandatory Access Control

MAC defines the accessibility of information in a consistent manner. In the MAC environment, the determination of access capacities is set into action beforehand. Unless the organization of information exchange is put into place by the administrators, users can't share the information. The administrators hold the responsibility for defining the changes in the information. They ensure the enforcement of stringent security measures.

To ensure effective operation of the MAC model, the perusal of the relationship existing between administrators and network designers must be done. The advantage offered by this model is its exhaustive functionality, enabling the detection and repair of security breaches. A well-designed MAC model allows outright control over the management of information, and if required, can lock down the network. The disadvantages accompanying the model are the integration of rigidness into it and the demand for the enactment of changes overtime. This model finds its applicability in the environments where the confidentiality of information is the crux of the matter.

Let's learn about the discretionary access control (DAC).

Discretionary Access Control

DAC model offers flexibility related to the exchange of information to the network users. It ensures dynamic exchange of information with other users. Despite the fact that this model offers a flexible environment, unauthorized information disclosure is always the likely possibility. Administrators struggle in the face of ensuring control over information access and the grant of access rights. The permission structure existing as "other" option with files in the Unix/Linux environment epitomizes the operability of DAC. The permission set in the Unix/Linux environment has been classified into three groups of user, i.e., owner, group, and other. The roles form the basis for associations of permissions between the owner and the group the respective owner belongs to, while those not falling under the purview of owner or the member of the owner's group come within the ambit of other. The permission set for this group is disparate with the other two, besides the exceptions of read, write, and execute.

Let's learn about the role-based access control (RBAC).

Role-Based Access Control

RBAC models put control over the information access from the viewpoint of organizational roles into perspective. The implementation of accessibility based on job function or responsibility is the gist of the RBAC model. The access to a specific information hinges upon the role incumbency. RBAC model offers flexibility, which is always greater than the MAC model, but less than the DAC model. The advantage that it incorporates is that it follows function-centric approach rather than individual centric. This model is appropriate in the environments exhibiting high turnover.

Let's learn about the rule-based access control.

Rule-Based Access Control

In rule-based access control, the decision making is dependent on the settings that have been saved into preconfigured security policies. These rules allow access to some people appearing in a list (an allow list) while deny access to others appearing in a different list (a true deny list). The list may contain usernames, IP addresses, or even domains. The operation of a rule-based model may carry out in concurrency with a role-based to further augment the flexibility.

2.4 Security Threats

There are numerous threats to security of applications and data. With the increasing use of the Internet and the advancing IT, applications are becoming increasingly vulnerable to threats that could be a malicious code, viruses, worms, etc.

Let us discuss some of the security threats in detail.

■ Viruses

A virus refers to piece of software that is designed and developed with the purpose of infecting a computer system and performs illicit operations. A virus infected system can hamper data stored on a hard drive, crash the OS, or get spread on a network. Some of the ways by which a virus gets transmitted to a system are:

- On using infected media, such as CDs or USB drives
- Through e-mails and accessing social websites
- As a part of another program

Different types of virus can be classified as follows:

- **Polymorphic:** Refers to the virus types that change from one form to another to avoid being detected. A system infected by a polymorphic virus displays a message and deletes the files available on the system. This virus involves the process of mutation which consists of encrypting its parts to avoid detection. Figure 22 shows polymorphic virus attack:

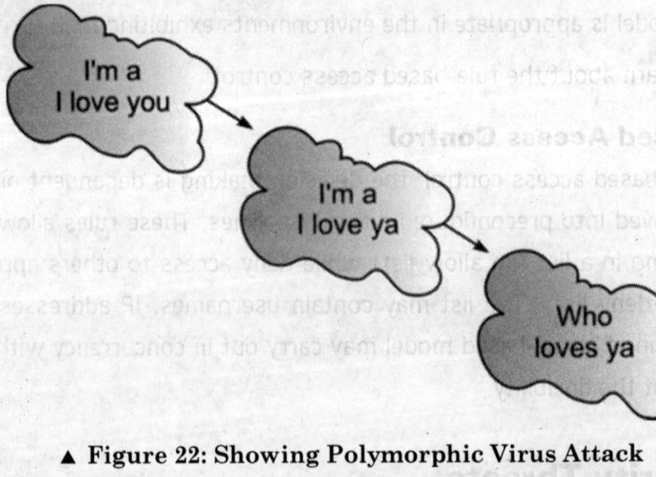

▲ **Figure 22: Showing Polymorphic Virus Attack**

- **Stealth:** Refers to a virus type that masks itself from application in order to avoid being detected. The stealth virus gets attached to the boot sector of a hard disk. The infected file is of different size than the original.

Figure 23 shows a stealth virus attack on the boot sector of a hard disk:

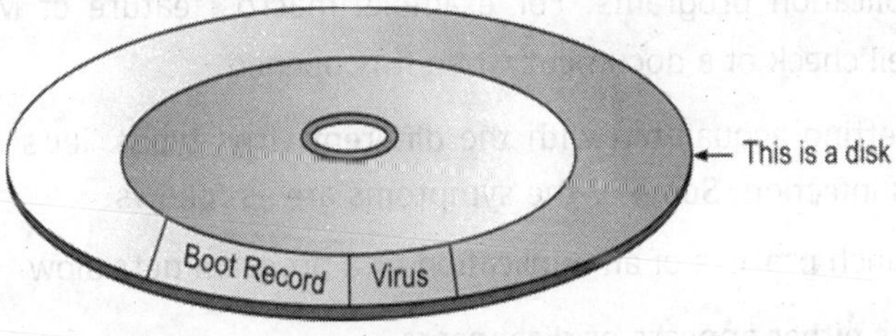

▲ **Figure 23: Showing Stealth Virus Attack**

- **Retroviruses:** Refer to the virus types that bypass installed antivirus software. The retrovirus is capable of making direct attack on an antivirus.
- **Multipartite:** Refers to a virus type that has the ability to react in multiple ways. The multipartite virus provides harm to a system in such a way that it infects boot sector and executable files. Figure 24 shows a multipartite virus attack:

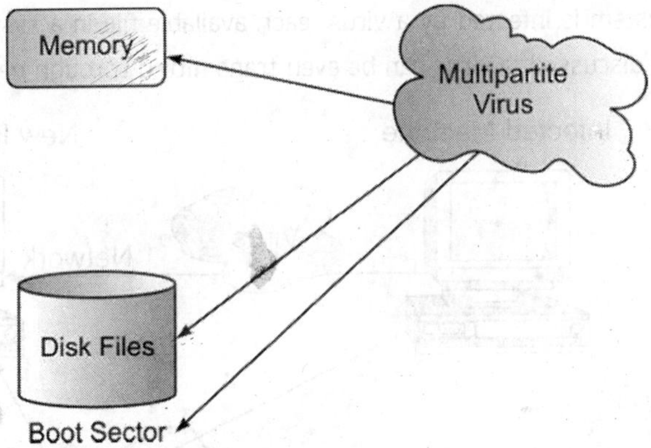

▲ **Figure 24: Showing Multipartite Virus Attack**

- **Armored:** Refers to a virus type that is difficult to detect. This virus type disables the virus debuggers or disassemblers from examining critical virus elements, as it is written in such a way that actual code designed to harm the computer is not directly visible.
- **Companion:** Refers to a virus type that gets spread by attaching itself with other programs. The companion virus when attached with legitimate programs gets saved with a different file extension and is saved in a temporary directory of a computer.
- **Phage:** Refers to a virus type that is responsible for modifications in other applications and programs. The phage virus harms the system in such a way that the only option to recover is to reinstall the infected programs.

- **Macro viruses:** Refer to the virus types that effect the enhancements available in application programs. For example, macros feature of MS Word enables automatic spell check of a document when it is opened.

After getting acquainted with the different virus types, let's get familiar with symptoms of virus infection. Some of the symptoms are as follows:

- Launch process of an application or a program gets slow
- Files either appears or disappears
- Size of the installed program gets changed automatically
- Interface of applications or programs might get change
- System gets shutdown or restart in an automatic manner
- Access to drives is restricted

The basic function of a virus is either to stop functioning of OS or spreading to other systems. When a system is infected by a virus, each available file in a system attaches itself with a virus. As already discussed, a virus can be even transmitted through network, as shown in Figure 25:

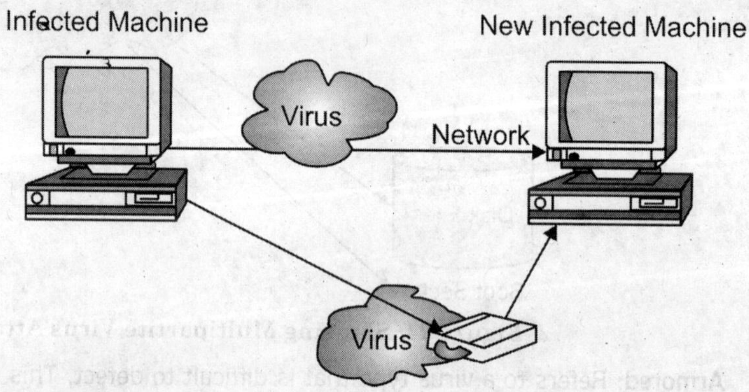

▲ **Figure 25: Showing Virus Transmission over a Network**

It is known that the other common method of spreading virus is through e-mail. When an e-mail is sent through an infected system, a virus file gets attached to an e-mail and transmits the virus on the system on which the e-mail is received, as shown in Figure 26:

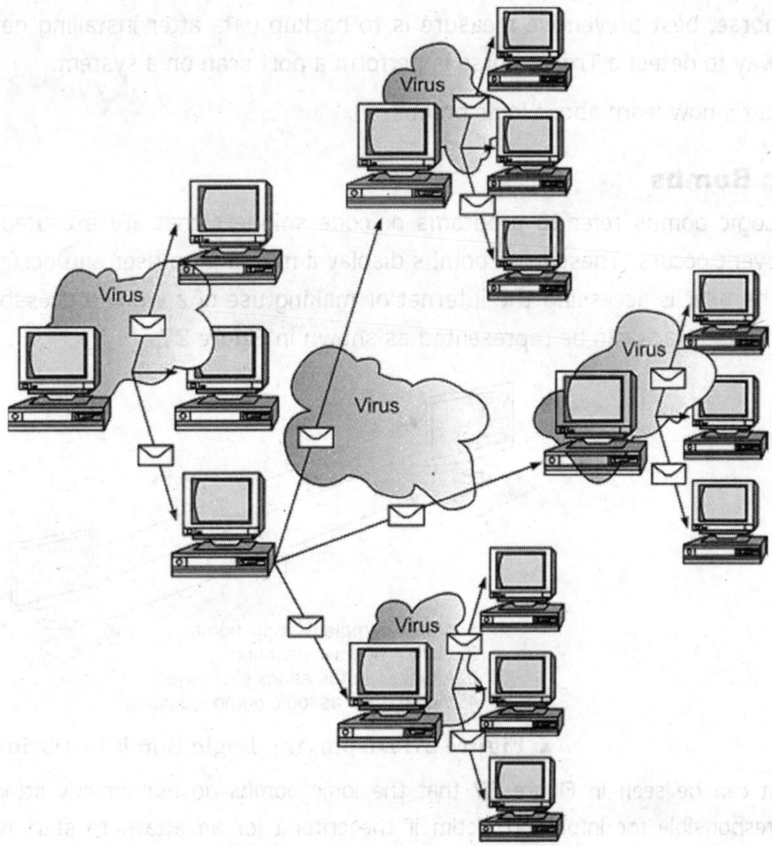

▲ **Figure 26: Showing Virus Transmission through E-mail**

In addition to these, virus can be easily transmitted to systems using USB drives. Apart from these, new viruses and threats are released frequently on timely basis, where many of them are just hoaxes. Some popular virus hoaxes are the Good Time and Irina viruses. Moving further, in addition to hoax, spam is also one of the main areas of concern. Spams are not considered to be a virus or hoax; they are referred as unwanted and unsolicited mails. There are two forms of SPAM, namely, Spam over Instant Messaging (SPIM) and Spam over Internet Telephony (SPIT).

Let's now get familiar with Trojan horses.

■ Trojan Horses

Trojan horses can be defined as programs that are transmitted to a system under disguise of any legitimate application or program, such as an attachment to a program or as part of an installation process. During installation, either a backdoor is created or the original program gets replaced by a Trojan horse. Due to difficulty in detection of a Trojan horse, best preventive measure is to backup data after installing new software. Another way to detect a Trojan horse is perform a port scan on a system.

Let's now learn about logic bombs.

■ Logic Bombs

Logic bombs refer to programs or code snippets that are executed when a pre-defined event occurs. These logic bombs display a message to user and occur at time when either the user is accessing the Internet or making use of a word processor application. A logic bomb attack can be represented as shown in Figure 27:

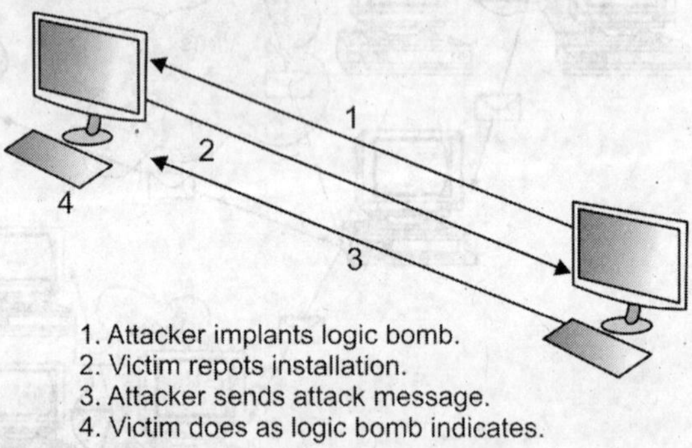

▲ **Figure 27: Displaying Logic Bomb Initiation**

It can be seen in Figure 27 that the logic bombs do not directly attack; however, they are responsible for informing victim if the criteria for an attack to start have been met. In the preceding figure, a message is being sent by a logic bomb that logic bombs are successfully loaded. This successful loading results in attacks, such as Distributed Denial of Service (DDoS).

Let's now learn about worms.

■ Worms

Worms can be defined as threats that are self-sufficient to replicate themselves and do not need any host application to get transmitted. Moreover, they are also capable of delivering a virus to a system. Earlier, the worms used to reside in the RAM of a target computer; however, nowadays, they can make use of TCP/IP, e-mail, or Internet services.

■ Antivirus Software

Antivirus software can be referred to as an application that can be used as a primary method for preventing malicious codes and viruses. The antivirus software is installed on a system and performs scan process to detect for virus, Trojan horse, or worm. In addition to these, the latest antivirus also scans cookies for harmful threats. Figure 28 shows an antivirus software interface:

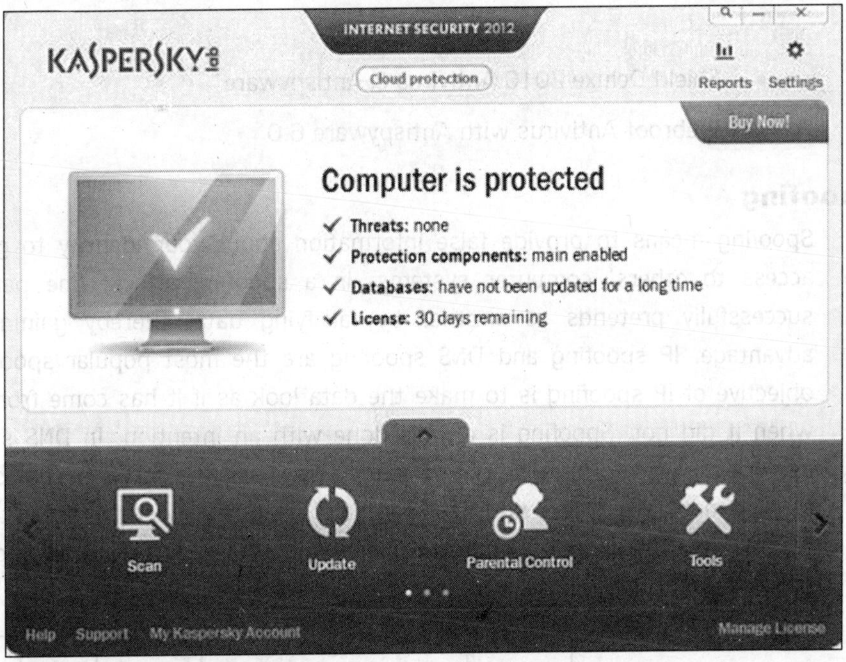

▲ **Figure 28: Showing Quick Heal Antivirus Interface**

Some of the ways to avoid getting infected by a virus is to maintain a database for all possible viruses and their solutions along with awareness of users. The following are several approaches to deploy antivirus software on your network:

- Placing antivirus client software on each client computer system in your network, and then an antivirus server automatically updates the antivirus client's software on a regular basis.
- Installing antivirus software on your mail server to scan all incoming mail for viruses and remove them before your network users ever see them.

The following is the list of some of the top antivirus software:

- Norton Antivirus 2010
- McAfee virus Scan Plus 2010
- Trend Micro Antivirus Internet Security 2010
- ESET NOD32 Antivirus
- BitDefender Antivirus 2010
- Kaspersky Antivirus 2010
- CA Antivirus Plus 2010

- Shield Deluxe 2010 Antivirus & Antispyware
- Webroot Antivirus with Antispyware 6.0

■ Spoofing

Spoofing means to provide false information about your identity to gain unauthorized access to others' computer systems. In a spoofing attack, one person or program successfully pretends as another by falsifying data, thereby gaining an illegitimate advantage. IP spoofing and DNS spoofing are the most popular spoofing attacks. The objective of IP spoofing is to make the data look as if it has come from a trusted host, when it did not. Spoofing is always done with an intention. In DNS spoofing, the DNS server is given information about a name server and the server assumes this information as legitimate, when it is not. This can send users to a website other than the one they wanted to visit. Figure 29 shows a spoofing attack occurring as a part of the logon process on a computer network:

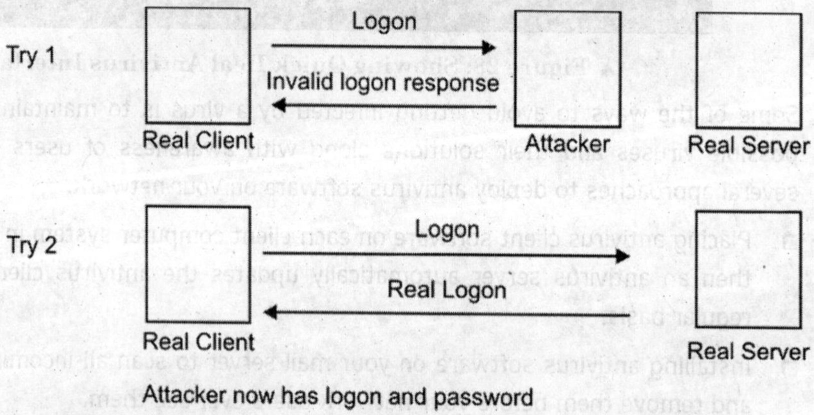

▲ **Figure 29: Displaying a Spoofing Attack during Logon**

The different types of spoofing are as follows:

- ❐ **IP spoofing:** Refers to connection hijacking through a fake IP address. IP spoofing is the action of masking a computer IP address so that it looks like it is authentic. During this masking process, the fake IP address sends what appears to be a malevolent message coupled with an IP address that appears to be authentic and trusted. In IP spoofing, IP headers are masked through a form of TCP in which spoofers discover and then manipulate vital information contained in the IP header, such as IP address and source and destination information.

- **Content spoofing:** Refers to a hacking technique used to lure a user on to a website that looks legitimate, but is actually an elaborate copy. Hackers looking to spoof content use dynamic HTML and frames to create a website with the expected URL and a similar appearance, and then prompt the user for personal information. Content spoofing is also common with e-mail alerts, account notifications, etc.
- **Caller ID spoofing:** Refers to the practice of causing the telephone network to display a number on the recipient's caller ID display which is not that of the actual originating station. The term is commonly used to describe situations in which the motivation is considered malicious by the speaker or writer. Just as e-mail spoofing can make it appear that a message came from any e-mail address the sender chooses, caller ID spoofing can make a call appear to have come from any phone number the caller wishes.
- **E-mail spoofing:** Refers to the forgery of an e-mail header so that the message appears to have originated from someone or somewhere other than the actual source. Distributors of spam often use spoofing in an attempt to get recipients to open, and possibly even respond to, their solicitations. Spoofing can be used legitimately. Classic examples of senders who might prefer to disguise the source of the e-mail include a sender reporting mistreatment by a spouse to a welfare agency or a "whistle-blower" who fears retaliation. However, spoofing anyone other than yourself is illegal in some jurisdictions. E-mail spoofing is possible because Simple Mail Transfer Protocol (SMTP), the main protocol used in sending e-mail, does not include an authentication mechanism. Although an SMTP service extension (specified in IETF RFC 2554) allows an SMTP client to negotiate a security level with a mail server, this precaution is not often taken. If the precaution is not taken, anyone with the requisite knowledge can connect to the server and use it to send messages. To send spoofed e-mail, senders insert commands in headers that will alter message information. It is possible to send a message that appears to be from anyone, anywhere, saying whatever the sender wants it to say. Thus, someone could send spoofed e-mail that appears to be from you with a message that you didn't write.

Trapdoor

Backdoor attacks, which are also known as back door, have two different meanings. While the original term backdoor attack defines troubleshooting and developer hooking into a system, the back door term is referred to as gaining access to a network. The backdoor attack lets malicious user to enter illicit code at the time of its execution. Moreover, a backdoor attack is primarily an access or a modification attack. However, it requires a user ID and password to gain administrative privileges. Some of the tools that are used to create backdoor attacks are Back Orifice and NetBus. Figure 30 shows an attack caused by using the backdoor program:

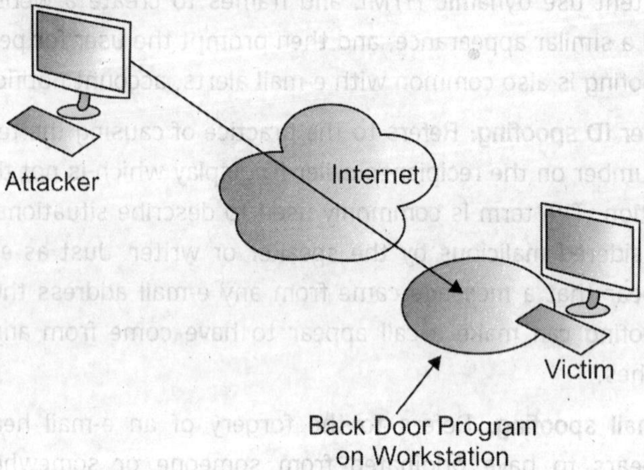

▲ **Figure 30: Showing Backdoor Attack**

▪ E-mail Virus

E-mail virus is one of the most common, highly effective, and potentially harmful programs forwarded as e-mail attachments to the e-mail users. E-mail viruses normally get activated as soon as you open them. These viruses are seemed to cause a lot of potential damages, including destruction of files on the computer system and re-mailing of the attachment to all the contacts in the list of the recipient.

You can defend yourself from e-mail viruses by taking the following measures:

1. Never opening attachments that are received from unknown senders or the attachments that you have no knowledge about
2. Having antivirus software installed on your system so that the attachments can be scanned before you can open them

In certain cases, firewalls activated by businesses have been successful in filtering out e-mails that might have some harmful contents. However, firewalls are not as effective technique as antiviruses.

▪ Macro Virus

A macro virus is a code that infects an application running on the system and then causes several actions to be performed with the start of the infected application or at the time of the infect application being triggered by some other activity. Most of the macro viruses hardly cause any harm, except incidents such as comic texts being inserted undesirably at some points of a line being written in a Microsoft Word document. These viruses are often forwarded in the form of an attachment to e-mails.

■ Malicious Software

A computer program is a sequence of symbols and instructions used to achieve a desired functionality. It is termed malicious when the sequence of instructions is used to intentionality have adverse effects on the computer system. This type of code is called **malicious code**, which is intended to harm, disrupt, or circumvent computer systems and network functions.

Malicious code is a new kind of threat in the form of an auto-executable application. It can be in the form of scripting languages, such as Java Applets, ActiveX controls, or various new programming languages designed to enhance Web pages.

Figure 31 shows the classification of malicious code:

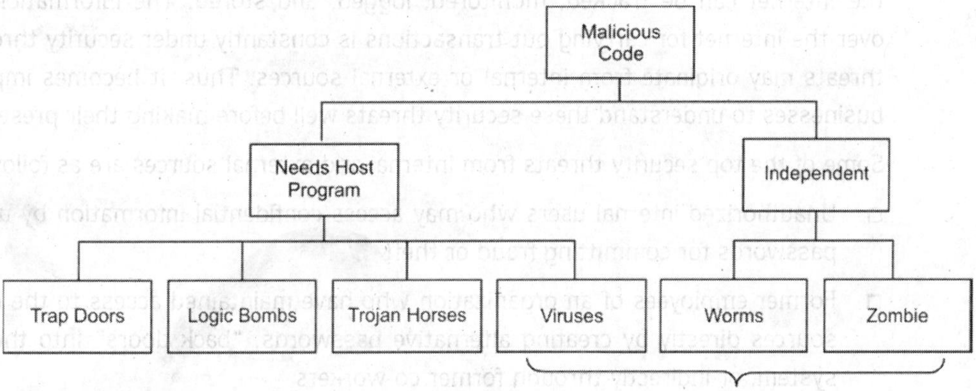

▲ Figure 31: Displaying the Classification of Malicious Code

Malicious code can be categorized into the following types:

- ❑ **Code that causes access violations**: Refers to the category of malicious code that tries to delete, steal, alter, or execute unauthorized files. It can steal passwords, files, and other confidential data.
- ❑ **Code that enables DoS attacks:** Refers to the category of malicious code that prevents the user from using the system. It may destroy the files that are open at the time of the attack.

Malicious codes are also called programmed threats. These threats include viruses, Trojan horses, logic bombs, and worms.

■ Denial-of-Service Attacks

DoS attack refers to an attempt that restricts access to the computer resources to its intended users or organizations. IP spoofing is almost used to defend against one of the most difficult attacks known as DoS. An attacker is not concerned with the proper transmission of packets; he/she is only concerned to occupy the resources and bandwidth. In addition, the attacker wishes to flood the victim with as many packets as possible in a short span of time. To increase the effectiveness of attack, the attackers spoof source IP addresses to make the process of tracing and stopping DoS as difficult as possible. Two types of DoS are ping of death and buffer flow. While the ping of death is responsible for system crash by sending large Internet Control Message Protocol (ICMP) packets than the system can handle, buffer overflow is responsible for putting more data on a buffer than it can hold.

2.5 Security Threats to E-Commerce

Internet, being a public domain, is open to all. Each and every transaction that occurs on the Internet can be tracked, monitored, logged, and stored. The information is shared over the Internet for carrying out transactions is constantly under security threats. These threats may originate from internal or external sources. Thus, it becomes imperative for businesses to understand these security threats well before making their presence online.

Some of the top security threats from internal and external sources are as follows:

- Unauthorized internal users who may access confidential information by using stolen passwords for committing fraud or theft
- Former employees of an organization who have maintained access to the information sources directly by creating alternative passwords, "back doors" into the computer system, or indirectly through former co-workers
- Weak access points in information infrastructure and security that can expose company information and trade secrets
- Management that undermines security may be the greatest risk to e-commerce
- Contractors, partners, consultants, etc. who take benefit of even limited access to important systems.

An increase in the sale of various antivirus software and subscription to e-mail virus protection indicate that people are increasingly becoming aware of these threats. Businesses can make it mandatory for their service providers and merchants to have firewalls, encryption, as well as testing and access policies as a condition of doing business with them. This will go a long way in providing a solid ground to e-commerce for flourishing.

Let us now learn about e-cash and e-payment scheme.

2.6 E-Cash and Electronic Payment System

The growth and widespread adoption of e-commerce as a new medium of trade and marketing by both large and small business organizations has emphasized the need of maintaining privacy, security, and safety in conducting online transactions. To ensure safe, error-free, and secure transactions, various methods of online payment have been adopted by the business organizations. Initially, in the traditional method of trading, the mode of payment was cash, cheque, and draft. However, in case of e-commerce, the two commonly used methods of making payment online are e-cash and e-payment. These two modes of payment allow the trading parties to conduct secure online transactions.

■ E-Cash

E-cash refers to electronic transfer of money in the form of a block of data representing money that is transferred online. The electronic transfer of money involves computer networks, Internet, and the digitally stored value system. E-cash bears a digital signature for authentication purposes and can be either sent over a network as data from sender to receiver or in the form of tokens exchanged for actual money transfer. E-cash is generally stored on computers or mobile devices in the form of software wallet programs. When a user needs to make a transaction, the wallet programs communicate with the bank or the e-cash issuer. The bank authenticates the user and after the authentication process is completed, it transfers the requested e-cash to the customer. The e-cash can then be paid to the seller using the wallet programs to complete the transaction. The e-cash company in turn charges a small amount from the merchants for each transaction.

Figure 32 shows how the e-cash mechanism works:

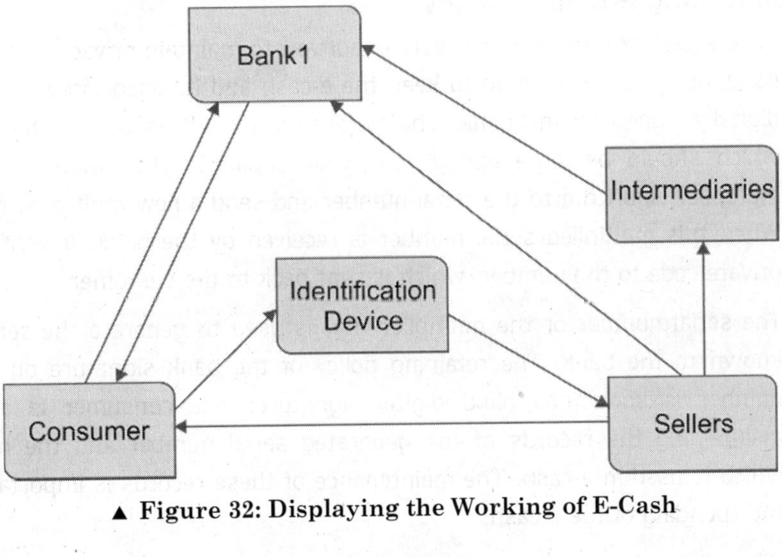

▲ **Figure 32: Displaying the Working of E-Cash**

Figure 32 shows the relationship between the consumer, bank, and seller involved in an e-cash transaction. The next section discusses about the problems associated with e-cash.

Describing the Problems in E-cash

With the use of e-cash, the transaction of money between consumers and sellers has become very fast; however, there are also some problems associated with its usage. The major problem is that the double spending of money by a consumer cannot be prevented or detected. Double spending is a mode in which there is a possibility to spend a token money twice. The bank provides some form of money as digital token or token money, and after spending this token, the consumer can reuse this token in another transaction. This is possible because after spending the token in a transaction, the token does not remove the data from its original holder.

The aforementioned problem can be solved partly by providing unique serial numbers to e-cash. The seller can verify the serial numbers with the bank to ensure that the serial number has not been used previously in any other transaction. The bank can match the serial number of the e-cash provided by the seller with other e-cash transactions. With the help of this validation process, the bank can prevent fraud transactions. In case of double spending, the banks can identify the token that is being reused to make a transaction.

Another problem with e-cash is money laundering, which is specified as an illegal transaction while generating an asset or a value services, such as tax evasion or false accounting.

Maintaining E-Cash Privacy

In an e-cash transaction, it is very important to maintain privacy. Therefore, the bank and its customers are required to keep the e-cash and its associated serial number, which is digitally signed by the bank. The serial number is selected by the customer randomly, which should be large enough to avoid duplicity. The customer can also apply the multiplier algorithm to the serial number and send a new multiplied number to the bank. When this multiplied serial number is received by the bank, it verifies it and assigns a private code to the number, which is sent back to the customer.

The serial number or the multiplier that is used to generate the serial number is never known to the bank. The retaining policy of the bank signature on the unknown serial number is known as blind digital signature. The consumer is also responsible for maintaining the records of the generated serial number and the multiplier algorithm, which is used in e-cash. The maintenance of these records is important to keep track on the spending of the e-cash.

When a consumer uses this e-cash to purchase goods, the serial number of the e-cash is transferred to the respective bank, which verifies the generated serial number and authenticates the consumer who is using the e-cash for the transaction. The bank stores the records of the transactions that are made using e-cash and uses these records to verify whether or not the e-cash is spent more than once.

Avoiding Double-Spending in E-cash

To avoid double-spending in e-cash, the bank has to maintain a record of the serial numbers of all incoming e-cash transactions. The process of identifying double-spent e-cash requires the use of non-editable software and cryptography algorithm. This implies that the identification details of a consumer, once maintained in the software for authentication purposes, cannot be edited further. The consumer's identity can be held in the software by encrypting the identity with a random secret key generated for each e-cash.

To prevent the double spending of e-cash, this encryption process is based on the two-part lock mechanism in which the parts of the lock can be opened with the secret key to determine the identity of the consumer. While transferring the e-cash to the seller, the identity of the consumer is also sent in the encrypted format. The seller then adds the information regarding the consumer to the e-cash, where one part of the two-part lock is opened up with the consumer's identity. Then the seller checks the e-cash with the bank to ensure that the money is not spent more than once. The bank, after carrying out the required verification, deposits the amount into the sellers account and stores the half-locked information of the consumer.

If a consumer tries to double-spend the e-cash with another seller, then the seller adds the half-locked part of the two-part lock and sends it to the bank for checking whether the money is double-spent or not. The bank then unlocks the other part of the two-part lock and combines both the parts together that reveal the consumer's identity. The same process is applied in case of sellers.

■ Electronic Payment Systems

There are several organizations that provide services for online monetary transactions. These services are called e-payment schemes, which are as follows:

- **Secure Electronic Payment Protocol/Secure Electronic Transaction (SEPP/SET)**: Uses digital signatures and user authentication for secured electronic payments. SEPP is an open specification for secure electronic payments over the Internet developed by the International Business Machines (IBM), Netscape, General Telephone & Electronics Corporation (GTE), CyberCash, and MasterCard. SEPP provides a usage of the Internet Keyed Payments Protocol (iKP) that is intended for HTTP transactions and adapted to bank card payments. SEPP messages are transmitted using Multipurpose Internet Mail Extensions (MIME) and are based on common ASN.1 syntax.

- **Secure courier electronic payment scheme:** Refers to the earliest payment scheme for secure payment between the users of banks and the Quicken home-banking program that uses SEPP. Secure courier scheme encrypts data and authenticates the individual consumers and the buyers at the time of electronic transactions. Many organizations are working with MasterCard, such as Netscape, IBM, Open Market, and GTE Corporation, and planning to use this technology for business.
- **CheckFree wallet:** Refers to an electronic payment service that enables consumers and buyers to make transactions in an easy and safe manner over the Internet. CheckFree wallet, based on the client/server architecture, uses the public-private key encryption technology that uses Rivest Shamir Adleman (RSA) data security and a large 768-bit key to secure sensitive payment data. CheckFree uses several mechanisms, such as CyberCash, Netscape's SSL, and VeriSign's Digital Identification (ID), for developing this system.
- **CyberCash:** Refers to a digital cash software system that guarantees payment by the buyers before the delivery of goods. CyberCash provides a secured mechanism to send the credit card information over the Internet as it encrypts the credit-card-related information. It uses a third party decryption for decrypting the transaction.

  Figure 33 shows the CyberCash e-payment process:

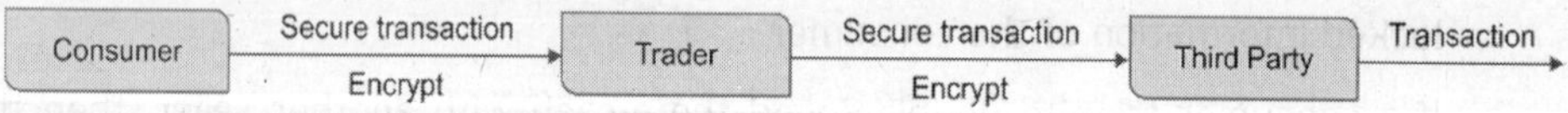

▲ **Figure 33: Displaying the CyberCash E-Payment Process**

- **VeriSign:** Refers to a technology that authenticates users by verifying the digital signature. IBM introduced the concept of digital ID into its Web browser and Internet connection Secure Server for Advanced Interactive eXecutive (AIX) and OS (OS)/2. IBM also adopted digital ID in its InfoMarket publishing network and clearinghouse.
- **DigiCash:** Refers to the e-cash based software that provides complete privacy. This type of system is currently used by Netherlands DigiCash NV. DigiCash enables the consumers to purchase goods over the Internet without using a credit card.

  The use of this kind of software where cash can be loaded into smart cards for electronic purchases are encouraged due to the threat of privacy loss. The greatest benefit of DigiCash is that it enables the organization to hold larger amount of money than credit cards.

2.7 Credit/Debit/Smart Cards

The evolution of credit card is also an important development in the banking sector. The person who owns a credit card can spend money whenever or wherever required within the limits fixed by the respective bank in which he/she holds an account. Credit card is similar to a postpaid card in which after reaching the given limit or completion of the due duration, the customer has to pay the credited amount. On the contrary, the debit cards are similar to prepaid cards, that is, some amount of money is deposited in the customer's account. Whenever the person uses the debit card to purchase something, the exact amount is deducted from the customer's bank account through Internet banking. To use a debit card, a person has to open an account with the bank that provides the debit card. A Personal Identification Number (PIN) is also issued to each customer along with the debit card. Whenever the debit card is used, the customer is identified by that PIN. When the customer purchases an item, he/she has to provide the PIN and the Internet security management authenticates that PIN. In this mode, a customer can never overspend as the transaction will be automatically aborted once the expenditure reaches its specified balance.

The smart card is a standard credit card-sized plastic card with an embedded microchip containing integrated circuits. It is often called an electronic wallet and provides not only memory capacity, but also computational capability capable of processing data. Smart cards can hold a large amount of information, ranging from personal to professional, such as medical health information and the information regarding any transaction made by the owner. The magnetic stripe of a smart card can store several hundred times more data than a conventional card. In addition, it is more reliable and secure than credit or debit cards and can perform tasks, such as authentication, identification, data storage, and application processing.

Let's now learn about e-commerce in India.

Information security plays an important role in the growth of e-commerce. It can be defined as a set of rules and regulations that the users follow online to ensure that the information they provide is not misused in any way. In other words, information security implies protection of information from illegal access or modification. For it to be successful, e-commerce must ensure the following factors:

- **Privacy:** The information provided by a user must be secured from other unknown users
- **Integrity:** The information sent by the user must not be tampered or altered

- **Authentication:** The sender and receiver of information must prove their identities to each another.
- **Non-repudiation:** It is the proof that the information was indeed received

2.8 Digital Signature

A digital signature or digital signature scheme is a mathematical approach used for authenticating a digital message or a document. Whenever a digital signature is assigned to a message, the recipient believes that the message is created by a known sender and has not been altered during transmission. Digital signatures are generally used in software distribution and financial transactions. Whenever a message is sent through an insecure network, an assurance that the message is sent by a claimed sender is given to the receiver through a properly implemented digital signature. The digital signatures are not much different from the traditional handwritten signatures. To standardize the use of digital signature, different organizations, such as the United States Government Printing Office (GPO), are publishing as well as releasing the electronic budgets. There are two main reasons for using digital signature, which are as follows:

- **Authenticity:** Refers to authenticating the sender and receiver. The use of digital signature authenticates the sources from where the message has been received, that is, it verifies the authenticity of the sender. Whenever the digital signature is associated with a specific user, it is used to identify the sender of the message because the authenticity of the sender/receiver is very important in the context of financial transactions. For example, in an online banking system, after a particular transaction, if a bank sends request to make changes in an account, the central office first checks the digital signature for authenticity of the message. If the central office is not convinced that the message is sent from the authorized bank, then it may not act on the request.
- **Security:** Assures that the messages are delivered securely without any security threats. This assures the sender and the receiver of a message that the message has not been altered by any unauthorized sources during transmission. Initially, you have learned about the process of encrypting the message to prevent its unauthorized access. However, the encryption process can only hide the contents of the message, which implies that the message is not being altered. In case of digital signatures, if any alteration is made in the message, the digital signature becomes invalid.

■ Requirements of Digital Signature System

A digital signature is a block of code which ensures that any data that is received originates from a specific user. It is used to simulate the security properties of a signature in digital form. You can use a digital signature when you want to distribute data and assure the recipient that the received data indeed comes from you. Signing data does not alter the data; it simply generates a digital signature string that you can send with the data. The benefit of using digital signatures is that they provide authentication and integrity to the messages sent. Authentication of data ensures that it is received from a trusted source, and integrity of data ensures that the received data has not been tampered during transmission.

■ Components of Digital Signature

Digital signatures are primarily used for the purpose of identity verification, user validation, and document authentication. These activities are subject to high-level security vulnerabilities, especially on the Internet. It is important for us to known the components of digital signatures so that we could understand the way it provides security.

A digital signature consists of the following components:

- **Name:** Refers to the name of the individual or organization. This is the necessary component and the rest of the components are optional. It is an important component as it prevents other individuals or organizations from being assigned with the same name.
- **Contact details:** Refer to the full contact details of the individual or organization, including e-mail address, telephone number, and other contact details.
- **Public key:** Refers to the public key of the individual or organization. This works as your secret identification number and is a part of the verification process. The signature also includes the expiry date of the public key that indicates the duration for which the digital signature is valid.
- **Serial number:** Refers to the serial number of the individual or organization that is used for digital identification.
- **Digital signature of the Certification Authority (CA):** Refers to the digital signature of the CA, which is a third party that has issued the digital certificate to the individual or organization.

■ Technical Issues

Digital signatures use 'public key cryptography'. They employ an algorithm that uses two different but mathematically related 'keys'; the first key is for creating a digital signature and is called the private key. It is known only to the signer. On the other hand, the second key is for verifying a digital signature. It is called the public key. When many people want to verify a signer's digital signature, the public key must be made available to all of them. Computer equipment and software are collectively called "asymmetric cryptosystem."

Use of digital signatures usually involves two processes, namely, digital signature creation and digital signature verification. Digital signature creation is performed by the signer. It uses a hash result which is computed from the signed message and the given private key. This hash result is unique.

Digital signature verification is performed by the receiver of the digital signature. A digital signature is verified by computing a new hash result of the original message using the same hash function that was used to create the digital signature. With the help of the public key and the new hash result thus obtained, the verifier checks:

1. Whether the digital signature was created using the corresponding private key.
2. Whether the newly computed hash result match with the original hash result. There are a number of asymmetric cryptosystems available in the market and they employ different algorithms and procedures to create and verify digital signatures. However, their overall pattern of operation is the same. The processes of creating a digital signature and verifying it satisfy many legal requirements because of the following reasons:
   - **Signer authentication:** A signer is verified by comparing the public and private key pair of a digital signature with that of an identified signer. If the match is found, the message is attributed to the signer. Thus, a digital signature cannot be forged unless the signer loses control of the private key either by losing it or divulging it.
   - **Message authentication:** The digital signatures also verify the signed message by comparing the hash results made during the signing and verification. They are able to authenticate the messages with greater accuracy than the paper signatures.
   - **Affirmative act:** Creating a digital signature requires the signer to use his/her private key. This alerts the signer to the fact that he/she is carrying out a transaction which may have legal consequences.
   - **Accuracy:** The creation and verification of a digital signature have proven to be quite accurate and is still a high level of assurance that the digital signature is genuinely the signer's.

Legal Issues

While making transactions on the Internet, you are potentially exposed to a number of legal frameworks simultaneously because you are entering into agreements with customers located anywhere in the world. In addition to this, a number of companies and consumers are still unaware of the legal constraints they may encounter by entering into electronic transactions.

Some major applications of digital signatures are as follows:

- Filing of income tax online
- Filing of license applications online
- Using digital signatures in banks and financial institutions
- Transferring funds from one bank to another in real time
- Booking railways tickets online
- Using digital signatures in e-procurement

2.9 Cryptography and Encryption

Cryptography ensures secure transfer of data over an unsecured network, such as the Internet. To ensure secure transmission, data is sent in such a way that it looks completely different from the original data. In cryptographic terms, data that is to be secured is called plaintext or cleartext and the data after encryption is called ciphertext. The process of converting a plaintext into ciphertext is called encryption, and the process of regenerating the plaintext from the ciphertext is called decryption.

A sender uses a key to encrypt a piece of data, which is then transmitted to the intended recipient. When the intended recipient receives the encrypted data, the recipient decrypts the data using a key. The key to encrypt and decrypt the data is decided prior to encrypting the data. This implies that if a user (including the recipient) does not have the pre-determined key, then the user cannot decrypt the data. Therefore, it is essential for the intended recipient to have the right key; otherwise, it is almost impossible to decrypt the received encrypted data. In this process, it is necessary that the data is transferred through a lossless channel (the channel using which the data is not lost during transmission) and there is a way for the receiver to decrypt the encrypted data and regenerate the original data. A graphical representation of how data is encrypted and decrypted is shown in Figure 34:

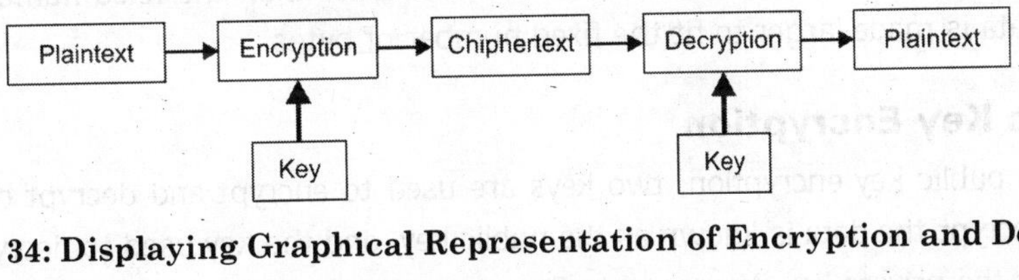

▲ **Figure 34: Displaying Graphical Representation of Encryption and Decryption**

The process of encrypting and decrypting data is done by using the following two encryption techniques:

- Private key (or secret key) encryption
- Public key encryption

Private Key Encryption

In private key (also known as secret key) encryption, a single key, called private key, is used for both encryption and decryption of data. The key is shared between the sender and the intended recipient, but is hidden from the remaining users on the network. The sender uses the private key to encrypt the data and then sends the encrypted data to the intended recipient over the network. When the intended recipient receives the encrypted data, the recipient uses the same key to decrypt the data. The sender and recipient both need to use the same key to encrypt and decrypt the data; any other key will not serve the purpose. Note that the sender and the intended recipient need to know the private key to be used for encryption and decryption. The sender and the intended recipient can share the private key by generating the key at the sender's end, encrypting it using publickey encryption, and sending it to the intended recipient. The need for sharing the key between the sender and the receiver of a message is the most vulnerable aspect of secret key encryption as the key can be disclosed to a hacker during the transmission of data. Note that the length of the secret key determines the strength of the encryption, that is, encryption that uses a longer key is more difficult to break than the one that uses a smaller key.

Secret key encryption is also known as symmetric encryption as encryption and decryption use the same key. The cryptography algorithms used for secret key (or symmetric) encryptions are known as symmetric algorithms. These algorithms are quite fast and therefore are suitable for encrypting and decrypting large amounts of data. Most of the symmetric algorithms are block ciphers as these algorithms encrypt a single block of data at a time. Block ciphers take a block of fixed number of bytes of the data and generate an output block of encrypted data. The fixed number of bytes that the block ciphers take may differ from one block cipher to another. For example, one block cipher may take an input block of 8 bytes and another may take an input block of 16 bytes. If the entire data is larger than this fixed number of bytes, then a block cipher encrypts one block at a time. However, if the data is smaller than the fixed number of bytes, then the data is made larger to fit the fixed number of bytes.

Public Key Encryption

In public key encryption, two keys are used to encrypt and decrypt data. The key used to encrypt the data is known as the public key, and the key used to decrypt the data is known as the private key. You need to first generate the public and private keys to use public key encryption. The public key is then made available to anybody who wants to send data. The sender can use the public key to encrypt the data and send the encrypted data to you. When you receive the encrypted data, you need to use the private key, which remains hidden from the sender, to decrypt the data. The public and private keys are related to each other in such a way that the data encrypted with a public key can be decrypted by using only the correct private key.

In publickey encryption, you need to first generate the public and private key pair on the systems of the two users who need to share data with each other in an encrypted form. When the sender and receiver need to authenticate and exchange data, they send their public keys to one another; however, they keep their private keys secret. The sender uses the receiver's public key to encrypt the data and send the encrypted data to the receiver, who, on receiving the encrypted data, uses the private key for decrypting the data.

■ Understanding Cryptanalysis

Cryptanalysis is the study of different methods to decrypt some encrypted data without the use of the decryption key. In other words, cryptanalysis is the science of retrieving plaintext from the ciphertext without the knowledge of the key or algorithm. It makes use of mathematics, probability, and powerful computing resources. It also requires some intuition, guesswork and general knowledge of the encrypted data. The person that performs cryptanalysis is called cryptanalyst. Cryptanalysis is the opposite of cryptography. In cryptography, the data is secured by encrypting it, whereas in cryptanalysis, attacks are performed on the data to uncover it.

Cryptanalysis involves weakening of ciphertext so that plaintext can be retrieved from it. The cryptanalyst tries to find a fault in the design or implementation of the cipher (the method used to encrypt data) so that the number of keys required in a brute force attack can be reduced. For example, if the data is encrypted with a symmetric-key algorithm that uses a key length of 128 bits, then a brute force attack would require trying all 2^{128} possible combinations to find the correct key for converting the ciphertext into plaintext. This is not possible with computing capabilities of today and of near future. However, a cryptanalysis of the cipher reduces the number of combinations required to find the correct key to 2^{40}. This makes the cipher weaker and the plaintext can be retrieved from the ciphertext with moderate computing resources.

Today, cryptanalysis is done in different areas and for different purposes. Governments use cryptanalysis to break the diplomatic and military transmissions of other governments. Companies developing security products send their products to cryptanalyst to test their security features. Hackers use cryptanalysis for performing illegal activities.

Let's now learn about code breaking methodologies.

■ Describing Code Breaking Methodologies

Code breaking methodologies refer to the general methods of decrypting some encrypted information. Some popular code breaking methodologies are as follows:

- **Brute force:** Represents a code breaking methodology in which an attacker simply tries every possible key until the correct key is discovered. In this methodology, the goal of the attacker is to obtain the correct key so that all the ciphertext can be easily converted into plaintext. With longer keys, performing brute force attacks becomes more difficult. However, the use of computers having high CPU speed enables brute force attacks possible. By networking a set of computers together and combining their strength, brute force attacks can be used to break long keys. Keys of 128 bit length are less likely to be broken with brute force attacks.
- **Frequency analysis:** Represents a code breaking methodology that involves calculation of letter frequencies and other patterns. In natural languages, such as English, French, and Russian, certain letters of the alphabet occur more frequently than others. For example, the letter e is likely to appear more number of times than any other letter in any sample of plaintext in English. Similarly, the letter pair th is the most common letter pair in English. The frequency analysis methodology assumes that the cipher has failed to hide these statistics. Analysis of ciphers with frequency analysis methodology is relatively easy.
- **Trickery and deceit:** Represents a code breaking methodology in which an attacker obtains the key through deception or theft. The man-in-the-middle attack (discussed in the next section) is an example of this methodology.

Let's now discuss cryptographic attacks.

■ Describing Cryptographic Attacks

Cryptographic attacks can be referred to as techniques of performing cryptanalysis. These attacks are based on what access the cryptanalyst has over the plaintext, ciphertext, and other aspects of the cryptographic attack. Some popular cryptographic attacks are as follows:

- **Ciphertext-only attack:** Refers to an attack in which the cryptanalyst has a piece of ciphertext (encrypted text) and has no knowledge of plaintext (unencrypted text). This attack is very difficult to perform as it involves the most difficult type of cryptanalysis and requires accurate guesswork of how the data would have been encrypted.
- **Chosen-ciphertext attack:** Refers to an attack in which the cryptanalyst selects some ciphertext and tries to find the matching plaintext. With this information, the cryptanalyst tries to find the key used for decryption.

- **Known-plaintext attack:** Represents an attack in which the cryptanalyst has the knowledge of a portion of the plaintext generated from the ciphertext. The cryptanalyst uses this information to extract the key used for encryption and recover the
encrypted text.
- **Chosen-plaintext attack:** Refers to an attack in which the cryptanalyst is able to produce ciphertext from some randomly selected plaintext; however, the cryptanalyst is not able to break the key that is used to produce the ciphertext. The cryptanalyst tries to break the key by comparing the entire ciphertext with the original plaintext.
- **Man-in-the-middle attack:** Refers to an attack in which the attacker (cryptanalyst) places a piece of surveillance software at the communication channel between the two users who want to exchange their keys for secure communication. Then the attacker exchanges keys with each of the users. The users assume that they are exchanging keys with each other, not with the attacker. In this way, the users unknowingly send keys to the attacker.
- **Replay attack:** Refers to an attack in which the attacker tries to fraudulently repeat or delay a valid data transmission. For example, a user A sends his/her password to another user B as the proof of his/her identity and a third user C somehow captures the password sent by user A. Now, when the users A and B have ended communication, user C connects to user B and sends the password of user A as the proof of identity and communicates with him/her as being user A.

Summary

The basic application of security of information and information systems has been discussed in this chapter. Then the chapter has explained that security of data means maintaining its CIA properties. You have learned about security technologies such as firewalls, VPN, IDS, and access control systems. You have explored the numerous threats to security of applications and data. Further, the chapter has discussed about security threats to e-commerce. It has also provided a brief explanation on electronic payment system such e-cash. The chapter has also explained about credit/debit/smart cards and digital signatures. Finally, you have learned about cryptography and encryption, including private, public, and secret keys encryption.

Exercises

■ Multiple Choice Questions

Q1. Third-party applications can be made more secure through:

a. Improvements in security of applications at the client side
b. Vendor collaboration
c. Application upgrades
d. All of the above

Ans. The correct option is d.

Q2. Data can be disposed by:

a. Handing over the storage devices to anyone
b. Shutting down the system that uses the storage device
c. Thrashing the storage devices into metal scrap
d. None of the above

Ans. The correct option is c.

Q3. Data backup is defined as:

a. An operation to secure an organization's database
b. An option to help recover some data files that are lost due to disasters or malicious activities
c. An option to provide continuous processing support
d. All of the above

Ans. The correct option is b.

Q4. Firewalls are used to:

a. Provide data backup facilities
b. Provide network integration facilities
c. Prevent hackers from accessing your computer through the Internet by blocking back doors or open ports that connect your computer with the Internet
d. All of the above

Ans. The correct option is c.

Q5. Firewalls are based on:

a. Open-source techniques to prevent network access
b. Proxy servers to control and monitor outbound traffic

c. Integrated network technique to allow the Internet users to interact with the systems of an organization

d. All of the above

Ans. The correct option is b.

Q6. VPN can be used to:

a. Prevent geographical locations from being connected

b. Weaken organizational security

c. Increase operational costs as compared to traditional WANs

d. Simplify network topology and provide telecommuter support

Ans. The correct option is d.

Q7. Viruses are normally used to:

a. Strengthen the security of a system

b. Cause harms to some files and storage media of a computer system

c. Enhance the security of individuals and organizations on the Internet

d. None of the above

Ans. The correct option is b.

Q8. Which of the following is a security threat to E-commerce?

a. Every person on the Internet

b. Unauthorized internal users who may access confidential information by stolen passwords

c. Every individual working in the concerned organization

d. All of the above

Ans. The correct option is b.

Q9. Which of the following is/are E-payment scheme(s)?

a. SEPP/SET Scheme

b. Secure Courier Electronic Payment

c. CheckFree wallet

d. All of the above

Ans. The correct option is d.

Q10. In the public-key encryption technique:

a. Two keys are used for identification, validation, and

b. Single key is used to verify and validate documents

verification of identity

c. No keys are used for validation, verification, and identification

d. All of the above

Ans. The correct option is a.

■ Subjective Type Questions

Q1. What are the considerations for data security in regards with data backup, archival, and disposal?

Q2. Discuss the various types of firewalls. How can we use firewalls to secure our applications?

Q3. What are security threats? Discuss the security threats to E-commerce.

Q4. What do you know about digital signature? How can we use it to authenticate and secure our digital documents?

Q5. What is public-key encryption? Discuss in detail.

03 Introduction to Security Measures

OBJECTIVES

- Secure information system development
- Application development security
- Information security governance and risk management
- Security architecture and design
- Security issues in hardware, data storage, and downloadable devices
- Physical security of IT assets
- Backup security measures

Security of assets, being seemingly the most crucial and challenging aspects for organizations today, requires greater managerial focus than other aspects. It is considered and as various surveys have proven, organizations having proper security measures are established to protect their assets and generate better revenue than organizations with no proper measures established for that. Security of information systems and applications is not the only things to be considered for organizations; they also need to emphasize on everything related to the security of the entire organization, including physical security of equipment, laptop, desktop, servers, etc. There are many challenges and issues encountered by organizations, and therefore, various security measures have been established. For example, your office may have 1,000 computer systems. You need to protect the systems from stealing, destruction, disasters, etc. All these require you to analyze the risk and the ways in which you can mitigate specific risks associated with certain things. You will be required to formulate proper strategies for the management and mitigation of risks. Also, you will need to prepare architecture for all security measures that are appropriate for the security of your assets. You will need to manage storage and downloadable device security as well as security of hardware. The physical security of your organization's Information Technology (IT) assets also has a requirement to be managed properly. In addition to all these security measures, it is imperative for you to think about the security of backup storage. Your backup is an extremely important part of your organization as all of the important data files have been stored as a backup. If the backup storage is destroyed, you cannot recover the crucial data once it is lost. So, managing the backup storage and applying proper measures for securing them are also the need of the hour.

This chapter discusses the development of secure information systems and security in application development. Then it explains to you about governance of information security and the management of risks. Further, you learn about security architecture and design to manage security risks. The chapter outlines the security issues related to hardware, storage of data, and downloadable devices. Toward the end, it discusses physical security of IT assets and the measures established to secure your backup data.

3.1 Secure Information System Development

Identification and planning followed by mitigation of risks are important processes for developing a secure information system. To manage risks properly, you have to find a balance between the different processes that include protecting organization's information and assets, costs incurred in applying security controls and in formulating strategies for round the clock security during the entire system development lifecycle, etc. The basic security considerations in the system development lifecycle are shown in Figure 1:

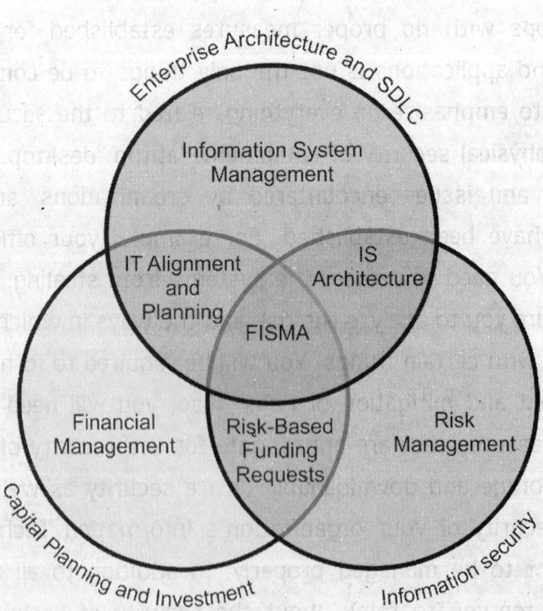

▲ Figure 1: Displaying Security Considerations

The best risk-management strategy is to find out the critical assets and operations for organization's business processes and then explore the possible vulnerabilities across systems in the organization. Security risks do not impact only a single area of operation. The entire organization may be affected due to a single vulnerability. So, you need to identify all the critical operations and assets, which can be done by planning for the system security and gathering insightful information from various business processes. This information helps you in determining the important operations, assets to support them, interdependencies among various operations, and the relationship between assets and business processes. After the criticality of business processes and assets has been analyzed, you can find out the impact of various operations on your organization's security. This process of analyzing the impact of vulnerabilities on business processes is called Business Impact Analysis (BIA), which helps to evaluate the impacts of disruption of important services on systems and assets related to those services. After the BIA is done, you can manage your organization's security on the basis of findings.

Secure information systems are developed by integrating risk analysis and management activities at the start of the System Development Lifecycle (SDLC) and continuing throughout, which means that security measures will be integrated into the system development operations involving planning, acquisition, building, and deployment of security of the system.

In this risk management-based approach, lifecycle management assures organization's management about considering every security-related aspect in each phase of development and helps in recording the decisions that are relevant to the organization's security. This documentation helps managers in checking their decisions by themselves and identifying the reasons for making a decision, which will enable the assessment of environment changes readily.

Organizations develop their information systems using various SDLC methodologies, which include waterfall model, prototype model, incremental model, spiral model, etc. Organizations select a particular model for developing their systems on the basis of many factors such as expected size of the system, its complexity, the schedule of development, and system's lifespan. Also, in a number of situations, organizations choose the SDLC model according to the definition given by the acquisition policy of the organization.

An SDLC has five phases: initial phase where expected size, complexity, and schedule are analyzed; development phase where system's design and coding is done; implementation phase where modules are tested and deployed; maintenance phase where the flaws in the system are corrected, users' feedbacks are taken and assessed, and changes based on recommendations of users are incorporated in the system; and disposal phase where legacy systems are replaced by fresh, reengineered systems. Security has an important role to play in every phase of this development lifecycle.

Figure 2 presents a conceptual view of the entire SDLC:

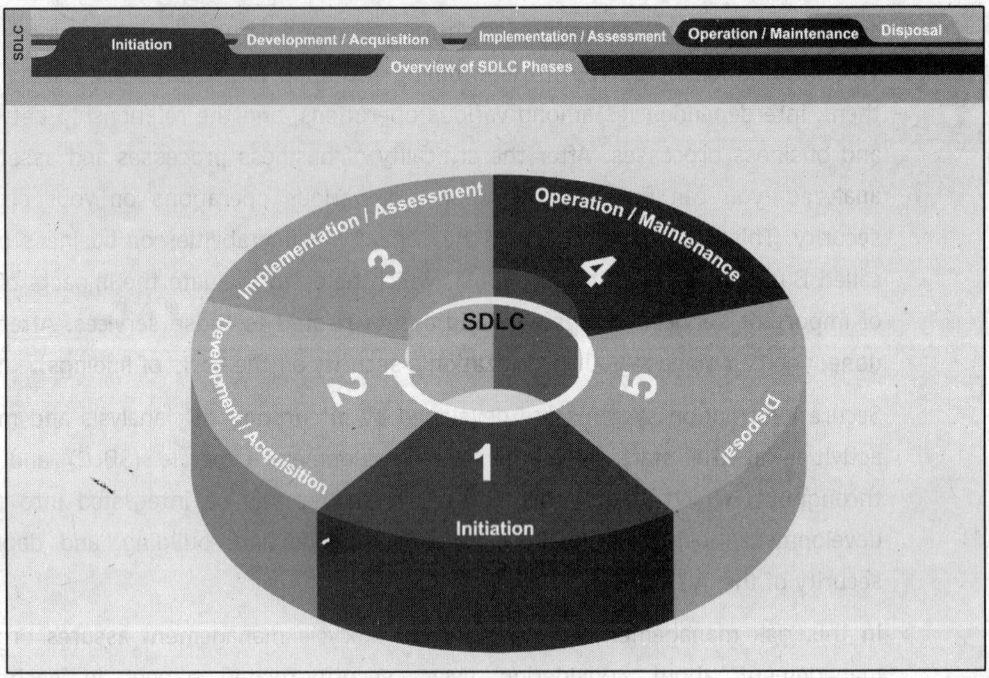

▲ **Figure 2: Displaying the Conceptual View of SDLC**

There are certain security-related considerations at every phase of the development lifecycle through which we can integrate the security aspects with the other business operations. Each phase has been represented by a figure containing specific details about the phase. Each figure includes a starting point that provides a brief idea about the individual phase; a control gates box that identifies points at which system evaluation will take place and the management will decide to continue the development process, change direction, or completely stop the development; and activities boxes that define primary security activities to be included in individual phases. The activities are further specialized as follows:

- **Description**: It includes a detailed overview of every activity including security-related considerations that are required to account for the given task. Description is represented by rectangular box marked as steps, such as Initiate Project-Security Planning and Categorize Information System.

- **Output**: It describes what will be delivered after a certain task is completed. It also includes artifacts and defines the suggested actions to be taken for forward/backward integration. Outputs are represented by boxes marked as "Outputs."
- **Synchronization**: It is a loop that accounts for feedbacks to ascertain the flexibility of the SDLC, which is to make sure that the communication is handled properly and tasks and deliverables are adapted as and when necessary. Synchronization is represented by the arrowed circles.
- **Interdependencies**: These are relationships between different tasks that ensure security measures are integrated without other IT processes affecting the system development process in a negative manner. Interdependencies are represented by arrows connecting boxes and loops.

Integrating Security at the Initial Phase

Initial phase is where the decision is taken to develop a system. In this phase, security considerations primarily involve business risks related to confidentiality, integrity, and availability. However, at this stage, apart from defining threats and possible security constraints for business, you need to consider privacy requirements also. There are many activities involved in this phase, which includes initiating project security planning, categorizing the information system, assessing the impact of privacy on business processes, assessing the business impact of an activity, etc. Figure 3 shows the security activities included in the initial phase of the SDLC:

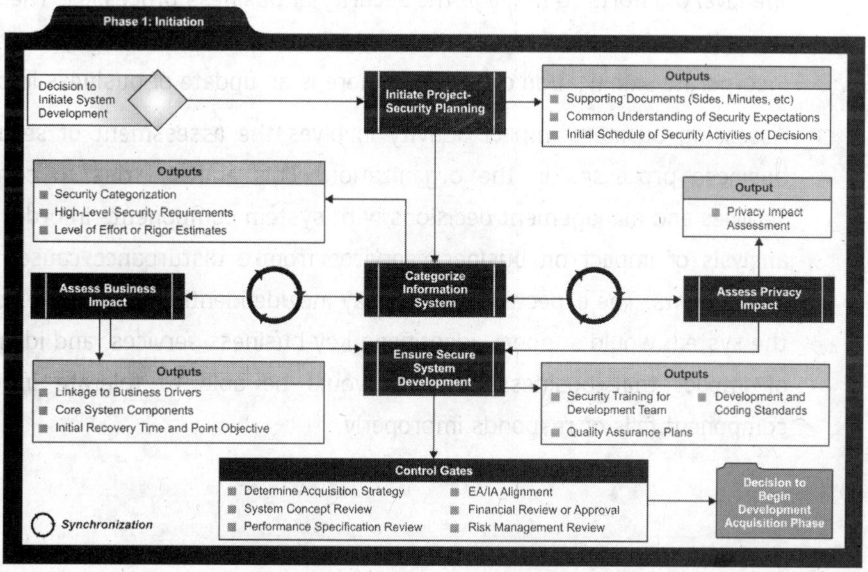

▲ **Figure 3: Showing Security Activities in the Initial Phase**

Analysis of risk and planning for countermeasures at this stage help in saving the cost and time required for system development. Basic control gates in this phase may include determining acquisition strategy, reviewing the system concept, aligning the enterprise architecture to comply with the standards, reviewing risk management, reviewing and getting finance approvals, reviewing performance specification, etc. There are several security activities in the initial phase and the expected outputs are defined accordingly. Security roles are identified, stakeholders are provided awareness for security, and project planning is done at this stage. The various security activities are defined in this phase, and accordingly, the expected outputs are finalized at this stage. The primary activities are described as follows:

- Initiating project security planning activity includes review documents, initial project schedule, a common understanding of system security expectations, etc., as outputs. It synchronizes various tasks by defining milestones and arranging meetings to discuss the security considerations and restrictions.
- Categorizing the information system activity is described as a way that promotes integration of security into business processes and provides base to standardize the security operations. It involves identifying the information that supports specific business decisions and evaluating their confidentiality, integrity, and availability. The key outputs include documentation of researches, important decision, and support information, listing of requirements to provide high-level security, and estimation of the level of efforts to manage the security of business processes. The synchronization requires review of categorization only in case information system that needs to incorporate signification changes or there is an update of business impact analysis.
- Assessing business impact activity involves the assessment of security on various business processes in the organization. This activity tries to correlate business services and management decisions with system components in order to facilitate the analysis of impact on business services from a disturbance caused to the system components. The expected outputs may include identification of lines of business that the system would support, identifying key business services, and identifying the level of impact that business services would be able to tolerate in case a system component fails or responds improperly.

- Assessing privacy impact activity involves defining and exploring the amount of private and confidential information that the system is expected to create, transmit, or store. This identification primarily takes place at the categorization stage where all the business processes, services, and security-related matters are considered. In this phase, the expected output mainly includes privacy impact analysis document that would contain details regarding the degree of privacy entailed to the information created, stored, and transmitted by the system.
- Ensuring the use of secure information system development process activity involves the description about how the information system would be developed securely. The outputs may include plans to provide the training regarding security implementation during the development phase; deliverables, techniques, and milestones that are planned for ensuring quality; and the development environment, coding standards, and development standards. The synchronization involves security testing and product evaluation so that the development process can be adjusted appropriately as per the requirements.

Integrating Security at the Development Phase

Development phase is where the shape of the information system is actually built. The security considerations specific to the development phase are as follows:

- Risk analysis conducted to help basic security controls to be applied
- Requirement analysis for the application of security risk countermeasures
- Test for ensuring that the functionality and security of the system are managed properly
- Initial document preparation for certifying and accrediting the system
- Security architecture design preparation

The main control gates in this phase include reviewing the architecture design, reviewing the functional tests, checking the status of the project and finance at middle point of development, reviewing risk-management operation, and reviewing the performance.

Primary security activities at the development stage of system development include risk assessment, security control selection and documentation, security architecture design preparation, security control development and engineering, security documentation development, and developmental, functional, and security testing.

Figure 4 shows the security activities included in the development phase of SDLC:

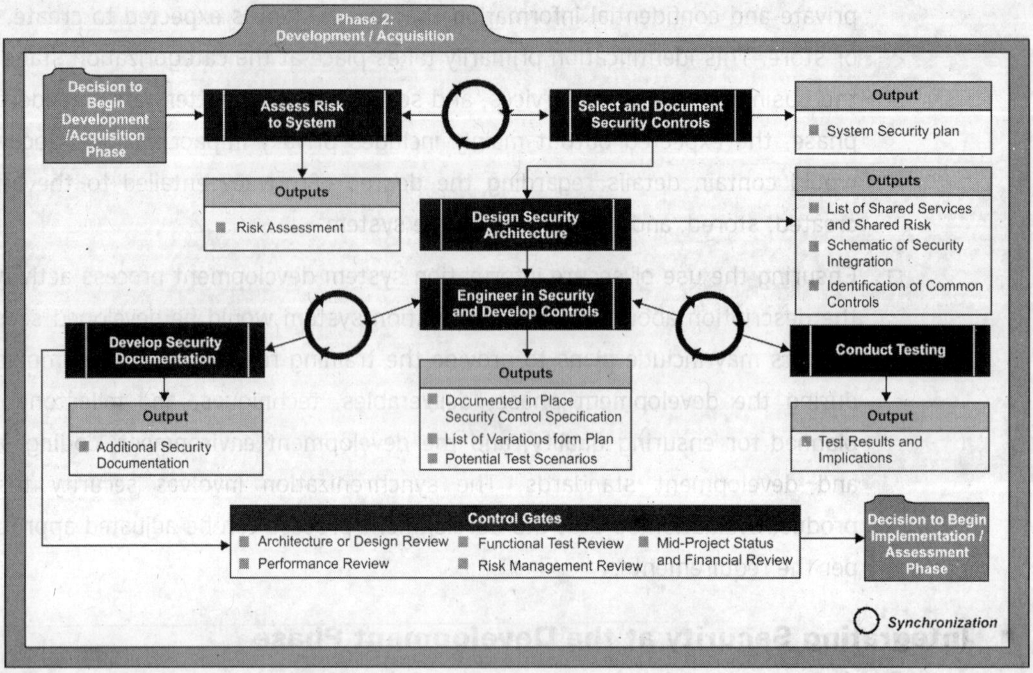

▲ **Figure 4: Showing the Security Activities in the Development Phase**

■ Integrating Security at the Implementation Phase

Implementation phase is where the system is installed and becomes operational. The evaluation of system is done on a continuous basis. In this phase, the basic security considerations are as follows:

- ❐ Integration of the information system into the operational environment
- ❐ Planning activities for certification of the system, conducing these activities, and testing security controls at the same time
- ❐ Completion of activities for accreditation of the system

In the implementation phase, the primarily involved control gates are as follows:

- ❐ Reviewing the readiness of the system for testing
- ❐ Reviewing confidentiality and availability
- ❐ Reviewing the final status of the project and finance
- ❐ Reviewing the readiness of the system for deployment

- Deciding about the Authorization Officer (AO)
- Deploying IT or getting approval for connection

Among the major activities related to the security of the system, creation of detailed plan for confidentiality and availability, integration of security into already existing environment and systems, assessment of system security, and authorization of information system are considered. Figure 5 shows the security activities that are included in the implementation phase of the SDLC:

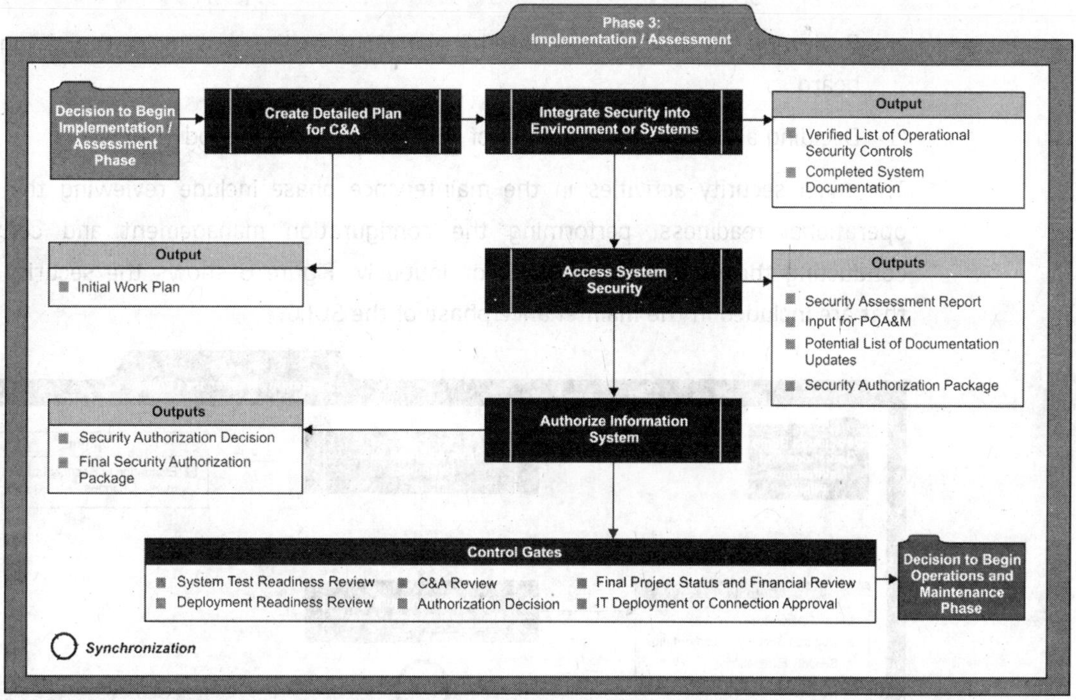

▲ **Figure 5: Showing the Security Activities in the Implementation Phase**

Integrating Security at the Maintenance Phase

Maintenance phase is where the system feedbacks are incorporated, improvements are made, and the system is continued to operate with some maintenance works going on constantly. Consistent efforts are put to enhance/modify the system so that the system is always up to the task. These modifications/enhancements are tested before they are introduced to the operational system. The continuous monitoring of the system is also done in this phase in order to keep the system up and running for fulfilling the development objectives. In this phase, the key considerations regarding the system security are as follows:

- Conducting a review to check the operational accuracy of the system
- Managing the system configuration
- Establishing processes and procedures in order to ensure that the system is up and running continuously while its operations are being monitored
- Performing the reauthorization according to the requirement

This phase includes several control gates. Some of the key control gates are as follows:

- Reviewing the readiness of the system for operational purposes
- Reviewing the changes proposed to be made in the system by the change control board
- Deciding about the accreditation of the system over a period of time

The main security activities in the maintenance phase include reviewing the system's operational readiness, performing the configuration management and control, and conducting the system monitoring continuously. Figure 6 shows the security activities that are included in the maintenance phase of the SDLC:

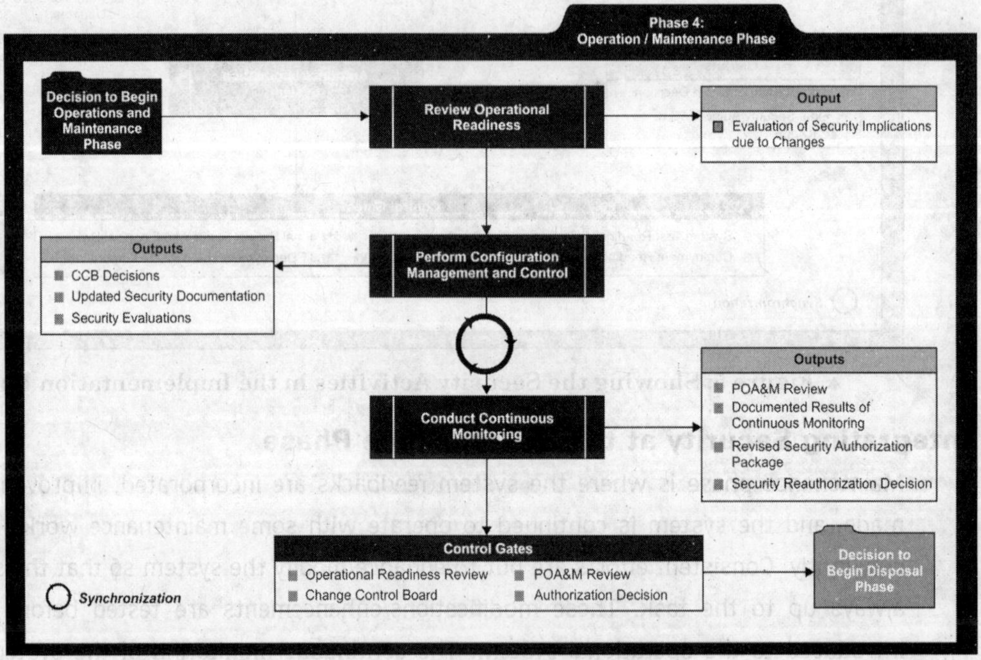

▲ **Figure 6: Showing the Security Activities in the Maintenance Phase**

Integrating Security at the Disposal Phase

Disposal phase is the final stage in the SDLC, and it is where the legacy systems are replaced by newer systems. The decision to replace the systems that have become obsolete for continuous operational purposes is taken by the management. After the management is convinced that the system can no longer operate properly, the system is finally disposed of, operations are transferred to newer or reengineered systems, and resources and assets are secured. Systems are not disposed of after a particular time, but the changing environmental, operational, and managerial conditions require older systems to be replaced by newer ones. The information regarding operations, management, and environment may still be important for the systems that will replace the older ones.

The disposal phase involves various activities to ensure that the replacement of systems is orderly and important information is saved. This helps in reactivating some parts or the overall information in future, if required. The primary security considerations in the disposal phase are as follows:

- Building and executing a plan for the disposal or transition of obsolete systems
- Archiving of the important information for the follow-on systems to work properly
- Cleaning the storage media and other supporting components
- Disposing the software and hardware components

In this final phase of the SDLC, the key control gates are as follows:

- Reviewing the closure of the system
- Reviewing the security of closure
- Checking the board that controls the change management process

Figure 7 shows the security activities that are included in the disposal phase of the SDLC:

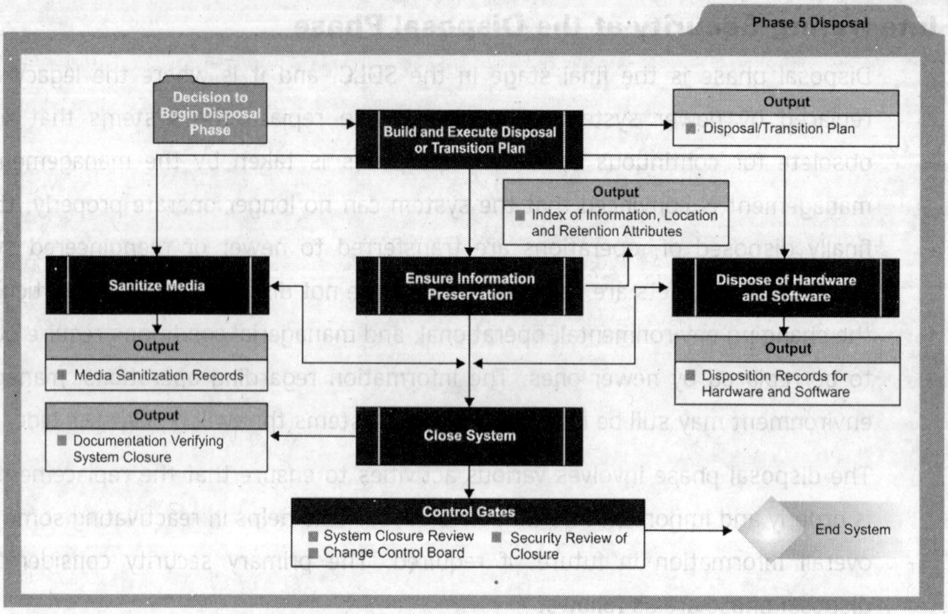

▲ **Figure 7: Showing the Security Activities in the Disposal Phase**

In addition to the specific security considerations in the different phases of the SDLC, some of the additional considerations regarding secure development of information systems include supply chain management and software assurance, following a service-oriented architecture to provide proper and secure services to clients, getting approvals and accreditations so that some of the security modules can be reused if required, finding solutions across organizations, and shifting technology and its migration on large basis. Development of data centers and provision of IT facilities and virtualization can also be taken as key security considerations when it comes to developing information systems securely.

3.2 Application Development Security

Information is available for organizations in the form of assets, which need to be used (collected, stored, shared, and deleted) in an intelligent manner. An intelligent use of information assets helps organizations in maintaining themselves ahead of their competitor organizations. Therefore, these assets need to be protected from any kind of threats that may result into breach of confidentiality, integrity, or availability of resources. Threats can harm the organization by disclosure of trade secrets and damage of organization's reputation. The organization may also lose its customer confidence.

An organization applies computer security measures to protect its information assets by selecting and applying a set of measures that will be appropriate for the security of information. The risk-management process in most of the organizations mainly involves reduction of vulnerabilities. This helps them mitigate the risk of financial or other kinds of losses.

Sharing of information assets in organizations is handled by computing services and applications that are mostly custom-developed for specific uses of the organizations. Most organizations facilitate development of these applications and services within their premises and allow them to be strongly interconnected with their networks, both intranet and the Internet. Interconnected nature of these applications provides growth opportunities for the organization, but also tends to be vulnerable for threats and attacks. To avoid loss of information assets, organizations must follow a secure application development strategy. However, most of the developers are less skilled to develop secure applications. Development of secure applications requires specific training for what the meaning of security is for an organization and for its applications, how secure code is written, and why it is needed to provide security to the applications.

In today's rapidly changing technological environment, we see some newer technologies emerging each year. People working on an earlier technology may continue working on them, but the newer technologies require new developers. Thus, with newer technologies and practices, there are newer developers as well. These developers need to be specifically trained to adapt to the new technology. If the training involves focus on secure application development strategy, organizations will mainly have only infrastructure issues to deal with when it comes to providing complete organizational security.

Some of the primary issues related to the secure development of applications are as follows:

- Less trained/skilled developers
- Less educational focus on secure development
- Difficulty of finding the right information related to specific security measures for particular applications or application development strategies

- Lifecycle systems considering security mostly in the last phases only
- Compilers, interpreters, and programming being unable to utilize the system resources in the best way possible

We cannot ignore security of information assets at any level. One of the most serious issues that information assets are facing is the theft of proprietary information, which causes financial losses.

The requirement of secure applications being created by the developers is more in the wake of all the issues of vulnerabilities for information assets. Although we have several security measures, such as antiviruses, IDS protection, firewalls, VPNs, etc., to secure the assets, yet reliability of such measures to provide full protection is always in question. If these measures can be compromised even a little, they will allow direct access to data and will result in potential loss of organization's assets. Therefore, we must develop secure applications so that the organization, its integrity, and its reputation are never compromised.

With the aforementioned issues for secure application development, it is still possible to develop applications that provide information security. We can do so by accepting a common framework that suffices certain basic requirements to information security. Such a common framework offers various benefits to developers and organizations. Some of the benefits are as follows:

- Developers can refer to the common standard provided in the framework to develop secure applications
- Strict guidelines and design principles included in the framework are time tested and universal
- Developers get a comprehensive view and understand security policy, programming language, and tools
- Organization can improve its development strategy to apply best methods, development efforts, standards and procedures, and security policy
- The view of the management becomes more objective towards considerations and mitigation of risks

This framework includes the following factors:

- **Foundation**: Foundation is the basic knowledge of the development procedure and security issues to consider before starting to develop the application
- **Principles**: Principles are the basic rules to be followed during the application development process
- **Design Guidelines**: Design guidelines include the best code implementation methods that are tested and have been proven successful over time

Secure applications can be developed by following certain specifications mentioned in this framework that contains foundation, principles, and design guidelines. It states the following points for each:

You must have the knowledge of the security policy and standards that you have to follow while developing your applications. You must also be aware of the guidelines, procedures, development methodology being used, preferred programming language to develop applications, and the compiler or interpreter. These points must be taken care of when dealing with the foundation part of the common application development framework.

When it comes to the specifications of principles part, you follow a set of rules to develop secure applications. Some of these rules include considering security as a part of design instead of taking it as an aftermath action, assuming the environment to present hostile conditions for the application to work properly, using standards that are open and known to all, minimizing the system elements that can be trusted and then securing them, providing the data at the source end rather than at the user end, providing restricted accesses to important sections of application, authenticating users of the application, leaving intact the security measures that are already in place, logging-monitoring-auditing, and applying secure measures for failure cases by planning it.

You can design a secure application only if you know that security of a system is a part of its design. If you are aware of the security measures that need to be placed right from the designing phase, you can develop secure applications. Your design should integrate security right from the start, not after the application is developed. There are certain design guidelines that must be followed in order to integrate security in the design phase. Some of these guidelines are as follows:

- **Validating inputs**: Implementation of security in application design must start from validation of inputs. You must be careful in programming for validating every input from the user. An attacker needs only a single chance to breach into your security barriers. This may allow him/her to access sensitive information used in the application. So, prevention of any unlawful activities by users requires you to check/validate inputs given to your application. The experiments in the user input must be restricted to the expected forms only. The problem arises when it is assumed that the format of input would be same as expected. The programmer should never trust the incoming input; instead, one must validate it before passing to the application. Also, inputs must not be too large in size even in the expected format and should be checked to be valid. Applying these best practices would help in reducing the risk for the information.

- **Handling exceptions**: Exception handling is particularly linked to the security of applications in cases of failure, which happens very often on encountering some unexpected action in computer systems. This failure may result into vulnerable conditions for both the system and the information assets. A system's operational status must not affect the security of data. To provide data security in such circumstances, you need to apply proper mechanisms to handle exceptions. The exceptional handling procedure is a standard way for the application to respond to run-time conditions of error, also called exceptions. You can use the built-in mechanism provided in most of the high-level programming languages. Exception handling provides classes and methods to control the flow of program if the execution context goes beyond the normal flow.
- **Applying cryptography**: Data security can be implemented through cryptographic algorithms that help us to manage the integrity, availability, and confidentiality of data. The most prominent issues with the implementation of cryptography are failure in using it appropriately, error in its proper implementation, defining custom cryptographic algorithms, assuming security by obscurity, etc. You should avoid these mistakes by trying to apply best practices for cryptographic implementation. You can use symmetric or asymmetric encryption algorithms to provide confidentiality, integrity, availability, and authentication.
- **Using random numbers**: Generating truly random numbers from computer is very difficult. Computers generate pseudo random numbers by using the random() function. These random numbers could be predictable and may prove to be a weak link for the security of the application. So, generating purely random numbers whenever required in applications is important. You need to be able to generate truly

random numbers. The natural means of random numbers include radioactive decay and fluctuations in thermal signatures.

3.3 Information Security Governance and Risk Management

Information security needs to be governed and managed properly because information has become one of the most crucial business drivers in recent years. According to the United States' National Institute for Standards and Technology (NIST):

"Information systems are subject to serious threats that can have adverse effects on organizational operations (i.e., missions, functions, image, or reputation), organizational assets, individuals, other organizations, and the Nation by exploiting both known and unknown vulnerabilities to compromise the confidentiality, integrity, or availability of the information being processed, stored, or transmitted by those systems. Threats to information and information systems can include purposeful attacks, environmental disruptions, and human/machine errors and result in great harm to the national and economic security interests of the Nation."

Going by the definition of threats and their consequences as given by NIST, we must protect all information assets from threats. We can do this only if managers at different levels in the organization are ready to take the security responsibilities. It should be the accountability of managers to provide protection to resources and manage risks in their domain. Organizations may face several types of risks where security risk is one of them. The operations in organizations must be highly interconnected and complex for risk management to be handled effectively. Risk management cannot be done by a single individual. However, participation of individuals helps in effectively mitigating the risk to a large extent.

Security governance and risk management should be a part of the overall organizational goals rather than a single, highly overlooked discipline. The key elements required for effectively managing the organizational security are as follows:

- Senior managers being assigned the responsibility of managing risks.

- Executives recognizing and understanding the risk for information security that can harm operations of the organization, its assets, individuals, reputation, and may be clients.
- Organization-wide risk tolerance level being established. This should include guidelines about what will be the impact of risk tolerance on the current decision-making processes.
- Risk management programs being implemented effectively throughout the organization where senior managers and executives are accountable for taking risk management decision and implementation.

The risk management process involves the following four activities:

1. **Framing:** Framing the risk means to sense a threat and inform all the related activities that execute in a sequential manner to be ready to control and avert a possible damage. In this activity, we analyze the possible risks associated with the security of information systems and the organization, and then we try to define certain actions for individual cases.
2. **Assessing:** Assessment of risk means to analyze the level of risks and the level of security provided with our organization and its information systems. The possible damages from a threat are also assessed in this activity.
3. **Monitoring:** Monitoring activity involves continuously checking the information system and keeping an eye on other threats and vulnerabilities that may be encountered by the organization. This will help you to define proper guidelines for the maintenance of security of your systems. Also, risk monitoring helps in analyzing whether the system is continuously secure or not.
4. **Responding:** Responding to the risks means to take preventive or corrective measures so that systems can be kept protected from any kind of threats, whether internal or external.

Figure 8 shows the process of information risk management:

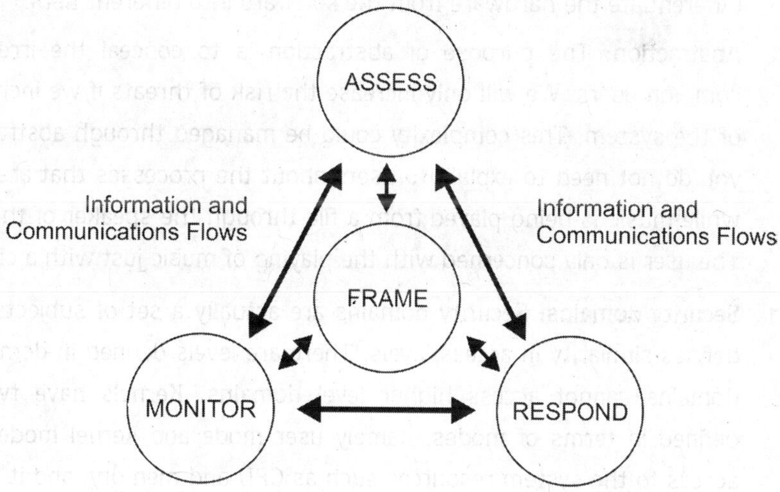

▲ **Figure 8: Showing the Risk Management Process**

In Figure 8, it can be seen that the flow of information starts by framing, and it communicates the information throughout the other processes, i.e., assessing, monitoring, and responding. These activities execute sequentially, which is to say that the framing of risk is the first activity followed by the assessment activity. After that, the monitoring will take place and finally the system will give response to the security risks.

3.4 Security Architecture and Design

The security architecture and design of a system means a bundle of the following components: the hardware, operating system, and software. It also includes a description of designing, architecting, and evaluating this system to provide security. Thus, the security architecture and design is explained in three parts, namely, the hardware and software part, the models, and the evaluation methods. Hardware and software part provides the way to design secure system, models part explains the way to maintain the security of this system, and evaluation part describes the level of security of a system.

■ Secure System Design

You can design a secure system by implementing software and hardware specifically and following some universal principles that include:

- **Layering:** Layering is a concept that arranges hardware, drivers for kernel and devices, operating system, and applications in a sequential order. Hardware is at the bottom layer and applications are at the top. The layering approach is used to differentiate the hardware from the software into different tiers.

- **Abstraction:** The purpose of abstraction is to conceal the irrelevant details from common users. We will only increase the risk of threats if we increase the complexity of the system. This complexity could be managed through abstraction. For example, you do not need to explain to users about the processes that are going on internally while music is being played from a file through the speaker of the computer system. The user is only concerned with the playing of music just with a click.
- **Security domains:** Security domains are actually a set of subjects and objects which defines similarity in access levels. There are levels defined in domains and lower level domains cannot access higher level domains. Kernels have two levels of access defined in terms of modes, namely user mode and kernel mode. The kernel allows access to the system resources such as CPU and memory, and it is considered as the most trusted part of the system
- **The ring model:** Ring model is, in fact, a layering of CPU hardware in four levels: Ring0, Ring1, Ring2, and Ring3. These layers are used, typically, in a sequence respectively by kernel, other OS components exceeding Ring0, Device drivers, and user applications. With the emergence of virtualization, Ring1 has been transformed as hypervisor mode and operates host OSs in Ring0 of the kernel.
- **Open-closed systems:** Open and closed systems are two different types of structures. Open systems are designed by employing open hardware and standards that may include hardware from a variety of vendors. For example, assembled systems are open systems. Close systems, on the other hand, only use proprietary hardware or software from specific vendor.

■ Secure Hardware System Architecture

The security architecture provides confidentiality, integrity, and availability to the system by including only the requisite hardware. The physical computer hardware that can be used to provide full system security is described in the secure system architecture. This includes not only the mother board, CPU, and memory, but also system buses and memory protection.

System unit is your system's case and the foundation on which all different components of your system are placed. Your system's case encapsulates all internal parts such as hard drives, motherboard, power supply, etc. The motherboard is a crucial part of the computer system hardware on which all the different components that form a computer system are based. These include CPU, memory slots, peripheral slots, Network Interface Card (NIC), etc.

Computer buses are the primary channels for each component to communicate effectively with another. All the communication that takes place between the CPU, memory, peripheral devices, and other components is based on these buses. An example of communication through computer buses is shown in Figure 9:

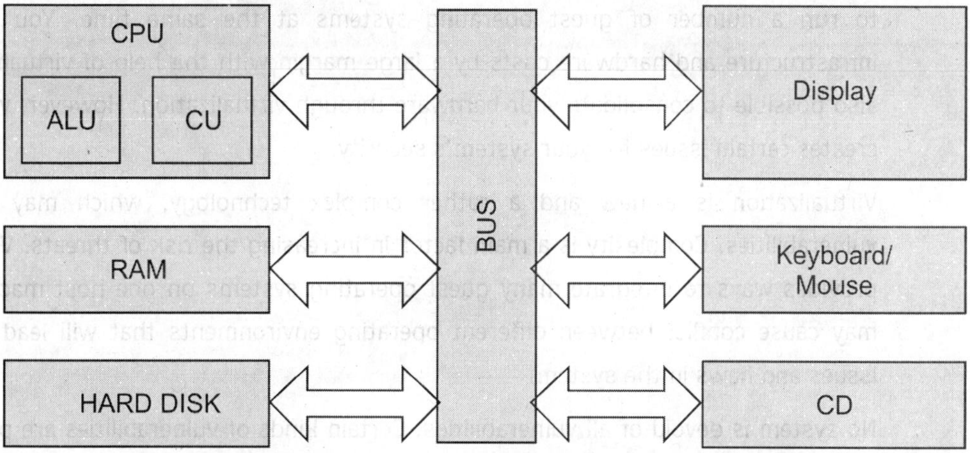

▲ **Figure 9: Showing Communication through Computer Buses**

Every processing activity is handled by the CPU of the computer system. CPU can be subdivided as Arithmetic and Logic Unit (ALU) and Control Unit (CU). Computer systems execute various processes at a time and all of them are handled by the CPU. Any computing or comparison activity is taken up by the ALU, and all the controlling and managing activities are taken up by the CU. Modern systems have CPUs that permit multitasking and multiprocessing, in addition to a number of other features.

Memory is always one of the most crucial aspects of every secure system. Everyone knows this fact that all the data is stored in the memory, which can be accessed randomly or sequentially. There are different types of memory that are categorized, most often, as Random Access Memory (RAM), Read Only Memory (ROM), and Cache memory. Additionally, we have a few other categories. However, those are less popular and less consequential. In recent years, virtual memory has also gained popularity because of the emergence of the virtualization technology as the leading technology domain worldwide.

■ Secure Operating System and Software Architecture

The secure hardware forms the base to provide security in the software and operating system. The architecture of the software and operating system is built on the secure hardware base. The secure operating system and software part includes the kernel that works as a reference monitor to mediate between subjects and objects; users and file permissions to restrict access to specific information only for a set of select users; and virtualization, which is an interesting technology that has emerged in recent years. Virtualization separates the software from the hardware by including a layer between them. This layer works as a platform that can be used by a single host operating system to run a number of guest operating systems at the same time. You can reduce infrastructure and hardware costs by a large margin with the help of virtualization. It is also possible to consolidate your hardware through virtualization. However, virtualization creates certain issues for your system's security.

Virtualization is a new and a rather complex technology, which may result into vulnerabilities. Complexity is a main factor in increasing the risk of threats. Virtualization provides ways to integrate many guest operating systems on one host machine, which may cause conflict between different operating environments that will lead to security issues and flaws in the system.

No system is devoid of all vulnerabilities. Certain kinds of vulnerabilities are part of every system. So, it is important to apply measures against specific threats and vulnerabilities that are known. There are various system threats that can cause harms for the system's confidentiality, availability, and integrity. To prevent attacks and threats from causing any kind of loss of data or service, we need to apply measures that include implementation of security models and their evaluation. This two-step process aims at securing a system completely, which is possible by applying the best security practices. Several models have been developed to provide and maintain fully secure design and architecture of systems. The models are followed up closely by the evaluation and standards so that the level of security provided within a system can be measured.

3.5 Security Issues in Hardware, Data Storage, and Downloadable Devices

It is paramount for every organization to protect its information assets. Securing computer systems means to protect all of its components that include hardware, software, storage devices, operating system, and peripheral devices. Each component has its own set of vulnerabilities. As an example, hardware parts can be stolen, destroyed, or otherwise used to harm the organization's security in terms of availability, integrity, and confidentiality. Securing assets needs specific measures to be employed by the organization. Security of every component of the computer system is equally important, but the issues for each of them are different. You need to be able to control your computer system completely so that the information assets can be protected. In this section, you will get a brief idea about security issues related to hardware, data storage, and peripheral devices. You will also be explained how to protect your assets.

■ Security Issues with Hardware

Hardware is the component on which the entire computer system is based. This includes the processor, hard drive, and monitor. You need to secure these devices by applying proper means of security. Hardware mainly faces security issues related to stealing, destruction, gaining unauthorized access, and breaching the security code of conduct. For instance, if an organization has given laptops to some of its employees, it can be possible that they are using their laptop for illegitimate activities, which result into threats for the organizations' data integrity and confidentiality. There can also be a case that the laptop is handed over to someone else to use and that person destroys some important or critical data, thereby causing threat for its availability. In all these cases, you must have proper usage protocols so that the hardware is not used in an unethical manner.

Any breach of the code of conduct needs proper security measures, such as placing the hardware within your controlled environment where you already have certain security measures in place, such as locks and access control mechanisms. However, your hardware may still be under the threat of breaching access rights. There are several attackers who may use different techniques to breach the security barrier, especially locks. Most of the time, attackers think in a way as shown in Figure 10:

▲ Figure 10: Showing an Attacker's Way of Thinking

To secure your hardware from such kinds of accesses, you can apply the following mechanisms: biometric access control, authentication tokens, Radio Frequency IDentification (RFID), etc. You also need to apply local intranet and Virtual Private Networks (VPNs) to provide complete security for your system. However, network routers are also subjected to eavesdropping and other kinds of attack that may harm your organization's internal security. You need to provide strong passwords and limited access to such devices. There are many different techniques that need to be used to secure your system's hardware, which is very difficult to protect.

■ Security Issues with Storage Devices

Data storage devices are used to save information. Devices such as Compact Disks (CD), Digital Versatile Disks (DVD), memory cards, flash drives, etc., can store information and be removed from the system to be kept at some other place. You can record crucial and confidential information on such devices for the purpose of data archival or maintenance of a data library. The information contained in data storage devices can be sensitive. So, protecting these devices from any external threat is extremely important. The threats to the security of data storage devices can be external or internal. For instance, if you have stored some data on a CD and some unauthenticated user gets access to that CD, he/she may use it unlawfully. This can create problems for data integrity and availability.

The main issues faced by data storage devices include their loss and theft, disposal, stealing of data, denial of data, malware introduction, etc. Your storage devices could be stolen by an external attacker who eyes to cause some harm for the security of your system's data. If the device has inbuilt security mechanisms, then it can be destroyed, thereby resulting in loss of some crucial data. If change of information is allowed in the data storage device, then a person may alter the data in such a way that it is no longer available for authenticated users. An individual may also introduce certain kind of malware to breach the security measures.

All these issues can be overcome by applying specific protection measures. You need to educate people and make them aware that any vulnerability left in a system can create a huge problem for the security. Explaining the importance of security to individuals will improve the understanding of people and thereby strengthen the security. You can take help from the advancing technology to protect your data storage devices and the information contained with them. In addition to that, you need to implement certain policies and procedures that provide an all-round security for the storage devices and data.

■ Security Issues with Downloadable (Peripheral) Devices

Peripheral devices are traditionally considered to be secured, and therefore, these devices can be vulnerable to security attacks. Some of the notable peripheral devices include:

- Universal Serial Bus (USB) drives
- USB patch cords that can be connected to a computer system using mini connectors or micro connectors
- Electronic notebooks that are similar to laptops but are limited in application
- Personal Digital Assistants (PDAs)

The issue with most of the downloadable devices is the threat that an external, unseen entity can create. You cannot easily detect threats to these devices. Therefore, they could be more vulnerable to security attacks in comparison with other devices/systems. Specific security measures should be applied to protect information from being damaged, stolen, or corrupted by internal or external threats. These devices are also vulnerable to theft and destruction. So, you need to protect these devices from various types of attacks on the security of data or information.

Most of the peripheral devices have very small size, and it is easy to hide them from people's eyes. However, if strong security measures are in place, you can protect these devices. The measures may include protection of data from theft, manipulation, or destruction; protection of the devices from being stolen or destroyed; and protection of the environment from undesired accesses.

3.6 Physical Security of IT Assets

Security of data and information assets is equally important. You need to apply all round security measures to be able to manage and secure your information properly. In this respect, physical security of your assets, especially the IT assets, is also very important. You can never imagine applying 100% security until you have proper physical security mechanisms in place. There are several issues that need to be countered in order to apply total security control. For example, you may need to use locks and other access control techniques to protect your assets from unwanted access.

Likewise, you may have to install detection systems to protect your assets from intruders and malicious watchers who can penetrate through other security mechanisms. Your systems need to function continuously, and they must always be up and running so that all business processes are working properly. You must understand the fact that the threats for your IT assets are in turn actually a threat for your organization's other processes.

You must be aware of the highly sensitive, important, and less sensitive information so that you can think of a good strategy for applying different levels of security controls in different cases. You must assess your risks properly, thereby deciding about the level of impact that a threat may cause for your system. When it comes to providing security to your IT assets, you should keep it as simple, coherent, and standardized as possible. The primary threats for the physical security are as follows:

- **Physical access exposure to human beings**: Organizations' own employees are one of the main factors to cause physical security threats, such as theft, fraud, accidents, and sabotage. Among the various reasons to these security concerns, the primary reasons are the accidental errors by human beings or tampering by unauthorized users who get undue control of a physical resource. Human factors not only include the insiders, but also the outside attackers who want to gain access to crucial information resources and try to breach confidentiality and integrity of the data and the organization. Human factor poses the greatest difficulty to the security control process when it comes to applying proper security measures. You must keep your systems password protected, but before that, you need to keep intruders or other outsiders out of the gate of your organization's building, restricted area, and computer systems overall. Also, you need to set proper standards for verification and validation of identity in order to prevent any kind of unethical control of your information assets.
- **Physical access exposure to natural disasters**: Natural disasters may destroy your computer systems or all data storage systems. They might even interrupt your network. Examples such as fire, lightening, or electric interruption may all be considered as physical threats in the form of natural disasters that may lead to data destruction, which will cause unavailability or disrupt the integrity.

To provide physical security of your IT assets, you need to use the following mechanisms:

a. **Physical access controls**: The physical access control measures can be applied in various forms, such as locks, biometric authentication systems, photo IDs, Entry logs, magnetic locks using electronic keycard, and computer terminal locks. The best advocated security control practices are prevention strategies. You will be able to restrict access to your assets at the first step even before an entry is granted. This will enable to have better control over your internal security mechanisms also.

An example of locking system to control physical access is shown in Figure 11:

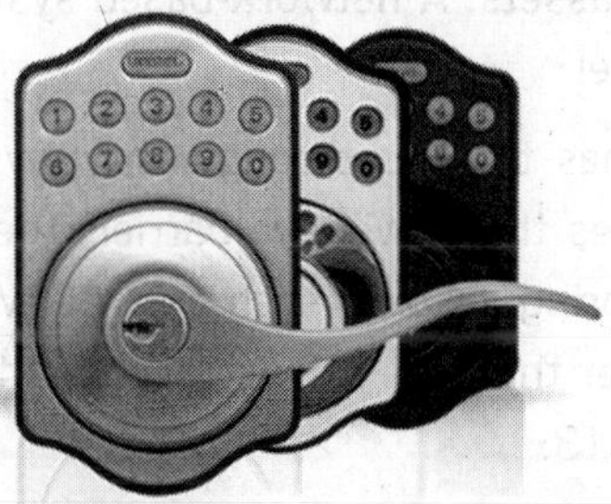

▲ **Figure 11: Showing Physical Access Control Locks**

b. **Electronic and visual surveillance systems – Closed Circuit Television (CCTV)**: Sometimes, even if you applied proper security and access control measures, some intruders may escape from human eyes or may breach other security restrictions. In such cases, applying electronic surveillance and visual detection mechanisms is considered a good security option. CCTV cameras and RFID sensor technologies are good ways to apply electronic means for the physical security of IT assets. Your assets can be protected only if you can prevent unauthorized access and unlawful activities, which is possible only through proper security mechanisms. CCTV cameras are also called the third eye because if human beings missed noticing some people entering a restricted zone, these cameras could capture the event and send the photo to the administrator who is connected through a local area network or Wi-Fi. These cameras are usually hidden from human views and record all the events taking place in a location where the cameras are placed. Figure 12 shows a CCTV camera monitoring system:

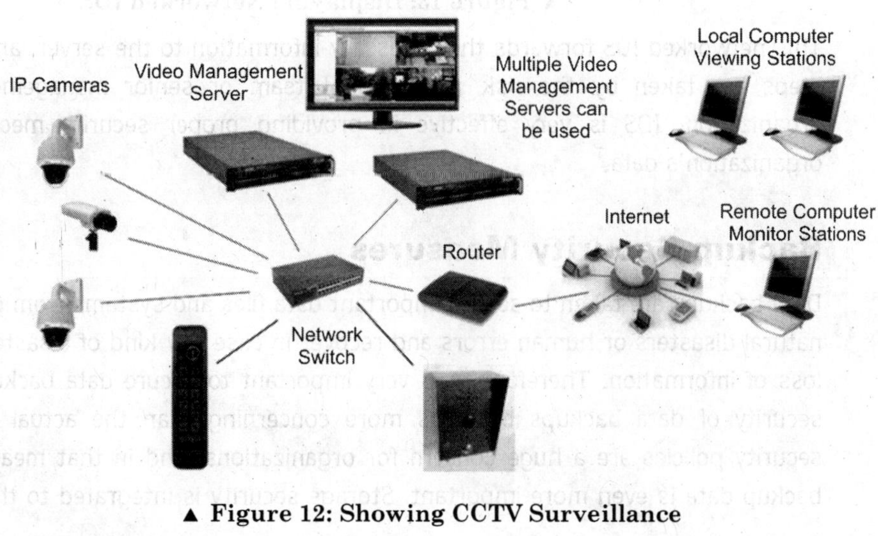

▲ **Figure 12: Showing CCTV Surveillance**

c. **Intrusion Detection Systems (IDS)**: IDS is a way of dealing with unauthorized access to information assets. A network-based system is established which functions in the following manner:

First, an attacker has to pass through the physical access prevention strategies. If one successfully breaches the preventive barrier, the threat is more concerning. In this case, an intrusion monitoring system, such as a CCTV camera, is used to analyze the activities of the attacker. After that, the IDS is placed, and it is connected to a network in a manner as shown in Figure 13:

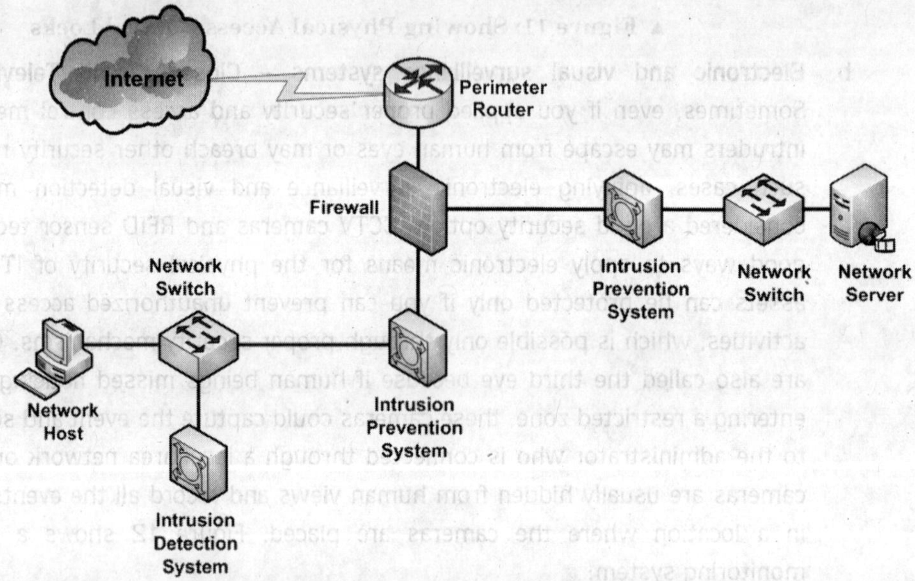

▲ **Figure 13: Displaying Networked IDS**

This networked IDS forwards the necessary information to the server, and all the further steps are taken by the risk management team or senior management team in an organization. IDS is very effective in providing proper security mechanisms for an organization's data.

3.7 Backup Security Measures

Data backups are taken to secure important data files and systems from being lost due to natural disasters or human errors and recover in case any kind of disaster has led to the loss of information. Therefore, it is very important to secure data backups. Sometimes, security of data backups becomes more concerning than the actual data files. Data security policies are a huge concern for organizations, and in that measure, securing a backup data is even more important. Storage security is integrated to the organizational security policy for the purpose that the joint efforts of security policies, tactical policies, and operational policies will make the organization's overall security stronger.

To maintain proper data backup security, an organization should implement the following practices:

a. **Assigning responsibility, authority, and accountability:** If accountability, responsibility, and authority are assigned properly to individual security personnel, the organizational security can be improved. The security of backup is not a separate task, but it is integrated to the overall protection of IT assets. If the data is extremely sensitive, individual roles and responsibilities should be divided.

b. **Assessing risks:** The risk management team must include assessment of data backup risk in the overall security policy for the organization. This will help in determining the impact of individual threats so that the backup security could be stronger.

c. **Developing data protection processes:** There should be separate measures established to protect the data being backed up. You cannot treat sensitive data and its backup in the same manner as you treat the ordinary or less sensitive information. Therefore, you need to devise strategies and explore ways for the protection of your backup data.

d. **Communicating the processes to the concerning people:** After you have developed strategies to secure the backup data, these processes need to be communicated to the other levels in your organization so that people who are concerned with the security of information can handle the processes properly. The communication should be clear and proper in order to avoid any compromise with information security and hence with the organization's security.

e. **Executing and testing the process:** After the processes to secure data are developed and communicated, it is the responsibilities of the management to execute and test the processes so that any misgivings can be easily analyzed and removed.

Thus, apart from all the security measures established to secure data, you must secure your backup data for recovering from failures and any kind of casualty or disaster. Security of all kinds of data is crucial in today's fiercely competitive world.

Data backup security provides a number of advantages. Some of them are listed as follows:

a. Close personal protection

b. Crowd control

c. Guard house personal

d. Alarm responses

e. Drug and explosive detection

f. Surveillance and private investigation

Summary

This chapter has explained about the development of secure information systems, development of secure applications, and governing guidelines and risk management processes. You have also studied about the security architecture and design mechanisms. Further, you have learned about the security issues related to hardware, storage devices, and peripheral devices. Moreover, you came to know about physical security of IT assets. In the end, the chapter has introduced you to the security measures that need to be taken to protect the data backup.

Exercises

■ Multiple Choice Questions

Q1. Secure information systems are developed by:

a. Integrating security with the system after it has been developed

b. Never integrating security with the information system

c. Keeping security as a separate action until the last step of the system development

d. Integrating risk analysis and management activities at the start of the system development lifecycle and continuing throughout the cycle

Ans. The correct option is d.

Q2. The security activities involved in each phase of SDLC are:

a. Description, dedication, encapsulation, and outputs

b. Description, synchronization, encryption, and outputs

c. Description, outputs, synchronization, and interdependencies

d. Interdependencies, synchronization, outputs, and action

Ans. The correct option is c.

Q3. Which of the following is a control gate in the development phase?

a. Authorizing the decision
b. Reviewing the architecture and design
c. Reviewing the confidentiality and availability
d. Reviewing the operational readiness

Ans. The correct option is b.

Q4. Which of the following sets is a set of concepts included in the common framework for developing secure applications?

a. Exploration, actions, and design guidelines
b. Foundation, exploration, and actions
c. Foundation, principles, and design guidelines
d. Actions, developments, and design guidelines

Ans. The correct option is c.

Q5. The risk management process involves:

a. Framing, deciding, executing, and deleting
b. Framing, assessing, monitoring, and responding
c. Monitoring, assessing, executing, and deleting
d. All of the above

Ans. The correct option is b.

Q6. Which of the following is used to provide physical security of IT assets?

a. Physical access control technique
b. CCTV surveillance technique
c. IDS technique
d. All of the above

Ans. The correct option is d.

Q7. Which of the following is a part of the security hardware system architecture?

a. Operating system
b. Peripheral devices and system buses
c. Microsoft Office's software components
d. None of the above

Ans. The correct option is b.

Q8. Which of the following is a part of the secure system design?

a. Layering
b. Abstraction
c. Security domains
d. All of the above

Ans. The correct option is d.

Q9. Which of the following is an issue faced by data storage devices?

a. Excessive data mounting
b. Theft, destruction, and damage
c. Too small size
d. All of the above

Ans. The correct option is b.

Q10. Data backup security can be implemented by:

a. Assigning accountability and responsibilities to the managers
b. Forcing the responsibilities on application developers
c. Applying firewalls
d. All of the above

Ans. The correct option is a.

■ Subjective Type Questions

Q1. Explain briefly the process of developing secure information systems.

Q2. Describe in brief the application development security.

Q3. What do you understand by security architecture and design?

Q4. What are the security issues related to hardware, data storage, and downloadable devices? Discuss.

Q5. What are the primary measures applied for the security of backup?

04 Introduction to Security Policies and Cyber Laws

OBJECTIVES

- Need for information security policy
- ISO Information security standards
- Various security policies and their review process
- Indian cyber law
- Objective and scope of the IT Act, 2000
- Intellectual property issues
- Intellectual-property-related legislation in India
- The Patent Law
- The copyright law
- The semiconductor law
- Software License

An information security policy is the documentation of organizational-level decisions on safeguarding information. While taking these decisions, managers face difficulty in making choices for resource allocation, competing objectives, and organization strategy related to safeguarding both technical and information resources and guiding employee behavior.

While designing an information security policy, it is ideal to understand that information is an asset and property of an organization. As such, information reaches beyond the territories of Information Technology (IT) and is present in all the areas of an organization. For effective results, an information security policy should be a part of the organization's asset management program and be organization wide.

There are various forms, styles, and kinds of security policies as there are different organizations, businesses, agencies, and universities. Apart from the various forms, each organization has a particular culture or mental model on the basis of which a policy should look and approve the document. The important aspect to be noted here is that each organization requires an information security policy.

The chapter begins with the need for security policies. Then it discusses about the International Standard Organization (ISO) information security standards. Further, you learn about various security policies and their review process. Apart from the security policies, the chapter also discusses about the Indian cyber law and the objective or scope of the IT Act, 2000. Next, it introduces you to the intellectual property issues and the Intellectual Property Related (IPR) legislation in India. Finally, the chapter explains the various laws such as patent, copyright, semiconductor, and software license.

4.1 Need for an Information Security Policy

From the software professional's perspective, the overall objective of an information security policy is to protect the integrity, confidentiality, and availability of information. It is true from the security perspective; however, not the organization objective. It is knowr that information is an asset and the property of an organization. As an asset, the management of an organization is expected to ensure that the appropriate levels of controls are in place to protect this resource.

An information security policy should be part of any organization's overall asset security policy. This policy is not defined to meet the security needs or audit requirements; it is a business process that allows management with the processes required to perform the fiduciary responsibility. The management of an organization is charged with a trust to ensure that adequate controls are in place to safeguard the asset of an enterprise. The security policies, standards, and procedures define a security program.
The information security professionals of an organization are responsible to implement security policies that depict the business and mission requirements of an organization.

Let's now discuss the information security standards defined by ISO.

4.2 Information Security Standards – ISO

It is known that security plays an important role in safeguarding the assets of an organization. As no single formula can guarantee 100% security, there is a requirement for a set of standards to ensure that the appropriate level of security is achieved, resources are utilized efficiently, and the best security practices are implemented. This section discusses the various standards and regulations available for information security.

The ISO, established in 1947, is a non-governmental international body that collaborates with the International Electrotechnical Commission (IEC) and the International Telecommunication Union (ITU). ISO has laid the following security standards:

- **ISO/IEC 27002:2005 (Code of practice for information security management)**: Refers to a code of practice for information security management which sets as a common basis and practical guideline for developing enterprise-level security standards and effective management practices.

  This standard specifies guidelines and best practices recommendations for the following ten security domains:

  - Security policy
  - Organization for information security
  - Asset management
  - Human resource security
  - Physical and environmental security
  - Communications and operations management
  - Access control
  - Information systems acquisition, development, and maintenance
  - Information security incident management
  - Business continuity management and compliance

- **ISO/IEC 27001:2005 (information security management system – requirements)**: Specifies the requirements for establishing, implementing, operating, monitoring, reviewing, maintaining, and improving a documented Information Security Management System (ISMS) within an organization. This standard allows an organization to select the adequate and proportionate security control to secure information assets. This standard is applicable for all types of organizations, including business enterprises, government agencies, etc.

  This standard defines a cyclic model known as "Plan-Do-Check-Act" (PDCA) model with the objective of establishing, implementing, monitoring, and improving the effectiveness of an enterprise's ISMS. The phases of the PDCA cycle are as follows:

  - The Plan phase to establish the ISMS
  - The Do phase to implement and operate the ISMS

- The Check phase to monitor and review the ISMS
- The Act phase to maintain and improve the ISMS

❒ **ISO/IEC 15408 (evaluation criteria for IT security)**: Consists of three parts: ISO/IEC 15408-1:2005 (introduction and general model), ISO/IEC 15408-2:2005 (security functional requirements), and ISO/IEC 15408-3:2005 (security assurance requirements). This standard helps an organization in evaluating, validating, and certifying the security assurance of a technology product against various factors such as security functional requirements specified in the standard.

❒ **ISO/IEC 1335 (IT Security Management)**: Consists of a series of guidelines for technical security control measures such as:

- The ISO/IEC 13335-1:2004 standard defines the concepts and models for information and communication technology security management
- The ISO/IEC TR 13335-3:1998 standard defines the techniques for the management of IT security
- The ISO/IEC TR 13335-4:2000 standard covers the selection of safeguards
- The ISO/IEC TR 13335-5:2001 covers management guidance on network security

4.3 Introducing Various Security Policies and Their Review Process

It has been discussed earlier that many organizations are required to develop and maintain specific security policies and procedures. Apart from designing a security policy, its review process is also essential to ensure that the policy is appropriate or adequate. Let's begin with a discussion on the following types of security policies and then focus on the review process:

❒ The World Wide Web (WWW) policy

❒ The e-mail security policy

❒ The corporate policy

This section also presents yet another sample security policy.

■ WWW Policy

The Internet is a network of networks providing various services such as sending e-mails, transferring files, login from remote systems, and WWW. The WWW is the universe of the

Internet-accessible information. While browsing the Internet, there are various risks, some of which are as follows:

- The software provided to the employees for business use can be used for any for-profit outside business activity or potentially embarrasses the company
- The software or documents downloaded over the WWW can contain virus
- The users of an organization while browsing the Internet can access sites containing offensive materials

To avoid such risks, the organization needs to define the WWW policy. Some examples of WWW policy are as follows:

- No offensive or harassing material may be made available through company websites
- No personal commercial advertising should be made available through company websites
- The personal material on or accessible from the website should be minimal
- No company confidential material should be made available
- Users of an organization should not be permitted to install or run Web servers

E-mail Security Policy

E-mails can be used not only to improve the communication between employees, but also to transmit proprietary information, harass other users, engage in illegal activities, and serve as evidence against the company in legal actions. E-mail is actually the electronic version of a postcard and requires special policy considerations from archiving to content guidelines. Therefore, the organizations should take various points into consideration while writing e-mail policies.

Generally, while creating an e-mail policy, the general rules and guidelines that users need to follow should appear first in the e-mail policy document. An organization can include the following "Ten Commandments of E-mail" while developing an e-mail policy:

1. You will [may be replaced may be complicated by readers] demonstrate the same respect thy gives to verbal communications.
2. You will check thy spelling, thy grammar, and read thine own message thrice before thou send it.

3. You will not forward any chain letter.
4. You will not transmit unsolicited mass e-mail (spam) unto anyone.
5. You will not send messages that are hateful, harassing, or threatening unto fellow users.
6. You will not send any message that supports illegal or unethical activities.
7. You will remember thine e-mail is the electronic equivalent of a post card and will not be used to transmit sensitive information.
8. You will not use thine email broadcasting facilities except for making appropriate announcements.
9. You will keep thy personal email use to a minimum.
10. You will keep thy policies and procedures sacred and help administrators protect them from abusers.

■ Corporate Policy

Corporate policy is the formal declaration of the principles and procedures according to which a company will operate. These principles or guidelines are laid down by the board of directors of a company or the senior management policy committee. A corporate policy comprises:

- ❒ Company's mission statement
- ❒ Company's objectives
- ❒ Principles on the basis of which strategic decisions are made

A corporate policy also lays down the factors for measuring performance and ensuring accountability at all levels of an organization. It is also known as company policy, which is defined after an analysis of all internal and external factors, affecting an organization's objectives, operations, and plans.

■ Sample Security Policy

Let's now look at the sample security policy. The template of the sample security policy is as follows:

1. Information security policy
    a. Purpose

   b. Aims and commitments
   c. Responsibilities
   d. Councils
   e. Heads of departments
   f. Users and external parties
2. Risk assessment and the classification of information
   a. Risk assessment of information held
   b. Personal data
3. Protection of information systems and assets
4. Protection of confidential information
   a. Storage
   b. Access
   c. Remote access
   d. Copying
   e. Disposal
   f. Use of portable devices or media
   g. Exchange of information and use of e-mail
   h. Cryptographic controls
   i. System planning and acceptance
   j. Backup
   k. Further information
   l. Hard copies
      i. Protective marking
      ii. Storage
      iii. Removal
      iv. Transmission
      v. Disposal

   j. Enforcement
   k. Compliance
   l. Other relevant university policies or guidance
   m. Contacts for further information
   n. Sample risk assessment
   o. Scope, criteria, and organization
      i. Scope
      ii. Criteria
5. Risk identification and analysis
   a. Assets
   b. Threats and risks
6. Appendix 1: Sample risk assessment
7. Glossary

■ Policy Review Process

Each policy created should be reviewed appropriately to ensure successful policy development. Figure 1 shows the six important steps to be performed while evaluating information
security policy:

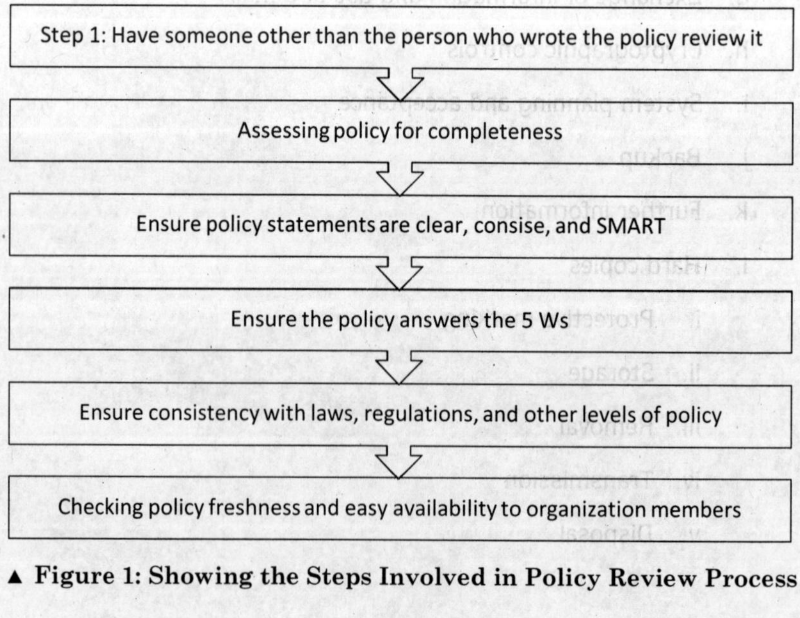

▲ **Figure 1: Showing the Steps Involved in Policy Review Process**

Let's discuss each of these steps in detail.

- **Step 1:** Having someone other than the person who wrote the policy review it: Generally, people tend to identify their own errors in a small percentage of time. Therefore, someone other than the person who created the policy should review and assess for mistakes. The policy reviewer should be aware about the organization fundamentals of information security and detail oriented for best results. Moreover, the person should be technically sound to review the policy for technical accuracy.

  The security policy should have an owner who has approved management responsibility for the development, review, and evaluation of the policy. Instead of the policy owner, the other person or team should be assigned the task to improvise the policy.

- **Step 2:** Assessing policy for completeness: The second step is divided into the following sub steps:
  - Assessing policy framework for completeness: Checks or examines the existence of standards and procedures supporting the policy set
  - Assessing policy elements for completeness: Checks or examines if the policy is not flawed due the lack of an element

- **Step 3:** Ensuring that policy statement is clear, concise, and SMART: SMART stands for specific, measurable, achievable, realistic, and time-bound. In this step, the policy reviewer ensures that the policy is clear, and simple language is used to ensure that it can be easily understood by everyone.

- **Step 4:** Ensuring that policy answers the 5 Ws: In this step, the reviewer checks whether the appropriate function is defined for the correct person in place. The reviewer also ensures when the actions will be accomplished. In other words, the policy should clearly explain the purpose, background, or policy statement.

- **Step 5:** Ensuring consistency with laws, regulations, and other levels of policy: In this step, the reviewer ensures that the policy is consistent with various laws and regulations; otherwise, the organization will face lawsuits. Also, the policy should ensure consistency with the laws and regulations of each country. During policy assessment, the policies are checked for consistency with lower and higher levels. Any discrepancy found should be resolved.

- **Step 6:** Checking policy freshness and easy availability to organization members: In this step, a policy is examined for provisions to keep it updated. This is important because an outdated policy can result into damage than good.

4.4 Introduction to Indian Cyber Law

Before indulging in any hacking activity, an ethical hacker must be familiar with the penalties of hacking a system. Prior to hacking a system, the ethical hacker must get a signed legal document from the target organization. Ethical hackers should know when and where to use their hacking skills and understand the consequences of misusing these skills.

Cybercrimes involve criminal activities, such as fraud, theft, forgery, and defamation, which are subject to the Indian Penal Code (IPC). In cybercrimes, a computer can be either used as a tool or a target object or both. In India, the unlawful use of computers has given birth to a new age of cybercrimes that are addressed by the IT Act, 2000. A separate set of laws, known as cyber laws or Internet laws, has been designed to regulate cybercrimes.

The two categories of cyber laws are as follows:

- **Computer as a target:** Specifies that a computer is used as a tool to attack other computers, such as virus and worm attacks
- **Computer as a weapon:** Specifies that a computer is used as a weapon to commit crimes, such as credit card frauds, cyber terrorism, and pornography

The IT Act, 2000 consists of 94 sections that are grouped into 13 chapters. It also includes four schedules. This Act was later amended in 2008, and it now includes 124 sections and 14 chapters. The amendments made in 2008 have replaced Schedules I and II and deleted Schedules III and IV.

The IT Act, 2000 addresses issues such as legal recognition of electronic records, legal recognition of digital signatures, secure electronic record, secure digital signature, and license to issue digital signature certificates. The IT Act, 2000 amended in 2008 has brought several additional new sections in it on offences such as cyber terrorism and data protection.

Need for Cyber Laws

With the growth of the Internet, various new systems have also developed, such as electronic commerce (for example, online marketing or online shopping) and electronic learning. Since these systems involve money transactions, there was an urgent need for some legal system to prevent frauds. This in turn led to the formulation of cyber laws.

Jurisprudence of Cyber Law

IT Act, 2000 is the primary source of cyber laws in India. It came into force on October 17, 2000. The Act was primarily brought up to provide legal recognition to electronic commerce and facilitate filing of electronic records with the Government. The Act also penalizes persons involved in cybercrimes and issues strict punishments (imprisonment terms up to 10 years and compensation up to 1 crore). A number of rules, regulations, orders, and acts were passed subsequently to complement the IT Act, 2000. They are as under:

- An executive order was passed on September 12, 2002. It contained instructions related to the provisions of the Act with regard to protected systems and application for the issuance of a Digital Signature Certificate. The IT (Removal of Difficulties) Order, 2002 was passed on September 19, 2002 in which minor errors in the Act were rectified.
- In 2002, the Negotiable Instruments (Amendments and Miscellaneous Provisions) Act, 2002 was passed, which amended the IT Act to introduce the concept of electronic cheques and truncated cheques. IT (Use of Electronic Records and Digital Signatures) Rules, 2004 was brought up in 2004 to provide the necessary legal framework for filing of documents with the Government issue of licenses by the Government and facilitated payment and receipt of fees to the Government bodies. Same day, the IT (Certifying Authorities) Rules, 2000 was enforced. It contained rules related to the eligibility, appointment, and working of Certifying Authorities (CAs). It also laid down the technical standards, procedures, and security methods to be used by a CA. The rules were subsequently amended in 2003, 2004 and 2006. IT (Certifying Authority) Regulations, 2001 was enforced on July 9, 2001. The regulations further added to the technical standards and procedures to be followed by a CA. It contained the following two important guidelines for CAs:
    - Guidelines for the submission of application for a license to operate as a CA under the IT Act. These guidelines were issued on July 9, 2001.

- Guidelines for the submission of certificates and certification revocation lists to the Controller of CAs for publishing in the National Repository of Digital Certificates. These guidelines were issued on December 16, 2002.

The Cyber Regulations Appellate Tribunal (CRAT) (Procedure) Rules, 2000 was also enforced on October 17, 2000. These rules provide for the appointment and working of the CRAT. The primary role of CRAT is to hear appeals against orders of the Adjudicating Officers. The CRAT (salary, allowances, and other terms and conditions of service of Presiding Officer) Rules, 2003 lay down the salary, allowances, and other terms for the Presiding Officer of the CRAT. IT (Other powers of Civil Court vested in Cyber Appellate Tribunal) Rules 2003 provide some additional powers to the CRAT.

The IT (Qualification and Experience of Adjudicating Officers and Manner of Holding Enquiry) Rules, 2003 were passed on March 17, 2003. These rules lay down the qualifications required for the recruitment of Adjudicating Officers. The chief responsibility of the Adjudicating Officers under the IT Act is to adjudicate on cases such as unauthorized access, unauthorized copying of data, spread of viruses, denial of service attacks, disruption of computers, computer manipulation, etc. These rules also lay down the manner and mode of inquiry and adjudication by these officers.

There were neither Adjudicating Officers nor any CRAT for almost two years even after the implementation of the IT Act. A public interest litigation was filed by the students of the Asian School of Cyber Laws in the Bombay High Court for the appointment of Adjudicating Officers and establishing CRAT. On October 9, 2002, the Bombay High Court ordered for the recruitment of Adjudicating Officers and constitution of CRAT. The court directed the Central Government to announce an appoint so as to make the public aware. Following this, the Central Government passed an order on March 23, 2003, which appointed the Secretary of Department of Information Technology of each State or Union Territories of India as the adjudicating officer for that State or Union Territory. The IT (Security Procedure) Rules, 2004were enforced on October 29, 2004. They deal with secure digital signatures and secure electronic records. Also relevant are the IT (Other Standards) Rules, 2003. An order related to blocking of websites was passed on February 27, 2003, This authorized the Computer Emergency Response Team (CERT-IND) to instruct the Department of Telecommunications (DoT) to block a particular website.

Several cybercrimes come under the ambit of the IPC such as forgery of electronic records, cyber frauds, destroying electronic evidence, etc. The IPC requires digital evidences as per the Indian Evidence Act for penalization purpose. The evidences must be proved in court. In cases where bank records are used as evidence, the provisions of the Bankers' Book Evidence Act (as amended by the IT Act) become relevant. There is also Reserve Bank of India Act (amended by the IT Act), which may become relevant in select cases. The Code of Criminal Procedure and the IT Act play an important role in the investigation and adjudication of cybercrimes in India. Let's now learn about objective and scope of the IT Act 2000.

4.5 Objective and Scope of the IT Act, 2000

The IT Act, 2000 consists of 94 sections that are grouped into 13 chapters. There are four schedules included in this IT Act. This Act was later amended in 2008, and now it includes 124 sections and 14 chapters. The amendments made in 2008 have replaced Schedules I and II and deleted Schedules III and IV. The IT Act, 2000 addresses issues, such as legal recognition of electronic records, legal recognition of digital signatures, secure electronic record, secure digital signature, and license to issue digital signature certificates. The IT Act, 2000 amended in 2008 has brought several additional new sections in it regarding offences, such as cyber terrorism and data protection.

India is the 12th country in the world to adopt cyber laws. The IT Act of India was legislated on May 17, 2000. The Act aims at the regulation of the use of IT. It aims mainly to legalize and regulate the system of electronic data interchange, electronic communication, and electronic commerce. This Act extends to the whole of India and also applies to any offence or contravention thereunder committed outside India by any person. The Act covers use of all the computer systems and networks located in India. Let us have a look on the main features of this Act:

- Chapter 1 of the Act deals with important definitions of the terms used in the regulation. It sets the scope of meaning of key terms of which the Act comprises.
- Chapter 2 covers regulations regarding digital signature. It provides legal recognition to digital signature.
- Chapter 3 deals with electronic governance. It legalizes the use of electronic records in government organizations and establishments.

- Chapter 4 involves attribution, acknowledgment, and dispatch of electronic records and their certifying authority.
- Chapter 5 comprises secure electronic records and secure digital signatures. It establishes the rules and regulations related to the electronic gazettes.
- Chapter 6 covers regulation of certifying authorities.
- Chapter 7 deals with digital signature and details its certification with the duties of subscribers.
- Chapter 8 involves duties of subscribers.
- Chapter 9 comprises penalties and adjudication by the cyber regulations appellate Tribunal. It covers penalty for damaging a computer or computer system.
- Chapter 10 details about the establishment of the CRAT to secure justice in such cases.
- Section 85 of the Act specifies the corporate social responsibility of a business. As per the Act, the directors and managers of a corporation are responsible to uphold the corporate responsibility with pursuance of law and IT ethics. Any violation of IT ethics or this law that is conducted with the knowledge of these authorities holds them responsible for not stopping it.

The Act contributes significantly in empowering organizations to fight against cybercrimes. It also protects the rights of consumers in carrying on with electronic business.

4.6 Intellectual Property Issues

Intellectual property refers to intangible property that has been created by individuals and corporates for their personal benefit or usage such as copyright, trade mark, patent, and digital data. It is created through human intelligence and mental efforts. It is therefore unethical to copy or steal the creativity and efforts of someone else. The technology that contributes to the creation and security of documents over the computer is the same that contributes in copying it easily. The dissemination of this copied document is also very quick and easy.

India is one of the signatories of the agreement that established the World Trade Organization (WTO). WTO came into force on January 1, 1995. The WTO Agreement consists of an agreement on Trade-Related Aspects of Intellectual Property Rights

(TRIPS). TRIPS prescribes the minimum standards to be adopted by the member countries within a stipulated timeframe regarding the following seven areas of intellectual property:

i. Copyright and related rights

ii. Trademarks

iii. Geographical indications

iv. Industrial designs

v. Patents

vi. Layout designs (Topographies) of integrated circuits

vii. Protection of undisclosed information

Let's now learn about intellectual-property-related legislation in India.

4.7 Overview of Intellectual-Property-Related Legislation in India

Intellectual property rights refer to the rights given to a person or an organization for their intellectual activity, i.e., creations of mind. This intellectual activity may be in the field of industry, science, literature, or any other artistic field. According to the Centre for Intellectual Property Rights, there are four major categories of Intellectual Property Rights in India, namely, Copyright, Patent, Trade Mark, and Design Protection.

Computer software come under the ambit of Copyright law and are protected by the Indian Copyright Act, 1957. The Indian Copyright Act was amended in 1994. These amendments came into effect from May 10, 1995. The main features of the Indian Copyright

Act are as follows:

- The Act specifies clearly the rights of a copyright holder
- The Act deals with the rentals of software
- The Act clearly states the rights of a user to make backup copies

Since software copyright violation can be carried out very easily by simply copying the software and since it is difficult in most cases to distinguish between an original software and a duplicate software, it had become utmost necessary to implement the Copyright Act. Some of the key features of the Act are as follows:

- Copying and distributing of copyrighted software without proper authorization is illegal according to section 14 of the Act
- The violator of the Act is liable to be tried under civil as well as criminal law
- A violator may be subjected to civil and criminal action for injunction, actual damages (which includes the profits, if any, made by the violator), or statutory damages per infringement
- The Act provides for strict punishment and/or heavy fines for any violation of software copyright
- According to Section 63 B, jail term of minimum 7 days can be given for a software copyright violation, which can be extended up to 3 years

Rationale behind Intellectual Property

To understand the rationale behind intellectual property, we must revisit the concept of *property* and the justification behind the protection of tangible property. In a capitalist society, such justification comes from two angles – labor and personality.

The justification from labor angle was put forward by Locke. According to Locke, a person creates property for himself and the State when he takes from the State what nature has provided as a common resource and mixes his labor with it. The State must encourage such people by rewarding them so that they remain innovative and perform better. Similar is the case with intellectual property. It involves both – innovation and value creation.

The society must encourage people to strive to be innovative and come up with creative solutions to generate wealth and welfare. Locke's idea of occurrence of commons in abundance in the primitive stage corresponds to the idea of intellectual property in modern day. This is public domain.

Another analogy can be drawn between tangible and intangible intellectual properties. All kinds of labor do not enjoy the same stature in society. Very good examples of this are slave labor and labor done by a housewife. The work done by slaves has never been counted as property generators. Similarly, even though the housewives are engaged whole day in some or the other activity of the household, their labor is not recognized as an economic activity. In the same way, the traditional knowledge and folklore do not get recognized as creation of knowledge, skill, or idea in the field of intellectual property.

The justification for IP from the *personality* angle is based on the belief that property represents the personality of a person. Hegel was the main advocate of this view who believed that property is the embodiment of one's personality. Property is a personal and private thing and needs to be protected. The same holds true for intellectual property also. However, this justification may apply differently to different subject matters. For example, the creations of mind in the field of creativity like art, music, or literature may reflect the personality of the creator, but software development, engineering designs, etc. do not support this justification. However, the personality justification has found place in the moral rights under the Copyright Act. These moral rights relate to preserving the integrity of the work against any change which has the potential of damaging either the reputation of the author or the message of his work.

Thus, none of the angles has been able to justify Intellectual Property Rights completely. Some intellectual properties derive their justification from the labor angle while others derive justification from the personality angle. Both the angles must be considered together for serving the entire gamut of intellectual property.

■ Underlying Premises of IP

IP is primarily the mental activity to produce some monetary benefits, and it is based on certain premises. You have the rights to own intellectual properly if you are generating any kind of wealth/welfare through your creative solutions. The IPRs are based on the following three premises:

1. Creative activities culminating in IP can be increased by proper encouragement and adequate economic incentives.
2. The creators of intellectual property should be rewarded in a just manner by giving appropriate economic benefit. This economic benefit can be ensured by granting them monopoly rights over their creation for a limited period of time.
3. The intellectual property regime ensures just economic rewards to creators of wealth and at the same time safeguards the interests of other entrepreneurs and the society at large.

■ Balancing the Rights of the Owner of the IP and the Society

Similar to any other right granted to us by our constitution, intellectual property rights are also not absolute but are limited by the rights of fellow citizens and the rights of the society. These rights are strongly guided by the considerations that the state has to provide an equal access to opportunities to all its citizens while protecting the intellectual property rights of individuals. Thus, it becomes the responsibility of the state to harmonize conflicting claims and maintain a balance.

IPRs are essentially negative rights that they stop others from copying or counterfeiting the intellectual property of an individual or organization. For example, in case of patents, if an invention is patented by a person for a certain time period and another person, working independently, makes the same invention, the person is expected to get a license from the first person to use his invention during that time period. But in cases of other IPRs like Copyright or Trademark, this absolute right can be made somewhat lenient to safeguard the rights of others.

The state seeks to safeguard the rights of other individuals by adopting mechanisms like limiting the period of IPRs and making preservation of life, environment, peace, and morality important factors in the grant of IPRs. The licenses can also be revoked in cases of abuse of IPR.

■ Enforcement of IPRS

While in most contracts, the rights and obligations of the contracting parties are clearly laid down, any disputes that may arise in connection with the contract can be resolved on the basis of the provisions in the contract itself. IPRs are different from these contracts in that they are aimed at excluding others from doing certain things as regards the IP even without the existence of a formal contract between them and the owner of the right. The purpose of IPRs will be served only when they can be implemented with speed and within reasonable cost.

The national laws provide the legal framework for dealing with the IPR violations. In addition to this, TRIPS agreement also provides certain guidelines to the member countries of WTO. These guidelines are related to the IPR enforcement and must be included in the IPR-related national laws. The TRIPS agreement also lays down certain conditions to be fulfilled for effective enforcement of IPRs. These conditions are as follows:

- ❐ The procedure of IPR enforcement should be fair and equitable
- ❐ It should be simple and not complicated

- It should be speedy
- The parties involved should enjoy the right to:
  - Be heard
  - Produce evidence
  - Get a written decision
  - Judicial review, etc.

The remedy granted by the court of law can be injunctive or a compensatory relief or the court may require the defendant to deposit the infringed material for destruction. This make the purpose of IPR enforcement quite clear to prevent infringements of property rights of people while safeguarding legitimate trade at the same time.

IP and Constitution of India

The Constitution of India mentions Patents, Inventions and Designs, Copyright, Trade Marks, and Merchandise under entry 49 of the Union list of matters, falling within the Union Government, for the purpose of legislation. There is no specific mention of intellectual property in the Constitution. Property, in the constitution, generally means tangible property. However, IP as a form of property can be put under Article 300A, which deals with property that can be entitled to a legal right.

It has been observed by experts that there may be situations where the Intellectual Property Right of a person, especially the Copyright, clashes with the fundamental right to freedom of speech and expression granted to all the citizens by the Constitution of India. The courts have always tried to safeguard the fundamental rights of the citizens, especially the freedom of speech and expression. Any other right that poses a threat to the freedom of speech and expression of people is likely to face challenges.

Let's now learn about patent.

4.8 Patent

A Patent is a monopoly right granted by the State to an inventor for a limited period of time in exchange for the public disclosure of the invention. The monopoly rights mean the right to make, use, license, or sell an invention to the exclusion of others. Once the term of patent expires, the invention comes into the public domain. In India, all patents are granted for period of 20 years.

The system of granting patents serves many purposes. If the invention is commercially utilized, the patent ensures just reward to the inventor in terms of money and recognition, thus paying the inventor for investing his time and effort, knowledge and skills, and money and other resources. For the society, the commercial exploitation of an invention means newer and better products, higher productivity, and more efficient means of production. The main objective of granting patents is to accelerate the technological and industrial development.

A patent system promotes technological innovation and its spread. This directly and indirectly affects the society, leading to better utilization of resources, development, growth, and prosperity. Thus, the number of patents filed and granted nationally and internationally is a good indicator of the growth of science and technology in a country.

Patents are granted by the State and hence have territorial applicability. It is valid only in the country that has granted the patent. There is no mechanism to obtain a global patent. A person is required to apply separately in all the countries where he/she may want his/her invention to be protected.

However, there exists a unified procedure for filing of patent applications in more than one country at the same time. This has been made possible by the Patent Cooperation Treaty (PCT) of the World Intellectual Property Organization (WIPO). Under this treaty, the applicant can file an application for patenting his/her invention in any one of the countries which is a member of the PCT. The application thus filed is called an International Application. This establishes a filing date, also called priority date, in all the other member countries. After this, the applicant has to follow the procedure for seeking patent in each country of his/her choice individually. This is because granting of patents is the prerogative of every state and there is no such thing as an international patent. There were 123 members of PCT as on October 15, 2003. India joined the PCT on December 7, 1998.

■ The Patent System

The practice of granting monopolies by patent is not a new concept and can be traced back to over 600 years. The term **patent** has originally come from the term *Letters Patent.* It was a grant given by the King or the Queen to individuals, mainly for inventions. This grant used to be certain rights or privileges which were presented in the form of an open document carrying the King's or the Queen's seal at the bottom.

In India, the patenting system is governed by Indian Patents Act, 1970. The Act was later amended by Patents (Amendment) Act, 1999 and Patents (Amendment) Act, 2002. The amendments came into force on May 2, 2003.

Patentable Invention

According to the Indian Patent Act, a patentable invention is defined as follows:

"A new product or process involving an inventive step and capable of industrial application."

Thus, an invention must fulfill the following three requirements for being considered as a patentable invention:

- **The invention must be 'new'**: Something that is already present and known is not patentable. An invention is considered new if it does not form a part of the already available knowledge on the date of filing the application. If the invention is disclosed, in any way, before filing the application for patent, it is disqualified from being 'new'. For example, an English inventor was denied grant of a patent for inventing an improved design of a ball point pen because he had mistakenly published the details of his invention even before filing the application for patent.
- **The invention must involve an 'inventive step'**: 'Inventive step' means that the invention must not be obvious or follow directly from something which is already known. An example of an inventive step could be rolling of metals without affecting their original characteristics but adding on other characteristics like increasing toughness, etc.
- **The invention must have 'industrial application'**: To be patentable, the invention has to be capable of industrial application. Industry here refers to any practical and useful activity which is not related to creative and aesthetic activity. It may or may not be related to the use of machineries and manufacturing.

Nonpatentable Invention

A patent that cannot be patented by an individual or an organization is termed as nonpatentable. There are a number of categories that are nonpatentable. Anything can be patented only if it is a fresh invention, and it causes no harm to the living beings in the world and follows the law.

The categories which cannot be patented under IPA are as follows:

- An invention, which is detrimental to public order, morality, environment, or health; for example, the invention of a new type of gambling machine.
- An invention related to atomic energy. In India, atomic energy is not a public domain. It is the sole responsibility of the Central Government. An invention which is against the laws of nature. A discovery of a scientific principle or the formulation of an abstract theory is not patentable on the grounds that it is not an invention.
- The discovery of a living thing or *non-living* substances or objects occurring in nature because it is not an invention.
- A substance obtained by a mere admixture of certain components or a process of producing such a mixture does not qualify as an inventive step and hence cannot be patented
- Arrangement or re-arrangement or duplication of known devices, where each functions independent of one another in a known way without changing the end results also does not qualify as an inventive step and hence is non-patentable.
- Traditional knowledge is non-patentable because they are not new and form a part of the prior knowledge or state of the art. A mathematical or business method or a computer programme or algorithms are not patentable as they follow logically from a known premise.

The following items also do not qualify as inventions as defined by the Indian Patents Act and are therefore not patentable:

- A method related to agriculture or horticulture
- Any process related to the medicinal, surgical, curative, prophylactic, diagnostic, therapeutic, or other treatment of human beings and animals
- Plants and animals in whole or part, excluding micro-organisms
- Seeds and biological processes for the production of plants and animals

The following two categories belong to other forms of intellectual property and hence are not subject matters of patents:

- A literary, dramatic, musical, or artistic work, including cinematographic work and television productions. This is covered by Copyright Act.

- Layout designs of integrated circuits. These are covered separately by the SICLD Act.

There are certain substances which do not come under patenting, but the process of manufacturing those substances can be patented. Some examples are as follows:

- Substances which could be used as food or medicine or drug.
- Substances which are prepared or produced by chemical processes such as biochemical, biotechnological, and microbiological processes. However, if the substance itself is used as a medicine or drug, it can be patented.

Computer programmes and microorganisms are two such areas where patent protection is increasingly sought. In India, computer programmes are protected under the Copyright Act, 1957.

Dr. Ananda Chakraborty was granted a patent in 1980 by the US Supreme Court. Hegenetically engineered bacterium, which could degrade oil spills. The bacterium did not exist naturally. This satisfied the criteria of novelty, non-obviousness, and industrial application which were necessary for an invention to be patentable. This was the first time in the history that a living entity was given the status of a product. In the modern days, biotechnology and genetics are emerging as major fields of research. Employment of living entities like microorganisms, viruses, genetic elements like DNA, RNA, enzymes, plant cell lines, animals, etc. has become inevitable and common in developing newer technologies in these areas. Since these are indispensable for the advancement of science and technology and possess huge potential for creating wealth and profits, it is imperative to grant intellectual property protection to them. However, the patent protection involving living entities do face serious ethical and legal issues. This can be understood from the fact that the USA has not been able to grant patent protection to the creation of the animal clone Dolly, the cloned sheep.

A point to remember in this context is that there exists a very thin line of distinction between 'discovery' and 'invention' in a number of cases in biotechnology. Thus, even though a discovery may relate to living entity, it may qualify as an invention. The definition of 'discovery' and 'invention' therefore needs to be reviewed so that the distinction between them is easy and unambiguous.

■ Procedure for Obtaining Patent

The application for getting a patent for an invention may be made by a person who is the true and first inventor of the invention (or his/her assignee) or by the legal representative of a deceased person, provided that he/she was entitled to file such an application by the deceased person before his/her death.

If the inventor is an employee in an organization, the inventions made by him/her during his/her employment would be patentable in his/her name. The ownership of the patent would, however, depend on the contract between the employee and his/her employer. In R&D organizations, normally, the ownership rights are retained by the employer while the patent is in the employee's name.

Let's now learn about copyright.

4.9 Copyright

Copyright is a form of protection provided to the authors of "original works of authorship." This is given in the fields of literature, dramatics, music, art, etc. This protection is applicable to published as well as unpublished works. In India, the Copyright protection is governed by the Indian Copyright Act, 1976. The Section 106of the Copyright Act, 1976 gives the following exclusive rights to the authors:

- To make copies of the work or to phonorecord it.
- To prepare derivative works based upon the original work.
- To distribute copies or phonorecords of the work to the public either by sale or rent or lease or lending, etc.
- To perform the work in public if the work is in the field of literature, music, dramatics, choreography, pantomimes, motion pictures, or any other audio visual work.
- To display the work publicly if the work is in the field of literature, music, dramatics, choreography, pantomimes, motion pictures or any other audiovisual work.
- If the work is related to sound recordings, he/she has a right to perform the work publicly by means of a digital audio transmission.
- In addition to these, authors of works of visual art may also have the rights of attribution and integrity according to section 106A of the Copyright Act, 1976.

- It is illegal for anyone to infringe any of the rights provided by the copyright.
- Act to the owner of copyright. These rights, however, are not unlimited in scope.

Some of the limitations defined by the Sections from 107 to 121 of the Copyright Act, 1976 are:

1. Doctrine of fair use is applied
2. Limited use of copyrighted work is permitted on the payment of specified royalties and compliance with statutory conditions

The Section 14 of the Copyright Act defines "copyright" as the exclusive right to do or authorize the doing of any of the following:

1. To reproduce a computer programme in any material form; including the storing of it on any medium by electronic means.

   Illustration 1

   Tanmay has the exclusive right to reproduce the School Management software on CD, DVD, and other storage media.

   Illustration 2

   Tanmay has the exclusive right to upload the School Management software onto his website.

2. To issue copies of the computer programme to the public.

   Illustration 1

   Tanmay has the exclusive right to provide the School Management software along with computer magazines so that the general public can use the software.

   Illustration 2

   Tanmay has the exclusive right to upload the School Management software onto his website so that people around the world can download it.

3. To performthe computer programme in public or communicate it to the public.

   Illustration 1

   Tanmay has the exclusive right to give a public demonstration of the workings of the School Management software.

4. To make any cinematograph film or sound recording in respect of the computer programme.

   Illustration 1

   Tanmay has the exclusive right to make a promotional film depicting the working of the School Management software.

   Illustration 2

   Tanmay has the exclusive right to make a promotional sound recording depicting the working of the School Management software.

5. To make any translation of the computer programme.

   Illustration 1

   Currently, the School Management software has all the menu commands and help files in English. Tanmay has the exclusive right to make a version of the School Management software that has the menu commands and help files in Hindi.

6. To make any adaptation of the work.

7. To do, in relation to a translation or an adaptation of the computer programme, any of the acts specified above.

8. To sell, give on hire, offer for sale, or offer for hire any copy of the computer programme.

   Illustration 1

   Tanmay has the exclusive right to offer the School Management software for sale.

   Illustration 2

   Tanmay has the exclusive right to act as an Application Service Provider for the School Management software; e.g., a user will be charged a small fee per month for using the School Management software.

Who can claim copyright?

In case works of authorship, the copyright is the property of the author who has created the work. Thus, the author or those who derive their rights through the author can claim copyright.

If the work was done by a hired person, the employer is considered the author and the copyright for the work goes to the employer. 'Work made for hire' has been defined by the Section 101 of the Copyright Act as:

1. a work prepared by an employee within the scope of his or her employment or
2. a work specially ordered or commissioned for use as:
   - a contribution to a collective work
   - a part of a motion picture or other audio-visual work
   - a translation
   - a supplementary work
   - a compilation
   - an instructional text
   - a test
   - answer material for a test
   - an atlas

if it is agreed between the parties in a written agreement that the work shall be considered as a work made for hire.

In case of a joint work, unless there is a contrary agreement, all the authors are the co-owners of the copyright. This is, however, not the case with collective works like publication of periodicals where each author contributes separately. The copyright for each contribution rests with the individual contributor.

Two general principles for copyright are as follows:

- Transfer of a work to a person does not by itself transfer the copyright with it
- Minors may claim copyright, but the laws of the state may regulate the business dealings involving copyrights owned by the minors

Copyright protects "original works of authorship" that are produced in a tangible form of expression. The work thus produced may be communicated with the help of a machine or device.

What Works are Protected?

Copyrightable works include the following categories:

1. Literary works
2. Musical works, including any accompanying words
3. Dramatic works, including any accompanying music
4. Pantomimes and choreographic works
5. Pictorial, graphic, and sculptural works
6. Motion pictures and other audiovisual works
7. Sound recordings
8. Architectural works

These categories need to be viewed broadly. For example, computer programs and most "compilations" may be registered as "literary works"; maps and architectural plans may be registered as "pictorial, graphic, and sculptural works."

What is not protected by copyright?

Several categories of material are generally not eligible for copyright protection. Some of these are:

- Works that have not been fixed in a tangible form of expression
- Titles, names, short phrases, and slogans; familiar symbols or designs; mere variations of typographic ornamentation, lettering, or coloring; mere listing of ingredients or contents
- Ideas, procedures, methods, systems, processes, concepts, principles, discoveries, or devices
- Works that consist of information that is a common property and that contains no original authorship; for example, standard calendars, height and weight charts, tape measures, etc.

How to secure a copyright?

Copyright is secured automatically upon creation.

Copyright is secured automatically when a work is created. A work is considered as "created" when it is fixed in a copy or a phonorecord for the first time.

"Copies" are defined as material objects from which a work can be read or visually perceived either directly or with the help of a machine or device, such as books, manuscripts, sheet music, film, videotape, or microfilm.

"Phonorecords" are material objects which contain fixations of sounds such as cassette tapes, CDs, or vinyl disks.

Thus, for example, a song (the "work") can be fixed in sheet music ("copies") or in phonograph disks ("phonorecords"),or both. If a work is prepared over a period of time, the part of the work that is fixed on a particular date constitutes the created work as of that date.

The Copyright Act, 1976 defines publication as follows:

- "Publication" is the distribution of copies or phonorecords of a work to the public by sale or other transfer of ownership, or by rental, lease, or lending. The offering to distribute copies or phonorecords to a group of persons for the purposes of further distribution, public performance, or public display constitutes publication. A public performance or display of a work does not by itself constitute a publication.
- Publication is no longer necessary for acquiring copyright as it was under Copyright Act,1909.

Copyright Registration

Copyright registration is a legal formality intended to make a public record of the basic facts of a particular copyright. However, registration is not a condition of copyright protection. Even though registration is not a requirement for protection, the copyright law provides several inducements or advantages to encourage copyright owners to make registration.

Some of the advantages are as follows:

- Registration establishes a public record of the copyright claim.
- Before an infringement suit may be filed in court, registration is necessary.
- If made before or within five years of publication, registration will establish prima facie evidence in the court of the validity of the copyright and of the facts stated in the certificate.
- If registration is made within three months after publication of the work or prior to an infringement of the work, statutory damages and attorney's fees will be available to the copyright owner in court actions. Otherwise, only an award of actual damages and profits is available to the copyright owner.

- Registration allows the owner of the copyright to record the registration with the U. S. Customs Service for protection against the importation of infringing copies. For additional information, visit the U. S. Customs and Border Protection website at www.cbp.gov/xp/cgov/import.
- Registration may be made at any time within the life of the copyright. Unlike the law before 1978, when a work has been registered in unpublished form, it is not necessary to make another registration when the work becomes published, although the copyright owner may register the published edition, if desired.

Let's now learn about law related to semiconductor layout and design.

4.10 Law Related to Semiconductor Layout and Design

The layoutdesign of a semiconductor integrated circuit refers to a layout of transistors and other circuitry elements which are connected through lead wires.

The Intellectual Property Rights in the field of SemiConductor Integrated Circuit Layout Design are protected by the Semiconductor Integrated Circuits Layout-Design (SICLD) Act, 2000. It provides the routes and mechanisms for the protection to all SemiConductor Integrated Circuit Layout Designs IPR applications which are filed in the registry in India.

The SICLD Act is being brought up in stages. The Act was first implemented on September 4, 2000. The rules under the Act were published on December 11, 2001. Sections 3 and 5 of the Act were implemented on October 1, 2004.

The main features of the SICLD Act, 2000 are as follows:

- The Act is applicable to the whole of India.
- The layout design of the integrated circuit chips are to be registered with the SICLD Registry for availing IPR protection.
- The Act lists the layoutdesigns of integrated circuits which can be registered it.
- It defines the duration for which the registration of layoutdesigns is valid.
- It lists the IPR rights which the registration provides to the person/organization.
- It specifies how the infringement of layoutdesigns occurs.
- It lays down the procedures for the assignment and transmission of the registered layoutdesigns.
- The Act provides the use of registered layout designs by the registered users. It provides that an Appellate Board can be used as a forum of redressal.
- It specifies how the royalties are to be handled.

- It provides the steps to be taken in cases of national emergency or extreme public urgency.
- It specifies penalty in cases of:
  - infringement of layout design
  - falsely representing a layout design as registered
  - improperly describing a place of business
  - falsification of entries in the register
  - forfeiture of goods
  - offences by companies
- The Act contains certain guidelines for agents.
- Lastly, the Act also provides for reciprocity with other recognized countries.

The SICLD Registry maintains a register of all the layout designs (which are registered with it) with the name, address, and other details of the proprietor. People are allowed to have a look at the registry after making the required payment.

The steps involved in the registration of a layout design with the Registry are as follows:

- The creator of the layout design needs to fill an application form and submit it at the SICLD Registry.
- The application may be accepted or rejected or accepted partially requiring certain modifications.
- The accepted applications are advertised within 14 days of acceptance and a 3 months wait period is given for filing of oppositions.
- In case opposition is filed in the 3 months wait period, a counter statement to the opposition can be filed within 2 months from the date of receipt of notice of opposition. A copy of the counter statement is also sent to the opposing party.
- The Registrar may take hearing with the parties and has the discretion to grant or reject the application of registration on the basis of conclusions of the hearing.
- Aggrieved party can appeal to the Appellate Board or in its absence to the Civil Court for relief on any ruling of the Registrar.

4.11 Software License

A software license is a contract law governing the use or redistribution of software. Software licenses are generally categorized into proprietary license and free-and-open source. A major difference between them is the terms defined for the distribution of the software for the end users. Generally, a software license grants an end user the permission to use one or more copies of software. Apart from providing rights and imposing restrictions on the use of software, software licenses typically contain provisions allocating liability and responsibility between the parties that enter into the license agreement.

Summary

The chapter has helped to explore the need for the security policies. It has provided a brief discussion on the ISO information security standards. Further, various security policies and their review process are discussed.

Apart from the security policies, the chapter also focused on the Indian cyber law and the objective or scope of the IT Act, 2000. Next, you were introduced to the intellectual property issues and the IPR legislation in India. Also, various laws such as patent, copyright, semiconductor, and software license were explained toward the end of the chapter.

Exercises

■ Multiple Choice Questions

Q1. Which of the following ISO standards sets as a common basis and practical guideline for developing enterprise-level security standards and effective management practices?

a. ISO/IEC 27002:2005 (Code of Practice for Information Security Management)

b. ISO/IEC 27001:2005 (Information Security Management System – Requirements)

c. ISO/IEC 15408 (Evaluation Criteria for IT Security)

d. ISO/IEC 1335 (IT Security Management)

Ans. The correct option is a.

Q2. Under which of the following steps the existence of standards and procedures supporting the policy set is checked?

a. Have someone other than the person who wrote the policy review it

b Assessing policy for completeness

c Ensure that policy statements are

d Ensure that the policy answers

clear, concise, and SMART	the 5 Ws

Ans. The correct option is b.

Q3. Which of the following chapters of the IT Act, 2000 deals with important definitions of the terms used in the regulation?

a. Chapter 1 b. Chapter 2

c. Chapter 3 d. Chapter 4

Ans. The correct option is a.

Q4. Which of the following refers to the rights given to a person or an organization for its intellectual activity, i.e., creations of mind?

a. Intellectual property rights b. Copyright act

c. Cyber law d. IPA

Ans. The correct option is a.

Q5. Under which of the following steps of the policy review process, a policy is examined for provisions to keep it updated?

a. Ensuring that policy statement is clear, concise, and SMART

b. Ensuring that policy answers the 5 Ws

c. Ensuring consistency with laws, regulations, and other levels of policy

d. Checking policy freshness and easy availability to organization members

Ans. The correct option is d.

Q6. Which of the following ISO standard covers management guidance on network security?

a. ISO/IEC TR 13335-5:2001 b. ISO/IEC TR 13335-4:2000

c. ISO/IEC TR 13335-3:1998 d. ISO/IEC 13335-1:2004

Ans. The correct option is a.

Q7. Which of the following is a form of protection which is provided to the authors of "original works of authorship"?

a. Copyright b. Patent

c. IPR d. Semiconductor layout and design

Ans. The correct option is a.

Q8. **Which of the following act aims at the regulation of the use of IT?**

a. IT Act, 2000 b. Copyright Act

c. Patent d. IPR

Ans. The correct option is a.

Q9. **Which of the following policy helps in avoiding the risk of browsing the Internet accessing sites containing offensive material?**

a. WWW policy b. E-mail security policy

c. Corporate policy d. All of the above

Ans. The correct option is a.

Q10. **Which of the following chapters details about the establishment of the Cyber Regulations Appellate Tribunal to secure justice in such cases?**

a. Chapter 10 b. Chapter 2

c. Chapter 3 d. Chapter 4

Ans. The correct option is a.

■ Subjective Questions

Q1. **Describe the intellectual property issues (IPR).**

Q2. **Write a short note on the Copyright act and the patent law.**

Q3. **Explain the semiconductor layout and design in detail.**

Q4 **Explain briefly the IT Act, 2000 and the coverage in each chapter.**

Q5. **Briefly explain the ISO standards to be considered while laying down the policies.**

Model Questions

Q1. What is Information System (IS)? How does IS relate to businesses and help them?

Ans. Information System (IS) was derived from IT, but it is not just a part of IT anymore. Today, IS has provided highly productive results, thus becoming more efficient. Essentially, it provides the necessary information for business operations. It has been designed to support all business functions. Currently, complex business functions get help from various types of IS to sustain and grow in the ever-changing business environment.

To understand an IS, it is logical to first understand the terms it is made up of, namely, information and system. Information can be defined as a well-structured data with a specific meaning. A system is an arrangement that takes input and provides output after completing the required process. In other words, IS can be defined as an arrangement that processes data and provides meaningful information. Essentially, it is a set of several components that process data to derive information. It can also be defined as a set of components that are interconnected to collect, store, process, generate, and disseminate information in order to ensure effective business functioning. This information supports decision making and helps in controlling various organizational departments and their functions. IS can be useful for both individual departments and for all departments collectively. Figure 1 shows the interrelationship between the components of an IS:

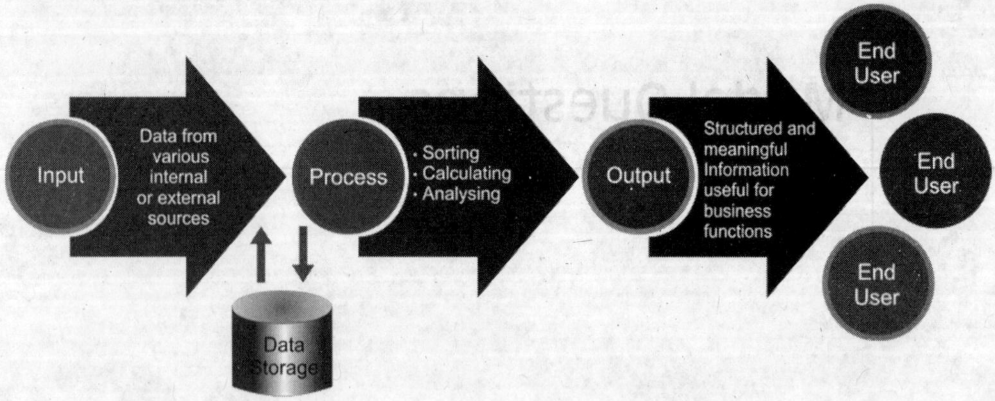

▲ **Figure 1: Displaying the IS Model**

The data for an IS can be collected from various inter-organization and intra-organization sources such as employees' personal details and competitors' performance. This data can be stored in both paper and electronic format. The processing of this data includes calculations, logical analysis, and other statistical methods, depending upon the information to be derived. After the data is processed, it is transformed into information. This information is disseminated to various end users to support their decision making, problem solving, strategy forming, and controlling functions in an organization.

For example, the data about individual sales by each sales associate in a month, the general sales target for each associate, and market sales trends for that month can be put to use. This data can be sorted, classified, calculated, and analyzed to produce information. This will provide information about the sales trends for that time period, gaps between the target and actual sales for individual associates, and the aggregate sales based on teams. The same data can be utilized to predict the next month's sales, target setting for the next month, strategy building for future sales, and the expected production level.

IS has become an integral part of business organizations. For example, those organizations involved in share trading are highly dependent on IS. Figure 2 shows how IS integrates various functions and users of an organization:

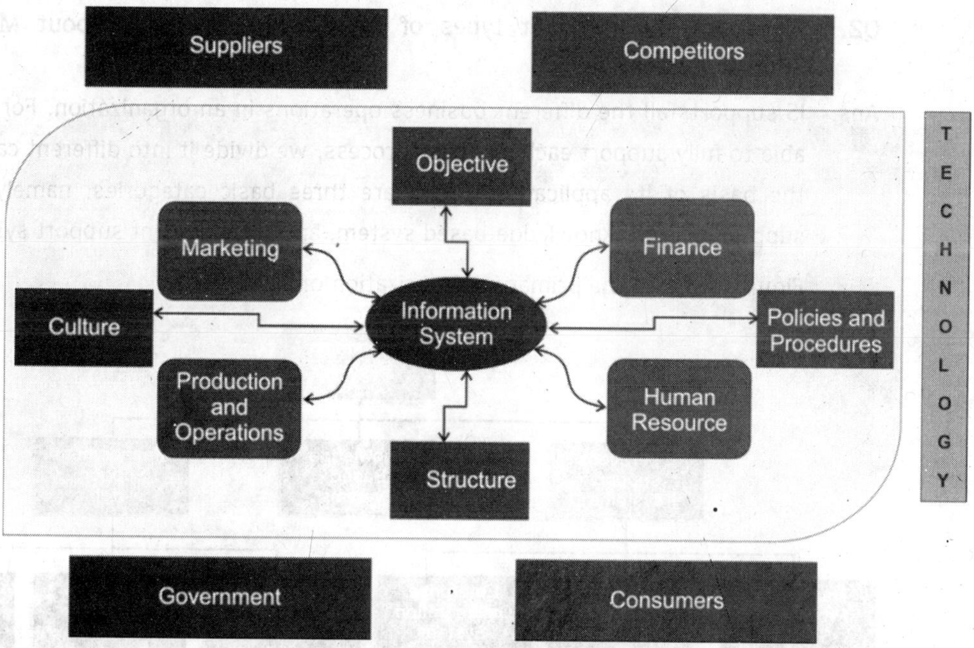

▲ **Figure 2: IS and Business Organization**

It can be seen in Figure 2 that IS has become a core component of a business organization. It plays a vital role in providing coordination between internal and external organizational factors. The internal organizational factors include various departments and organizational behavioral factors such as culture, objectives, structure, policies, and procedures. The external organizational factors include suppliers, competitors, consumers, and legal system.

IS supports the following business processes:

- **Operations support process:** Use of IS in various business processes at the operational level. For example, running of plant and machinery for production and purchase of material. Organizations certainly depend on IS for productive business processes.
- **Decision support process:** Use of IS for business decision making. IS provides useful and relevant information after processing data from various inter and intra-organizational sources. This information helps in effective decision making and logical functioning of a business.
- **Strategic support process:** Gaining competitive advantage by providing critical information to management at the top level. With the help of information on various inter and intra-organizational factors, management can work on various business strategies to improve productivity and profit. For example, quick delivery of orders by Domino's Pizza without unnecessary delay.

Q2. **What are the different types of IS? Discuss in detail about Management Support System.**

Ans. IS supports all the different business operations in an organization. For an IS to be able to fully support each business process, we divide it into different categories on the basis of its application. There are three basic categories, namely, operation support system, knowledge-based system, and management support system.

Figure 3 shows the primary categorization of an IS:

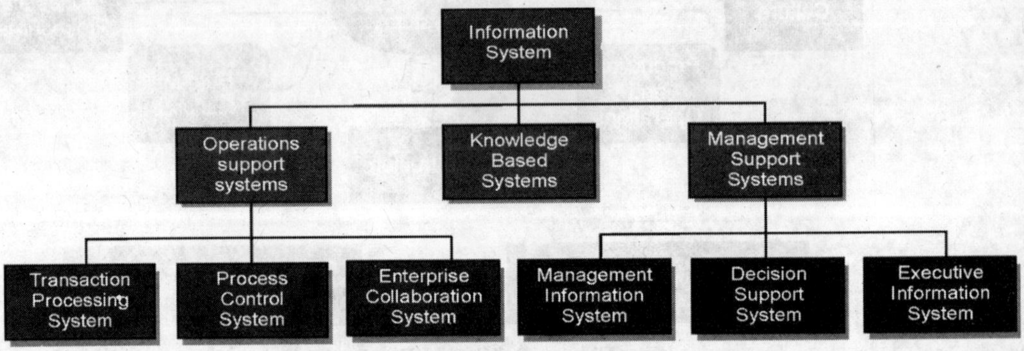

▲ **Figure 3: Displaying the Classification of IS**

A Management Support System (MSS) provides useful information to managers for decision making and control. The different types of MSS are as follows:

- **Management Information System (MIS)**: Provides information on various business aspects to managers. It generates information for monitoring performance and maintaining coordination. For example, a production manager can check the report of cost and time of production for the previous year so that he/she can take effective production decisions for the current year.
- **Decision Support System (DSS)**: Supports managerial decision making. For example, a sales manager can set sales targets for the coming year by considering the existing market conditions.
- **Executive Information System (EIS)**: Provides critical information to the executive and top-level managers for making strategic decisions. It provides statistical representation of information. For example, an executive can check for a brand image by looking at the graphs representing customers' preferences and the sales of competitive brands in the last five years.

Q3. What are the approaches followed in developing IS? Explain one of the approaches in brief.

Ans. Development of IS, similar to the application development procedure, has various approaches. The suitability of an approach depends upon the specific input conditions, preference of approach, and development objective. You can follow any of the different approaches, based on your requirements, for an effective IS development. The main approaches are listed as follows:

- Waterfall model
- Prototyping model
- Evolutionary model
- Spiral model
- Incremental model

Spiral model is a further improvement in the system development. It is a combination of the features of the waterfall and prototype models. This idea was given by Boehm, a computer professional. Similar to the evolutionary model, this model also adapts to repetitive improvement, as shown in Figure 4:

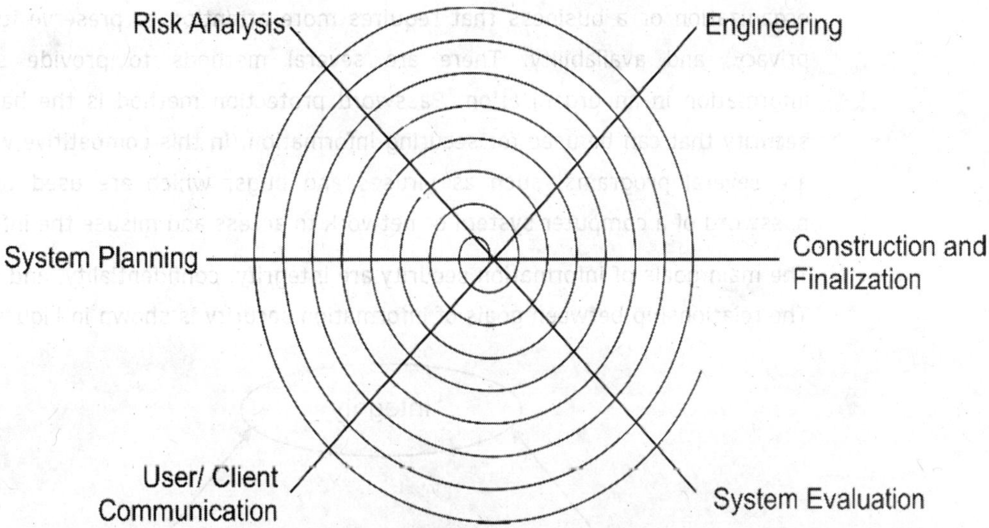

▲ **Figure 4: Showing the Spiral Model**

The following phases are included in the spiral model of system development:

- **User/client communication:** Interaction with the client or users of the system to identify the requirements and specifications in the system

- **System planning:** Planning the system to be developed and preparing a rough draft and schedule of the development process
- **Risk analysis:** Identifying the problems in the plan and developing solutions to check them
- **Engineering:** Involves system hardware and software design, coding, and testing the system
- **Construction and finalization:** Involves system building and testing to release it for use
- **System evaluation:** Evaluation by user or client to use the system
- All these phases are repeated in the process of system development until users approve the system.

Q4. What is the meaning of information security? Discuss about the goals of information security and the relationship between these goals.

Ans. Information security refers to the protection of information. In other words, it is the process of securing, protecting, and safeguarding the information from an unauthorized access, use, and modification. Information is an important part of an organization or a business that requires more attention to preserve its integrity, privacy, and availability. There are several methods to provide security to information in an organization. Password protection method is the basic level of security that can be used for securing information. In this competitive world, there are several programs, such as viruses and bugs, which are used to hack the password of a computer system or network to access and misuse the information.

The main goals of information security are integrity, confidentiality, and availability. The relationship between goals of information security is shown in Figure 5:

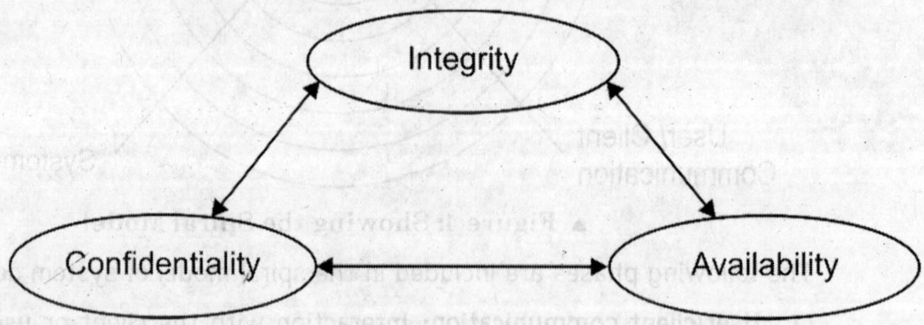

▲ **Figure 5: Displaying the Relationship between Goals of Information Security**

The goals of information security are explained as follows:

- **Confidentiality:** Refers to the process of securing information from unauthorized access. Confidentiality ensures that only an authorized person can access the network resources to get the valuable information provided on the network. A good example where confidentiality of information plays an important role is the credit card transaction. When we use a credit card to pay our dues through a computer.system, the credit card number is transmitted over the network in encrypted form so that other persons cannot read the information.
- **Integrity:** Refers to the accuracy of information or data. In other words, integrity means securing the information from unauthorized modification. Data integrity and data accuracy are related to each other, but this is not always possible that both of these co-exist. For example, you may have entered incorrect data in the network, but it is possible to have data integrity in such a scenario. The data can only be modified by an authorized user.
- **Availability:** States that information must be available when it is needed. The information is said to be available if the following conditions are satisfied:
  - It is provided on time
  - The fault tolerance exists in the computer system or network
  - There is a fair allocation of resources over the network
  - There is a concurrency control management in database
  - There is a deadlock management in database

Q5. What is Information Assurance (IA)? Differentiate between information security and IA. Also describe the three dimensional IA model.

Ans. Information Assurance (IA) is the term related to the management of risks associated with the information system of an organization. IA is defined as the set of measures applied to protect information systems and the information of an organization. It ensures availability, integrity, authentication, confidentiality, and non-repudiation of an organization's information and IS. IA ensures these critical security functions by providing the restoration capability to IS with the measures that include protecting the system from potential risks, detecting possible risks, and reacting to the vulnerable situations.

IA is, in fact, the management of risks in relation of processing, transmitting, or storing data or information. Most of the people are unable to differentiate between IA and information security, which means to protect information and information systems from accessing, misusing, disclosing, disrupting, destructing, and modifying in an unlawful manner. Information security has a limited scope as compared to IA, which is wide and covers all the measures for protecting information. The differences between IA and information security are presented in Table 3:

Table 3: Difference between Information Security and IA

IA	Information Security
Focuses mainly on strategy	Focuses primarily on tools and tactics
Covers information management and protection in a larger domain	Gives importance and priority to technology and operations
Keeps focus on the overall risk management for the security of an organization	Concentrates on applications and infrastructure developed to provide security

IA, on one hand, includes the measures to ensure that the overall security of an organization is maintained. On the other hand, information security includes use of tools and techniques so that the infrastructure and applications of an organization are secured from potential threats. It has three goals that are established for maintaining the security in an organization. These goals are called CIA, abbreviated from Confidentiality-Integrity-Availability.

IA, as per the definition given by the Information Systems Security Committee (NSTISSC), includes:

- "Information operations (IO) that protect and defend information and information systems by ensuring their availability, integrity, authentication, confidentiality, and non-repudiation. This includes providing for restoration of information systems by incorporating protection, detection, and reaction capabilities."

IA is not limited to protection only, but it expands to the point of taking offensive measures also in order to secure the information systems and the information. The scope of IA is very widespread, as shown Figure 6:

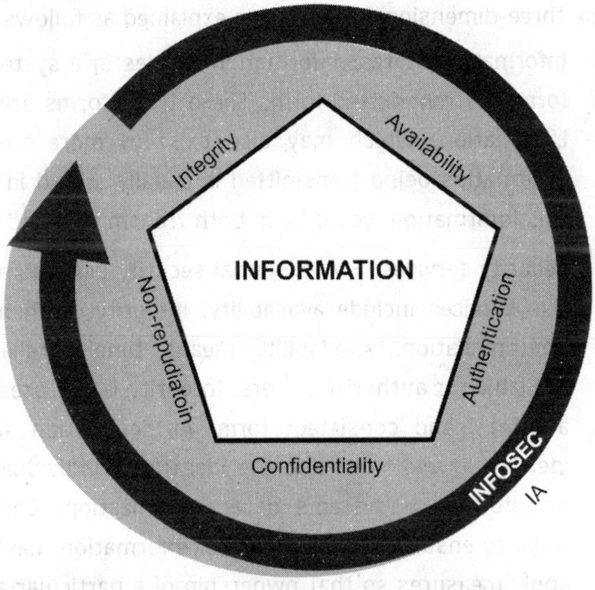

▲ **Figure 6: Displaying the Scope of IA**

IA is not a single discipline, as stated earlier. It covers multiple dimensions. Three-dimensional IA model includes information states, security services, and security countermeasures that are established over time. This model can be represented as shown in Figure 7:

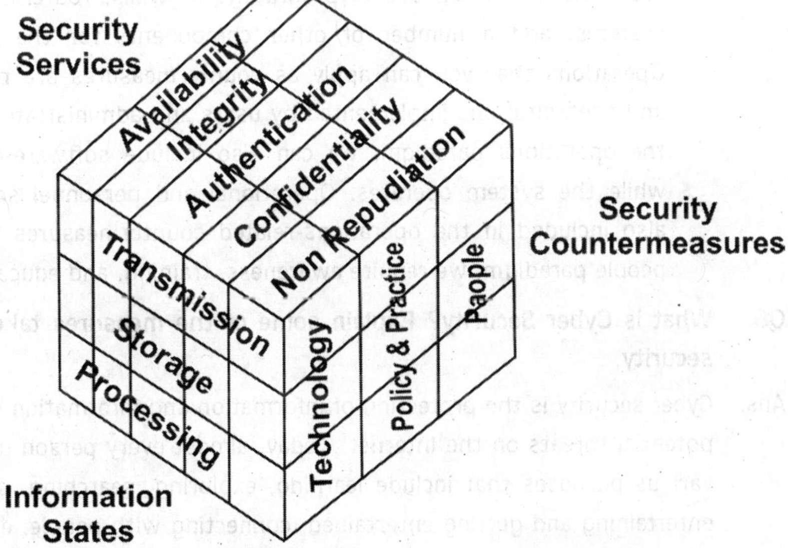

▲ **Figure 7: Showing Three-Dimensional IA Model**

The three-dimensional IA model is explained as follows:

- **Information states:** Information resides in a system in stored form, processed form, or transmitted form. These three forms are referred to as the states of information, which may also exist in more than one state. For example, information being transmitted is usually stored in disks at the sender end. So, this information would be in both transmitted and stored states.
- **Security services:** Five essential security services are provided in the IA model. The services include availability, integrity, authentication, confidentiality, and nonrepudiation. Availability means timely, reliable data access facility is available for authorized users. Integrity is the presence of data in its complete, accurate, and consistent form. Authentication services define measures for identifying and validating the identity of individuals to access the information or information systems of an organization. Confidentiality services provide ways to ensure non-disclosure of information. Lastly, nonrepudiation means to apply measures so that ownership of a particular action cannot be denied later by the individual who took the action.
- **Security countermeasures:** After the risks are assessed and analyzed, it is time to react. Your systems must include certain countermeasures for maintaining the security and IA. These security countermeasures are applied against vulnerabilities through technology, people, and operations. In terms of technology, you can use cryptography, firewalls, routers, intrusion detection systems, and a number of other components for the maintenance of IA. Operations that you can apply as countermeasures are policies, procedures, and configurations implemented by users and administrators of the system. In the operations paradigm, we can also include software-defined conventions while the system operates. Operational and personnel security domains are also included in the operations-related countermeasures for security. In the people paradigm, we require awareness, training, and education.

Q6. What is Cyber Security? Explain some of the measures taken to ensure cyber security.

Ans. Cyber security is the protection of information and information systems against the potential threats on the Internet. Today, almost every person uses the Internet for various purposes that include learning, exploring, searching, sharing information, entertaining and getting entertained, connecting with people, etc. All these involve pleasure and value, but the potential vulnerabilities cannot be overlooked. The Internet can be very valuable if used responsibly. However, it may be extremely harmful in case some unlawful, indecent actions are taken by using the Internet. Cyber security is the ability to protect yourself and your cyberspace (or the Internet) from the attacks caused through the Internet.

People on the Internet do not know everything about security. Considering this as a weapon, one can attack another person (who has limited knowledge about the use of the Internet) through viruses (a program written to cause harms to a system) and can steal their identity through phishing (an act of convincing people to provide confidential details such as passwords and PINs) or spyware (a program that is created to read the personal information of a person from their accounts or systems). You must protect yourself from such kind of attacks. People may launch viruses through e-mails or blog posts. For example, if you like a specific game and you shared this information on your social networks, someone who wants to access your personal data may send you an e-mail with a link to download the new version of the game and advertising himself/herself as a person from the company that developed the game. After you have downloaded the software from the given link, the software starts forwarding your personal information to the individual who sent you the link. There can also be other methods to launch such kinds of attacks that are known as phishing.

In order to protect yourself from such types of attacks, you must be aware of the ways in which the attacks may harm you. Also, you need to be careful about what kind of data you are sharing on the Internet, what kinds of people are connected to you through the Internet, and what types of people may use the information shared by you. Confidential information should never be shared on the Internet. Your likes, dislikes, and the preference for particular things should be known only to the people you trust. Protecting from viruses and phishing is one of the most difficult things when it comes to the harms caused by the Internet.

People steal identity for criminal purposes that may prove harmful for victims of the identity theft. The financial crime is one of the most noted consequences of identity theft. Consider someone who knows the PIN of your ATM card and the ATM card number. He/she might use this information for online purposes and funds transfer for his/her benefits. Therefore, no secret and confidential information should be shared with anyone on the Internet however dear they are.

To protect yourself from viruses and spyware, you need to have your firewalls and antivirus software up to date. Antivirus software and firewalls are very effective ways to keep yourself protected from cyber attacks, but installing too many security software programs harms your system's performance. The privacy and the security settings in your Web browser must not expose your system to any potential threats on the Internet.

Today, online advertising has become a way to go for business. Catchy phrases and various offers are used to drag people into the business domains. However, the activities have their potential misgivings. People who are not well aware of cyber attacks may get trapped by some malicious people. Advertisements might contain a spyware or a software application that can be run on computer systems. Such software can damage another application already running on the system or can send information from the system to the person who advertises with these programs. This may harm individual privacy and application security. One must protect oneself from all such kinds of advertisements or attacks.

If you are sharing important information about yourself, that information may be taken by advertisers who want to know the maximum they can about you. This information can be crucial for their purpose. Advertises can send cookies on the Web browsers so that they could record the online behavior of user, and advertisement on the basis of behaviors might be sent. These could be harmful for your individual security and the security of your applications. You must therefore check all new e-mails independently and ignore advertisements that you have no concerns with. You must keep privacy and security settings of your browser that asks you to run or ignore cookies from sites. This can help you avoid tracking of activities on the Internet and Web.

Some applications and mobile phones are designed to store user information. You, as users, are not allowed to deny storage of the information, such as the unique ID of your device. These information may be used by advertisers to send user-specific advertisements, which may cause harm for individuals and applications.

Development and prominence of social networking sites in the Internet era has been one of the most noted developments. People use social networks to connect with people, share thoughts and preferences, stay in touch, and for various other purposes. You must note that the Internet has nothing private. Whatever you share on the Internet can be used globally. Therefore, you must be careful while projecting your views and giving details about yourself through the Internet.

Cyberbullying has been seen as one of the most common offenses online. A lot of people use the Internet to stalk other people, harass them, and assault and extort sexually. People may hide real identities easily on the Internet. Some people use this trick to exploit children and girls. A number of complaints all around the world about sexual offenses, sending of texts to arouse sexual feelings, calling on cell phone to disturb the peace of mind, etc. are some of the actions of cyberbullies. Cyberbullying is considered as a crime all over the world because these activities may cost victims their life. Irreparable damages can be resulted from all such incidents. Some other ways to chat with strange people are also included under cyberbullying. These activities include chatting through mobile applications (WhatsApp and Hike, for example), consoles of video games, and anonymous chat rooms.

As a solution from being bullied online, people can use information sharing and empowerment of the family members, guide children of the family, apply a set of rules for children to use the Internet safely, and giving tips on texting and cyberbullying. Teenage girls or boys are the most vulnerable to cyberbullying. They can be easily misguided. Also, children may trust people easily, leading to sexual exploitation, harassment, and stalking. In the process of tolerating such kinds of incidents, the victims may have to lose their lives. So, protection against online predation and cyberbullying is a must these days when it comes to cyber security.

Q7. What, according to you, are the main threats for E-commerce security?

Ans. E-commerce involves all kinds of transactions that are done over the Internet, including sale, purchase, and exchange of products, services, and information. Internet is a public domain and, hence, it is open to all. Each and every transaction that occurs on the Internet can be tracked, monitored, logged, and stored. Information shared over the Internet for carrying out transactions is constantly under security threats. These threats may originate from internal or external sources. Thus, it becomes imperative for businesses to understand the threats before making available their products, services, and data online. Some of the main security threats for E-commerce from internal and external sources include the following:

- Unauthorized internal users who may access confidential information by using stolen passwords for committing fraud or theft
- Former employees of an organization who have maintained access to the information sources directly by creating alternative passwords, "back doors" into the computer system, or indirectly through former co-workers
- Weak access points in information infrastructure and security that can expose company information and trade secrets

- Management that undermines security may be the greatest risk to e-commerce
- Contractors, partners, consultants, etc. who take benefit of even limited access to important systems.

An increase in the sale of various antivirus software and subscription to e-mail virus protection indicate that people are increasingly becoming aware of these threats. Businesses can make it mandatory for their service providers and merchants to have firewalls, encryption, as well as testing and access policies as a condition of doing business with them. This will go a long way in providing a solid ground to e-commerce for flourishing.

Q8. Explain in detail the two common modes of paying money online, i.e., E-cash and E-payment.

Ans. The growth and widespread adoption of e-commerce as a new medium of trade and marketing by both large and small business organizations has emphasized the need of maintaining privacy, security, and safety in conducting online transactions. To ensure safe, error-free, and secure transactions, various methods of online payment have been adopted by the business organizations. Initially, in the traditional method of trading, the mode of payment was cash, cheque, and draft. However, in case of e-commerce, the two commonly used methods of making payment online are e-cash and e-payment. These two modes of payment allow the trading parties to conduct secure online transactions.

E-cash refers to electronic transfer of money in the form of a block of data representing money that is transferred online. The electronic transfer of money involves computer networks, Internet, and the digitally stored value system. E-cash bears a digital signature for authentication purposes and can be either sent over a network as data from sender to receiver or in the form of tokens exchanged for actual money transfer. E-cash is generally stored on computers or mobile devices in the form of software wallet programs. When a user needs to make a transaction, the wallet programs communicate with the bank or the e-cash issuer. The bank authenticates the user and after the authentication process is completed, it transfers the requested e-cash to the customer. The e-cash can then be paid to the seller using the wallet programs to complete the transaction. The e-cash company in turn charges a small amount from the merchants for each transaction.

Figure 8 shows how the e-cash mechanism works:

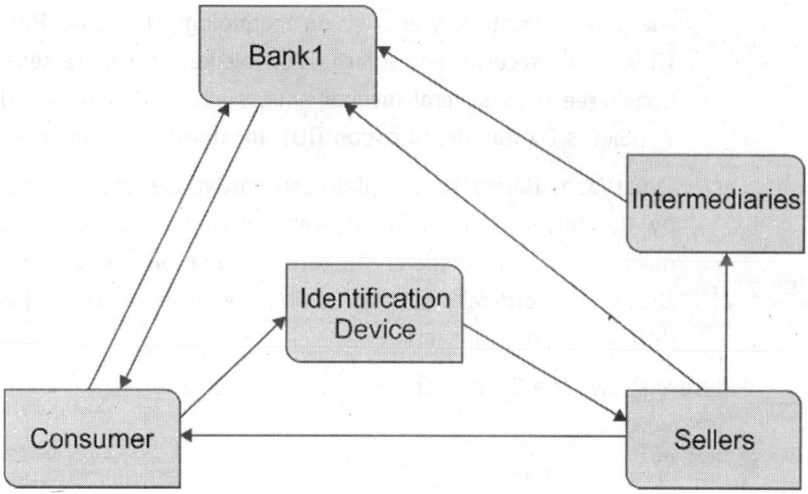

▲ **Figure 8: Displaying the Working of E-Cash**

Figure 8 shows the relationship between the consumer, bank, and seller involved in an e-cash transaction.

There are several organizations that provide services for online monetary transactions. These services are called e-payment schemes, which are as follows:

- **Secure Electronic Payment Protocol/Secure Electronic Transaction (SEPP/SET):** Uses digital signatures and user authentication for secured electronic payments. SEPP is an open specification for secure electronic payments over the Internet developed by the International Business Machines (IBM), Netscape, General Telephone & Electronics Corporation (GTE), CyberCash, and MasterCard. SEPP provides a usage of the Internet Keyed Payments Protocol (iKP) that is intended for HTTP transactions and adapted to bank card payments. SEPP messages are transmitted using Multipurpose Internet Mail Extensions (MIME) and are based on common ASN.1 syntax.
- **Secure courier electronic payment scheme:** Refers to the earliest payment scheme for secure payment between the users of banks and the Quicken home-banking program that uses SEPP. Secure courier scheme encrypts data and authenticates the individual consumers and the buyers at the time of electronic transactions. Many organizations are working with MasterCard, such as Netscape, IBM, Open Market, and GTE Corporation, and planning to use this technology for business.
- **CheckFree wallet:** Refers to an electronic payment service that enables consumers and buyers to make transactions in an easy and safe manner over the Internet. CheckFree wallet, based on the client/server architecture, uses

the public-private key encryption technology that uses Rivest Shamir Adleman (RSA) data security and a large 768-bit key to secure sensitive payment data. CheckFree uses several mechanisms, such as CyberCash, Netscape's SSL, and VeriSign's Digital Identification (ID), for developing this system.

- **CyberCash:** Refers to a digital cash software system that guarantees payment by the buyers before the delivery of goods. CyberCash provides a secured mechanism to send the credit card information over the Internet as it encrypts the credit-card-related information. It uses a third party decryption for decrypting the transaction.

Figure 9 shows the CyberCash e-payment process:

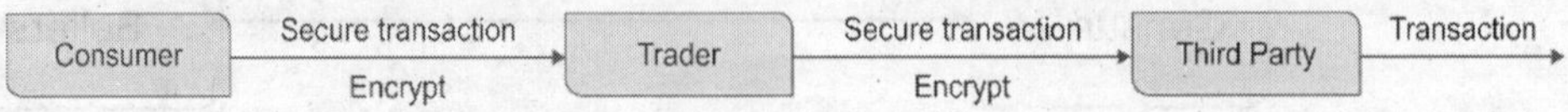

▲ **Figure 9: Displaying the CyberCash E-Payment Process**

- **VeriSign:** Refers to a technology that authenticates users by verifying the digital signature. IBM introduced the concept of digital ID into its Web browser and Internet connection Secure Server for Advanced Interactive eXecutive (AIX) and OS (OS)/2. IBM also adopted digital ID in its InfoMarket publishing network and clearinghouse.
- **DigiCash:** Refers to the e-cash based software that provides complete privacy. This type of system is currently used by Netherlands DigiCash NV. DigiCash enables the consumers to purchase goods over the Internet without using a credit card.

The use of this kind of software where cash can be loaded into smart cards for electronic purchases are encouraged due to the threat of privacy loss. The greatest benefit of DigiCash is that it enables the organization to hold larger amount of money than credit cards.

Q9. What do you understand by access control to information systems? How is authentication different from identification? Also differentiate between authentication and authorization.

Ans. Access control is a mechanism that defines and controls access rights for individuals who can use specific resources in the OS. In other words, you can say that access control is a security feature through which the system permits or revokes the right to access any data and resource in a system. The permission to access a resource is called authorization. Access control systems include:

- **File permissions:** Refer to the access control in which the user can create, read, edit, or delete on a file server
- **Program permissions:** Refer to the access control in which the user can execute a program on an application server
- **Data rights permissions:** Refer to the access control in which the user can retrieve or update information in a database

Identification and authentication both are similar terms with a little difference, that is, identification refers to the process of labeling and recognizing a user, whereas authentication refers to the process of verifying whether the user is a valid user or not. These terms are used in access control, which means controlling the access of users over the network resources and information. In these processes, the user provides his/her credentials to a computer or a network, which identifies the user. If the user credentials are correct, the user gains access to the computers or network resources. However, if the user credentials are incorrect, the user's request to access the network resources is rejected. In this way, you can protect your network from unauthorized access and modification.

Authentication processes or methods are password based or PIN, smart card, token, or an identification device, and fingerprints or retinal pattern.

SFA checks one set of values at a time; hence, it is the basic form of authentication. SFA implements authentication by using the combination of username and password. In the logon process, the usernames and passwords are used as a unique identifier. The username and password are unique identifiers for a logon process.

In the logon process, computer systems first identify the user by identification. Most of the systems identify the user by using the user ID and password. The information about user ID and password is passed to all the connections either as a plain text or in an encrypted form.

Then the logon process identifies the OS or the network.

The logon and password process is shown in Figure 10:

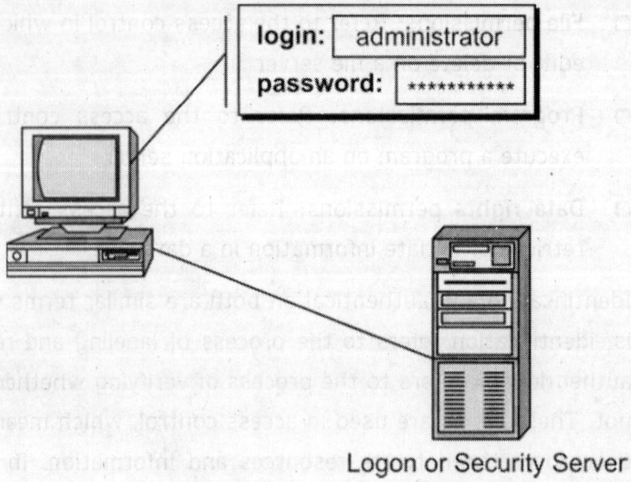

▲ **Figure 10: Displaying the Logon and Password Process**

In the logon process, the OS compares the username and password information to the stored information in the security server, and then accepts and denies the logon attempt.

The process in which more than one party authenticates each other is called mutual authentication. In mutual authentication, the client needs to prove its identity to a server, and the server needs to prove its identity to the client before any data communication on the client-to-server connection.

Q10. What are the primary mechanisms used for controlling access to information systems?

Ans. There are three main types of access control mechanisms used are:

- Mandatory Access Control (MAC)
- Discretionary Access Control (DAC)
- Role-Based Access Control (RBAC)

MAC defines the accessibility of information in a consistent manner. In the MAC environment, the determination of access capacities is set into action beforehand. Unless the organization of information exchange is put into place by the administrators, users can't share the information. The administrators hold the responsibility for defining the changes in the information. They ensure the enforcement of stringent security measures.

To ensure effective operation of the MAC model, the perusal of the relationship existing between administrators and network designers must be done. The advantage offered by this model is its exhaustive functionality, enabling the detection and repair of security breaches. A well-designed MAC model allows outright control over the management of information, and if required, can lock down the network. The disadvantages accompanying the model are the integration of rigidness into it and the demand for the enactment of changes overtime. This model finds its applicability in the environments where the confidentiality of information is the crux of the matter.

DAC model offers flexibility related to the exchange of information to the network users. It ensures dynamic exchange of information with other users. Despite the fact that this model offers a flexible environment, unauthorized information disclosure is always the likely possibility. Administrators struggle in the face of ensuring control over information access and the grant of access rights. The permission structure existing as "other" option with files in the Unix/Linux environment epitomizes the operability of DAC. The permission set in the Unix/Linux environment has been classified into three groups of user, i.e., owner, group, and other. The roles form the basis for associations of permissions between the owner and the group the respective owner belongs to, while those not falling under the purview of owner or the member of the owner's group come within the ambit of other. The permission set for this group is disparate with the other two, besides the exceptions of read, write, and execute.

RBAC models put control over the information access from the viewpoint of organizational roles into perspective. The implementation of accessibility based on job function or responsibility is the gist of the RBAC model. The access to a specific information hinges upon the role incumbency. RBAC model offers flexibility, which is always greater than the MAC model, but less than the DAC model. The advantage that it incorporates is that it follows function-centric approach rather than individual centric. This model is appropriate in the environments exhibiting high turnover.

Q11. What are the primary considerations for data security? Discuss.

Ans. Security of data means maintaining its Confidentiality-Integrity-Availability (CIA) properties. Ensuring data security needs certain points to be considered. These considerations are related to data backup, archival, and disposal. Let us discuss these data security considerations in detail.

To manage data properly, we must consider data backup, which is primarily used for the purpose of data security against any kind of accidents or loss of data due to some malicious activities. In case of casualties resulting into loss of data, you can restore the original data from your backup. Backup of data is nothing, but the storage of a snapshot of data at certain points. You can take regular backups of data so that it remains in the latest stages, and in case your data is lost due to some reason, you could restore the most recent form of data. Data backup is seen as an essential part of data management operations. Some reasons for data to be lost due to accidents or malicious activities are as follows:

- Failure of hardware or faults in the hardware system
- Fault in the media or software
- Hacking of data or infection of viruses causing loss of data
- Failure of power, resulting in data loss
- Erroneous human activities, such as changes in or deletion of files

The preceding are the primary reasons for an accidental or malicious loss of data. Therefore, your data backup strategy should be based mainly on the considerations such as current state and quality of your hardware and software, local situations regarding supply of power, the value of your data, and levels of risk that you think are appropriate given that the situation at your place remains the same.

Data, considerably the most valuable asset in an organization, may or may not be in active use. Some parts may be crucial for future references, but may not be actively used anymore. Therefore, most organizations move the currently inactive parts of data to a separate storage location in order to reduce complexity and keep active parts of data fresh. This process of separating older (or currently inactive) data from currently active, new, and fresh data is known as archival of data. The separated older data is moved to a different storage device so that the data can be retained for a long time and referenced whenever required. Figure 11 shows the typical data archival strategy used by most organizations (archive obsolete data):

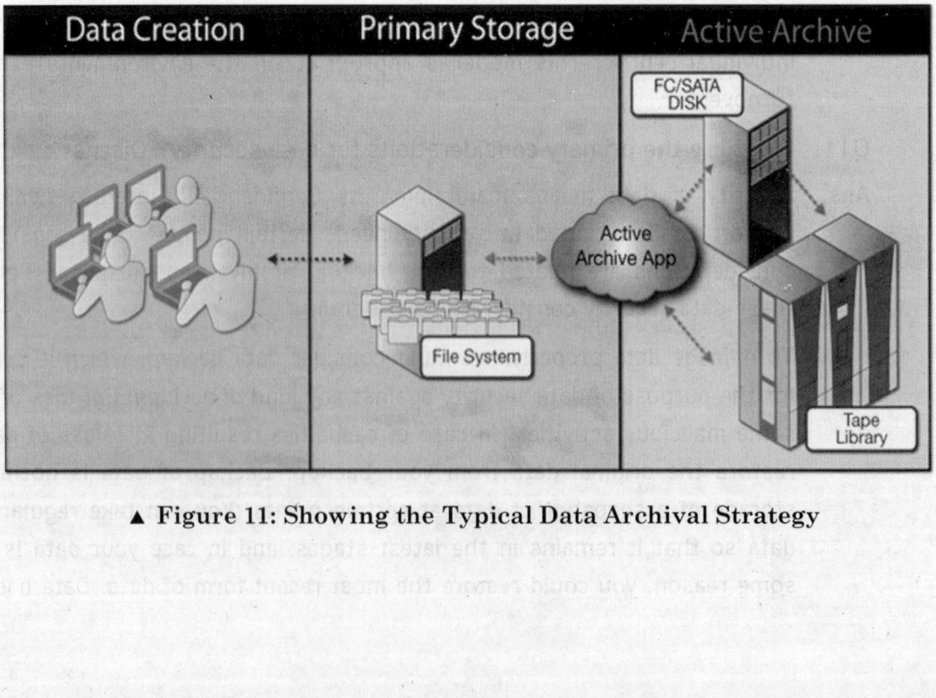

▲ **Figure 11: Showing the Typical Data Archival Strategy**

Archival of data is not the same as data backup, which is storage of data that can be used later to recover data lost due to disaster or malicious activities such as hacking. Data archiving requires retaining data that has become obsolete for current purposes but can be required, at a later stage, for reference. The process of data archival requires moving selected part of data to a different storage media in order to reduce cost, save storage space in the online system, reduce access complexity, and improve system performance. The information that should be preserved can be identified efficiently by most of the products that are used for the purpose of data archival. These products define various criteria for the identification of information to be retained as archive. The criteria can be defined by the user or the archiving products may take metadata for files and contexts of objects as defining criteria to select the information to be archived. Archived data is stored according to the object context and indexed so that finding them becomes easy whenever required in future.

Records being rarely changed or accessed and important but less accessed information are most suitable data for archival. Nowadays, organizations use data archival to preserve historical information for a long time duration, which helps them reduce the requirements to induct huge storage media in online systems and to backup large amounts of data. Archival of data ensures proper maintenance of records so that they can be produced as evidence when referenced later. An archiving storage system is reliable and supports current activities. These systems store records in a well-managed form so that we can use and understand the records in future. Archived data can be used in businesses or may be produced as evidence in matters having legal consequences. You can also use archived data for historical researches and for accountability to your business stakeholders, both internal and external.

Data disposal is an act of permanently deleting or destroying the data stored in a media. Sometimes, we may require destroying the data permanently for some security or compliance reasons. Data, undoubtedly, is an asset of great value for organizations. However, at some point, its destruction is inevitable. Whenever legacy or obsolete systems and devices are replaced, removal of data stored in those systems and devices at present is a must. Also, your business must comply with the federal policy legislation, which requires you to destroy some of your data after a definite time period. You cannot destroy data just by sending items into the trash. Destruction of data requires you to take measures beyond this. Data sent to trash can be recovered easily.

Destruction of data means to completely wipe out the data from the storage media. This process of wiping out the data completely is known as data disposal. The National Institute of Standards and Technology (NIST) describes three primary ways in which data can be disposed. These methods are overwriting hard drive, degaussing the hard drive and backup tape, and destroying the storage media. The overwriting method means rewriting all the areas of hard drives, degaussing means demagnetizing all areas of storage on hard drives and backup tapes, and destroying storage media means demolishing the storage media itself.

Q12. What are the different technologies used for the security of data and application? Explain the vulnerabilities associated with VPN.

Ans. Data and application security has become one of the most prominent issues; therefore, we must take care while applying security measures properly. We have a variety of technologies that enable security of application and data in an organization. Use of firewalls, VPN, Intrusion Detection System (IDS), and access control systems are among the few ways to keep data secure.

Firewall is a part of a computer system or network that is designed to inspect incoming and outgoing network traffic and alter the traffic flow by dropping or passing certain packets. It is designed to block unauthorized access while permitting authorized communications. Firewall is a device or a set of devices that is configured to permit or deny network transmissions on the basis of certain rules and criteria. A firewall inspects all the messages that enter or leave the company's Intranet and blocks those that do not meet the specified security criteria. It analyzes the incoming data to determine the IP address of the machine from which it is coming and the content that it contains. Next, the firewall checks if the content is compliant with the rules that you have already configured. It also analyzes the information at the application level and determines whether or not the application should send or receive data through the port with which you are connected.

A firewall also prevents computer hackers from accessing your computer through the Internet by blocking back doors or open ports that connect your computer with the Internet. This protects your system from being attacked by viruses from the Internet.

You can implement a firewall in your system in any form—hardware, software, or a combination of both.

Figure 12 shows a hardware firewall:

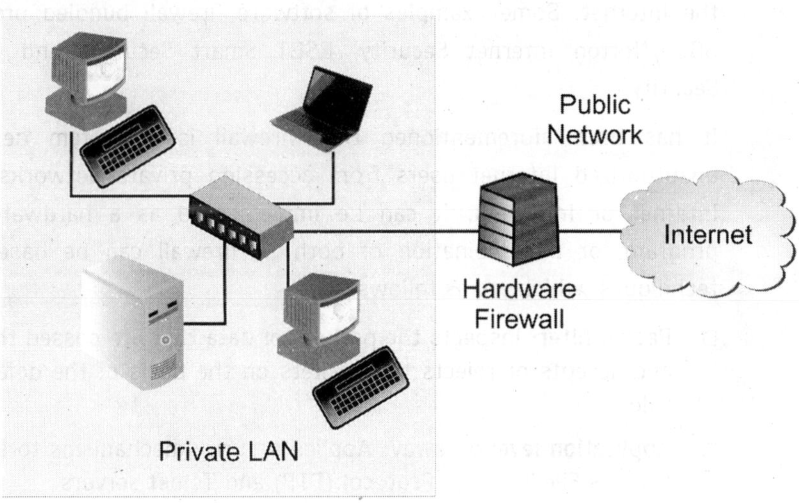

▲ **Figure 12: Showing a Hardware Firewall**

The hardware firewall is a physical piece of equipment that is kept between the Internet and your LAN network. An example of a hardware firewall is a broadband router. This kind of firewall can protect multiple computer systems that are connected to it simultaneously.

The software firewall is a software program that is installed on your computer. It also works in the same way as the hardware firewall by monitoring and blocking information that comes to your computer through the Internet.

Figure 13 shows a software firewall:

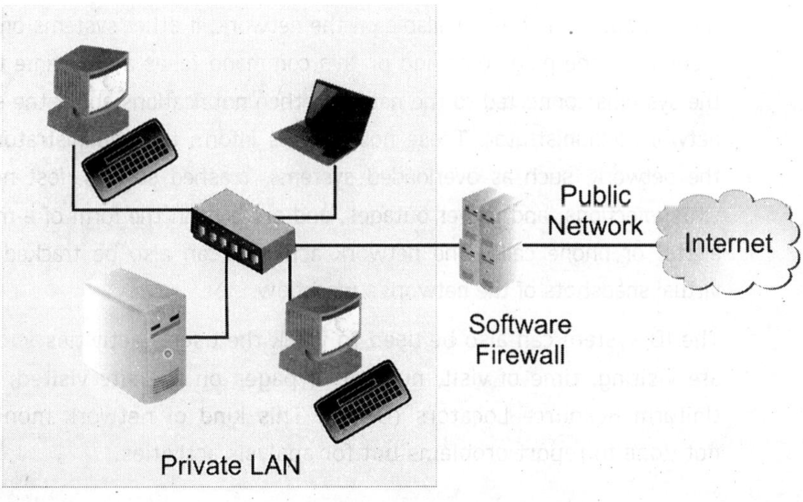

▲ **Figure 13: Showing a Software Firewall**

You can either install a software firewall from a computer disk or download it from the Internet. Some examples of software firewall bundled programs are Norton 360, Norton Internet Security, ESET Smart Security, and Kaspersky Internet Security.

It has been aforementioned that firewall is a system designed to prevent unauthorized Internet users from accessing private networks connected to the Internet or Intranets. It can be implemented as a hardware device, software program, or a combination of both. A firewall can be based on a variety of techniques, which are as follows:

- **Packet filter:** Inspects the packets of data that are passed through the network and accepts or rejects the packets on the basis of the default or user-defined rules.
- **Application-level gateway:** Applies security mechanisms to specific applications such as File Transfer Protocol (FTP) and Telnet servers.
- **Circuit-level gateway:** Applies security mechanisms after establishing a TCP or an UDP connection.
- **Proxy server:** Checks all messages that enter or leave a network. It helps in hiding the real network addresses.

Network monitoring refers to the process of tracking the activities that are being performed in the network. This task of monitoring the activities of a network can be assigned to a specific computer or a set of computers. The computer that acts as a network monitoring system must always be kept on and consists of strong power lines and backup generators.

The system performing the task of monitoring the network sends a ping command to all the computers that are available on the network. If other systems on the network do not respond to the ping command or this command takes a long time to execute on any of the systems connected to the network, then notifications about the same are sent to the network administrator. These notifications inform the administrator about problems in the network, such as overloaded systems, crashed servers, lost network connections, virus infections, and power outages, and are sent in the form of e-mail messages, pager alerts, or phone calls. The network activities can also be tracked by regularly taking virtual snapshots of the network's workflow.

The ID system can also be used to track the user's activities such as websites they are visiting, time of visit, number of pages on the site visited, and entry and exit Uniform Resource Locators (URLs). This kind of network monitoring is generally not done to report problems but for analysis activities.

An intrusion detection system always has a sensor as its core element that is used to detect intrusions. The data received by these sensors is obtained from various sources such as IDS knowledge database, syslog, and audit trails.

Figure 14 shows a sample IDS system:

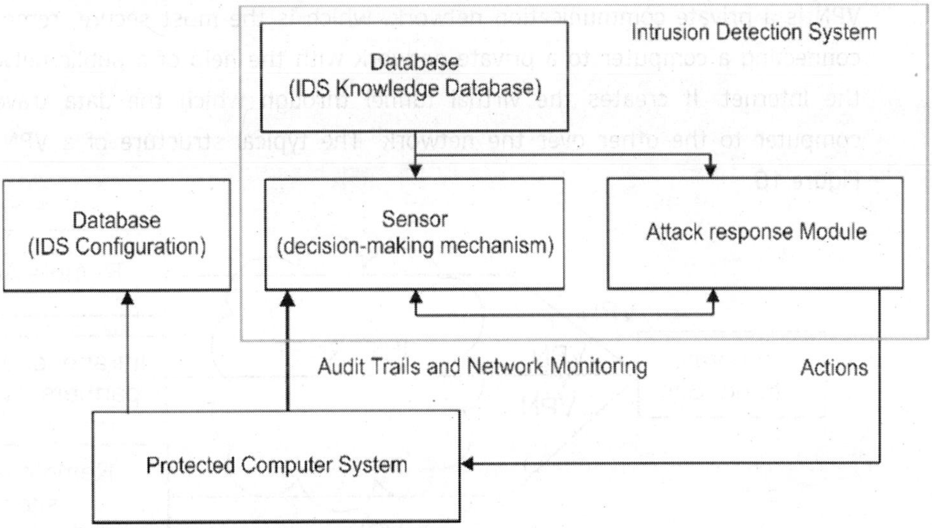

▲ **Figure 14: Showing a Sample IDS**

Figure 15 shows the integration of different components with the sensor:

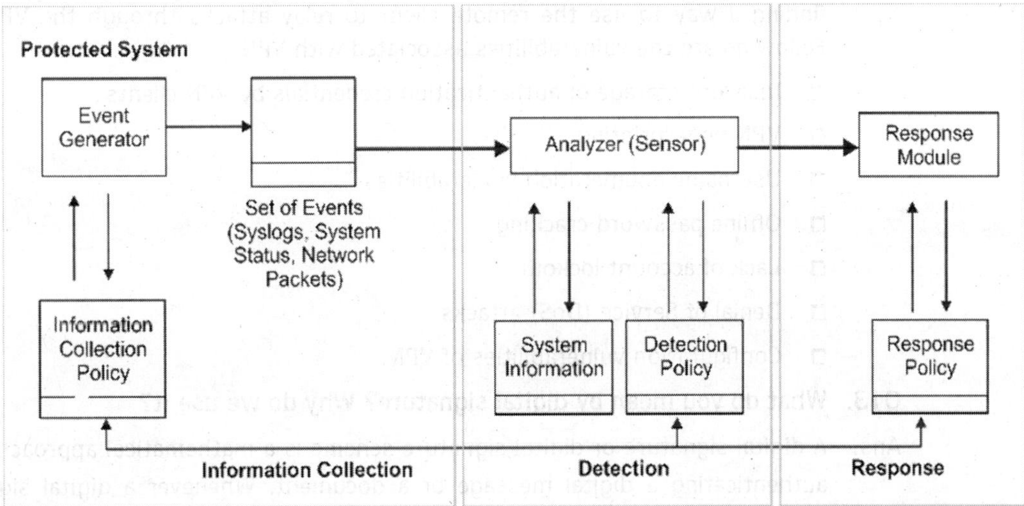

▲ **Figure 15: Showing the IDS Components**

Depending on the functionality and architecture, an IDS system can be of different types, such as NIDS or HIDS. In addition, there are IDSs that work similar to antivirus software, looking for specific signatures of known threats to protect the network even before an attack. Some IDSs detect malicious activities by comparing traffic patterns against a baseline and look for anomalies, whereas some IDSs come into action in response to a detected threat.

VPN is a private communication network, which is the most secure, remote method of connecting a computer to a private network with the help of a public network, such as the Internet. It creates the virtual tunnel through which the data travels from one computer to the other over the network. The typical structure of a VPN is shown in Figure 16:

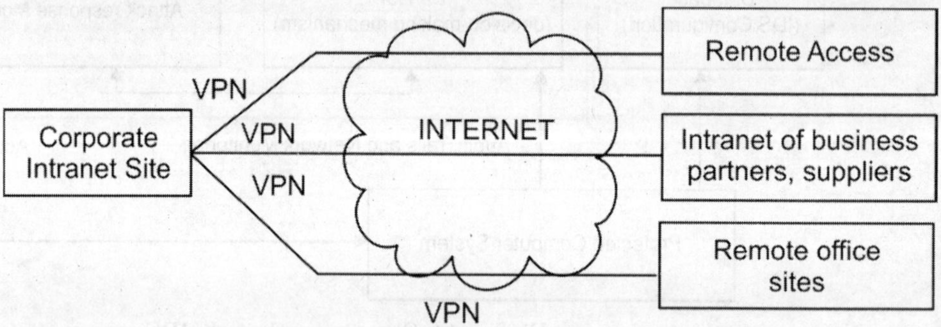

▲ **Figure 16: Showing the Structure of a VPN**

The data travelling through the virtual tunnel offers an attacker with a chance of finding a way to use the remote client to relay attacks through the VPN tunnel. Following are the vulnerabilities associated with VPN:

- Insecure storage of authentication credentials by VPN clients
- VPN fingerprinting
- Username enumeration vulnerabilities
- Offline password cracking
- Lack of account lockout
- Denial of Service (DoS) attacks
- Configuration vulnerabilities of VPN

Q13. What do you mean by digital signature? Why do we use it?

Ans. A digital signature or digital signature scheme is a mathematical approach used for authenticating a digital message or a document. Whenever a digital signature is assigned to a message, the recipient believes that the message is created by a known sender and has not been altered during transmission. Digital signatures are generally used in software distribution and financial transactions. Whenever a message is sent through an insecure network, an assurance that the message is sent by a claimed sender is given to the receiver through a properly implemented digital signature. The digital signatures are not much different from the traditional handwritten signatures. To standardize the use of digital signature, different organizations, such as the United States Government Printing Office (GPO), are publishing as well as releasing the electronic budgets. There are two main reasons for using digital signature, which are as follows:

- **Authenticity:** Refers to authenticating the sender and receiver. The use of digital signature authenticates the sources from where the message has been received, that is, it verifies the authenticity of the sender. Whenever the digital signature is associated with a specific user, it is used to identify the sender of the message because the authenticity of the sender/receiver is very important in the context of financial transactions. For example, in an online banking system, after a particular transaction, if a bank sends request to make changes in an account, the central office first checks the digital signature for authenticity of the message. If the central office is not convinced that the message is sent from the authorized bank, then it may not act on the request.
- **Security:** Assures that the messages are delivered securely without any security threats. This assures the sender and the receiver of a message that the message has not been altered by any unauthorized sources during transmission. Initially, you have learned about the process of encrypting the message to prevent its unauthorized access. However, the encryption process can only hide the contents of the message, which implies that the message is not being altered. In case of digital signatures, if any alteration is made in the message, the digital signature becomes invalid.

A digital signature is a block of code which ensures that any data that is received originates from a specific user. It is used to simulate the security properties of a signature in digital form. You can use a digital signature when you want to distribute data and assure the recipient that the received data indeed comes from you. Signing data does not alter the data; it simply generates a digital signature string that you can send with the data. The benefit of using digital signatures is that they provide authentication and integrity to the messages sent. Authentication of data ensures that it is received from a trusted source, and integrity of data ensures that the received data has not been tampered during transmission.

Q14. What is cryptographic attacks? Explain in detail.

Ans. Cryptographic attacks can be referred to as techniques of performing cryptanalysis. These attacks are based on what access the cryptanalyst has over the plaintext, ciphertext, and other aspects of the cryptographic attack. Some popular cryptographic attacks are as follows:

- **Ciphertext-only attack:** Refers to an attack in which the cryptanalyst has a piece of ciphertext (encrypted text) and has no knowledge of plaintext (unencrypted text). This attack is very difficult to perform as it involves the most difficult type of cryptanalysis and requires accurate guesswork of how the data would have been encrypted.
- **Chosen-ciphertext attack:** Refers to an attack in which the cryptanalyst selects some ciphertext and tries to find the matching plaintext. With this information, the cryptanalyst tries to find the key used for decryption.
- **Known-plaintext attack:** Represents an attack in which the cryptanalyst has the knowledge of a portion of the plaintext generated from the ciphertext. The cryptanalyst uses this information to extract the key used for encryption and recover the encrypted text.
- **Chosen-plaintext attack:** Refers to an attack in which the cryptanalyst is able to produce ciphertext from some randomly selected plaintext; however, the cryptanalyst is not able to break the key that is used to produce the ciphertext. The cryptanalyst tries to break the key by comparing the entire ciphertext with the original plaintext.
- **Man-in-the-middle attack:** Refers to an attack in which the attacker (cryptanalyst) places a piece of surveillance software at the communication channel between the two users who want to exchange their keys for secure communication. Then the attacker exchanges keys with each of the users. The users assume that they are exchanging keys with each other, not with the attacker. In this way, the users unknowingly send keys to the attacker.
- **Replay attack:** Refers to an attack in which the attacker tries to fraudulently repeat or delay a valid data transmission. For example, a user A sends his/her password to another user B as the proof of his/her identity and a third user C somehow captures the password sent by user A. Now, when the users A and B have ended communication, user C connects to user B and sends the password

of user A as the proof of identity and communicates with him/her as being user A.

Q15. What is the process of developing secure information systems? Discuss about main security considerations in developing secure information systems?

Ans. Secure information system development involves a number of processes. Some important processes include identification, planning, and mitigation of risks. To manage risks properly, you have to find a balance between the different processes that include protecting organization's information and assets, costs incurred in applying security controls and in formulating strategies for round the clock security during the entire system development lifecycle, etc. The basic security considerations in the system development lifecycle are shown in Figure 17:

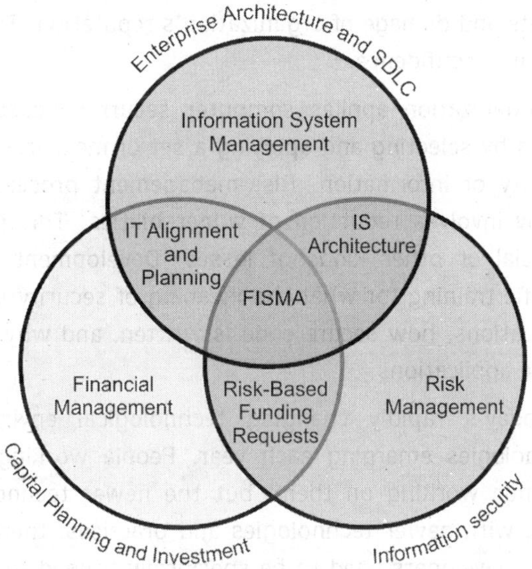

▲ **Figure 17: Displaying Security Considerations**

The best risk-management strategy is to find out the critical assets and operations for organization's business processes and then explore the possible vulnerabilities across systems in the organization. Security risks do not impact only a single area of operation. The entire organization may be affected due to a single vulnerability. So, you need to identify all the critical operations and assets, which can be done by planning for the system security and gathering insightful information from various business processes. This information helps you in determining the important operations, assets to support them, interdependencies among various operations, and the relationship between assets and business processes. After the criticality of business processes and assets has been analyzed, you can find out the impact of various operations on your organization's security. This process of analyzing the impact of vulnerabilities on business processes is called Business Impact Analysis (BIA), which helps to evaluate the impacts of disruption of important services on systems and assets related to those services. After the BIA is done, you can manage your organization's security on the basis of findings.

Q16. What is security in developing applications? What are the primary issues related to the secure development of applications?

Ans. Information is available for organizations in the form of assets, which need to be used (collected, stored, shared, and deleted) in an intelligent manner. An intelligent use of information assets helps organizations in maintaining themselves ahead of their competitor organizations. Therefore, these assets need to be protected from any kind of threats that may result into breach of confidentiality, integrity, or availability of resources. Threats can harm the organization by disclosure of trade secrets and damage of organization's reputation. The organization may also lose its customer confidence.

An organization applies computer security measures to protect its information assets by selecting and applying a set of measures that will be appropriate for the security of information. Risk-management process in most of the organizations mainly involves reduction of vulnerabilities. This helps them mitigate the risk of financial or other kinds of losses. Development of secure applications requires specific training for what the meaning of security is for an organization and for its applications, how secure code is written, and why it is needed to provide security to the applications.

In today's rapidly changing technological environment, we see some newer technologies emerging each year. People working on an earlier technology may continue working on them, but the newer technologies require new developers. Thus, with newer technologies and practices, there are newer developers as well. These developers need to be specifically trained to adapt to the new technology. If the training involves focus on secure application development strategy, organizations will mainly have only infrastructure issues to deal with when it comes to providing complete organizational security.

Some of the primary issues related to the secure development of applications are as follows:

- Less trained/skilled developers
- Less educational focus on secure development
- Difficulty of finding the right information related to specific security measures for particular applications or application development strategies
- Lifecycle systems considering security mostly in the last phases only

- Compilers, interpreters, and programming being unable to utilize the system resources in the best way possible

Q17. What are the activities involved in the process of management of risks related to information assets of an organization?

Ans. The risk management process involves the following four activities:

1. Framing: Framing the risk means to sense a threat and inform all the related activities that execute in a sequential manner to be ready to control and avert a possible damage. In this activity, we analyze the possible risks associated with the security of information systems and the organization, and then we try to define certain actions for individual cases.
2. Assessing: Assessment of risk means to analyze the level of risks and the level of security provided with our organization and its information systems. The possible damages from a threat are also assessed in this activity.
3. Monitoring: Monitoring activity involves continuously checking the information system and keeping an eye on other threats and vulnerabilities that may be encountered by the organization. This will help you to define proper guidelines for the maintenance of security of your systems. Also, risk monitoring helps in analyzing whether the system is continuously secure or not.
4. Responding: Responding to the risks means to take preventive or corrective measures so that systems can be kept protected from any kind of threats, whether internal or external.

Figure 18 shows the process of information risk management:

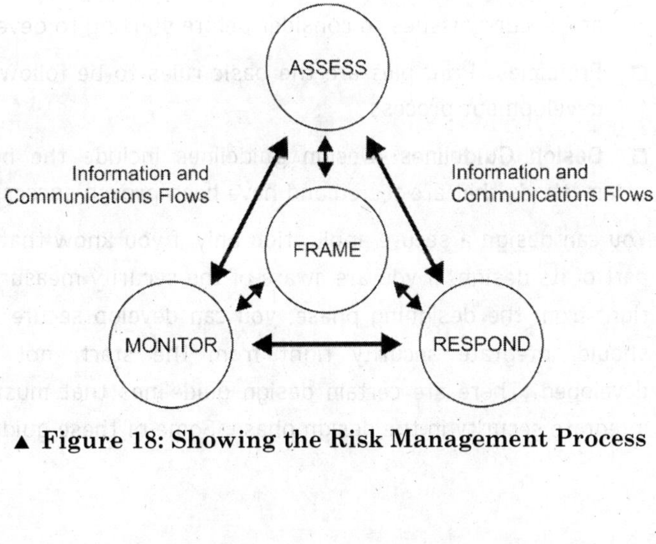

▲ **Figure 18: Showing the Risk Management Process**

In Figure 18, it can be seen that the flow of information starts by framing, and it communicates the information throughout the other processes, i.e., assessing, monitoring, and responding. These activities execute sequentially, which is to say that the framing of risk is the first activity followed by the assessment activity. After that, the monitoring will take place and finally the system will give response to the security risks.

Q18. What are the benefits of the common framework used for developing secure applications and what are the factors of this framework? Explain in detail about design guidelines.

Ans. We can develop application providing information security by accepting a common framework, which includes certain guidelines that are useful in developing secure applications. The main benefits of this framework are as follows:

- Developers can refer to the common standard provided in the framework to develop secure applications
- Strict guidelines and design principles included in the framework are time tested and universal
- Developers get a comprehensive view and understand security policy, programming language, and tools
- Organization can improve its development strategy to apply best methods, development efforts, standards and procedures, and security policy
- The view of the management becomes more objective towards considerations and mitigation of risks

The common framework includes the following factors:

- **Foundation**: Foundation is the basic knowledge of the development procedure and security issues to consider before starting to develop the application
- **Principles**: Principles are the basic rules to be followed during the application development process
- **Design Guidelines**: Design guidelines include the best code implementation methods that are tested and have been proven successful over time

You can design a secure application only if you know that security of a system is a part of its design. If you are aware of the security measures that need to be placed right from the designing phase, you can develop secure applications. Your design should integrate security right from the start, not after the application is developed. There are certain design guidelines that must be followed in order to integrate security in the design phase. Some of these guidelines are as follows:

- **Validating inputs:** Implementation of security in application design must start from validation of inputs. You must be careful in programming for validating every input from the user. An attacker needs only a single chance to breach into your security barriers. This may allow him/her to access sensitive information used in the application. So, prevention of any unlawful activities by users requires you to check/validate inputs given to your application. The experiments in the user input must be restricted to the expected forms only. The problem arises when it is assumed that the format of input would be same as expected. The programmer should never trust the incoming input; instead, one must validate it before passing to the application. Also, inputs must not be too large in size even in the expected format and should be checked to be valid. Applying these best practices would help in reducing the risk for the information.
- **Handling exceptions**: Exception handling is particularly linked to the security of applications in cases of failure, which happens very often on encountering some unexpected action in computer systems. This failure may result into vulnerable conditions for both the system and the information assets. A system's operational status must not affect the security of data. To provide data security in such circumstances, you need to apply proper mechanisms to handle exceptions. The exceptional handling procedure is a standard way for the application to respond to run-time conditions of error, also called exceptions. You can use the built-in mechanism provided in most of the high-level programming languages. Exception handling provides classes and methods to control the flow of program if the execution context goes beyond the normal flow.
- **Applying cryptography**: Data security can be implemented through cryptographic algorithms that help us to manage the integrity, availability, and confidentiality of data. The most prominent issues with the implementation of cryptography are failure in using it appropriately, error in its proper implementation, defining custom cryptographic algorithms, assuming security by obscurity, etc. You should avoid these mistakes by trying to apply best practices for cryptographic implementation. You can use symmetric or asymmetric encryption algorithms to provide confidentiality, integrity, availability, and authentication.
- **Using random numbers**: Generating truly random numbers from computer is very difficult. Computers generate pseudo random numbers by using the random() function. These random numbers could be predictable and may prove to be a weak link for the security of the application. So, generating purely random numbers whenever required in applications is important. You need to

be able to generate truly random numbers. The natural means of random numbers include radioactive decay and fluctuations in thermal signatures.

Q19. What is security architecture and design? How can we design a secure system?

Ans. The security architecture and design of a system means a bundle of the following components: the hardware, operating system, and software. It also includes a description of designing, architecting, and evaluating this system to provide security. Thus, the security architecture and design is explained in three parts, namely, the hardware and software part, the models, and the evaluation methods. Hardware and software part provides the way to design secure system, models part explains the way to maintain the security of this system, and evaluation part describes the level of security of a system.

You can design a secure system by implementing software and hardware specifically and following some universal principles that include:

- **Layering:** Layering is a concept that arranges hardware, drivers for kernel and devices, operating system, and applications in a sequential order. Hardware is at the bottom layer and applications are at the top. The layering approach is used to differentiate the hardware from the software into different tiers.
- **Abstraction:** The purpose of abstraction is to conceal the irrelevant details from common users. We will only increase the risk of threats if we increase the complexity of the system. This complexity could be managed through abstraction. For example, you do not need to explain to users about the processes that are going on internally while music is being played from a file through the speaker of the computer system. The user is only concerned with the playing of music just with a click.
- **Security domains:** Security domains are actually a set of subjects and objects which defines similarity in access levels. There are levels defined in domains and lower level domains cannot access higher level domains. Kernels have two levels of access defined in terms of modes, namely user mode and kernel mode. The kernel allows access to the system resources such as CPU and memory, and it is considered as the most trusted part of the system
- **The ring model:** Ring model is, in fact, a layering of CPU hardware in four levels: Ring0, Ring1, Ring2, and Ring3. These layers are used, typically, in a sequence respectively by kernel, other OS components exceeding Ring0, Device drivers, and user applications. With the emergence of virtualization, Ring1 has been transformed as hypervisor mode and operates host OSs in Ring0 of the kernel.
- **Open-closed systems:** Open and closed systems are two different types of structures. Open systems are designed by employing open hardware and

standards that may include hardware from a variety of vendors. For example, assembled systems are open systems. Close systems, on the other hand, only use proprietary hardware or software from specific vendor.

Q20. What are the security issues with storage devices and peripheral devices?

Ans. Data storage devices are used to save information. Devices such as Compact Disks (CD), Digital Versatile Disks (DVD), memory cards, flash drives, etc., can store information and be removed from the system to be kept at some other place. You can record crucial and confidential information on such devices for the purpose of data archival or maintenance of a data library. The information contained in data storage devices can be sensitive. So, protecting these devices from any external threat is extremely important. The threats to the security of data storage devices can be external or internal. For instance, if you have stored some data on a CD and some unauthenticated user gets access to that CD, he/she may use it unlawfully. This can create problems for data integrity and availability.

The main issues faced by data storage devices include their loss and theft, disposal, stealing of data, denial of data, malware introduction, etc. Your storage devices could be stolen by an external attacker who eyes to cause some harm for the security of your system's data. If the device has inbuilt security mechanisms, then it can be destroyed, thereby resulting in loss of some crucial data. If change of information is allowed in the data storage device, then a person may alter the data in such a way that it is no longer available for authenticated users. An individual may also introduce certain kind of malware to breach the security measures.

All these issues can be overcome by applying specific protection measures. You need to educate people and make them aware that any vulnerability left in a system can create a huge problem for the security. Explaining the importance of security to individuals will improve the understanding of people and thereby strengthen the security. You can take help from the advancing technology to protect your data storage devices and the information contained with them. In addition to that, you need to implement certain policies and procedures that provide an all-round security for the storage devices and data.

Peripheral devices are traditionally considered to be secured, and therefore, these devices can be vulnerable to security attacks. Some of the notable peripheral devices include:

- Universal Serial Bus (USB) drives
- USB patch cords that can be connected to a computer system using mini connectors or micro connectors
- Electronic notebooks that are similar to laptops but are limited in application
- Personal Digital Assistants (PDAs)

The issue with most of the downloadable devices is the threat that an external, unseen entity can create. You cannot easily detect threats to these devices. Therefore, they could be more vulnerable to security attacks in comparison with other devices/systems. Specific security measures should be applied to protect information from being damaged, stolen, or corrupted by internal or external threats. These devices are also vulnerable to theft and destruction. So, you need to protect these devices from various types of attacks on the security of data or information.

Most of the peripheral devices have very small size, and it is easy to hide them from people's eyes. However, if strong security measures are in place, you can protect these devices. The measures may include protection of data from theft, manipulation, or destruction; protection of the devices from being stolen or destroyed; and protection of the environment from undesired accesses.

Q21. What are the measures taken to secure data backup? What practices should an organization apply in order to secure backups?

Ans. Data backups are taken to secure important data files and systems from being lost due to natural disasters or human errors and recover in case any kind of disaster has led to the loss of information. Therefore, it is very important to secure data backups. Sometimes, security of data backups becomes more concerning than the actual data files. Data security policies are a huge concern for organizations, and in that measure, securing a backup data is even more important. Storage security is integrated to the organizational security policy for the purpose that the joint efforts of security policies, tactical policies, and operational policies will make the organization's overall security stronger.

To maintain proper data backup security, an organization should implement the following practices:

a. **Assigning responsibility, authority, and accountability:** If accountability, responsibility, and authority are assigned properly to individual security personnel, the organizational security can be improved. The security of backup is not a separate task, but it is integrated to the overall protection of IT assets. If the data is extremely sensitive, individual roles and responsibilities should be divided.

b. **Assessing risks:** The risk management team must include assessment of data backup risk in the overall security policy for the organization. This will help in determining the impact of individual threats so that the backup security could be stronger.

c. **Developing data protection processes:** There should be separate measures established to protect the data being backed up. You cannot treat sensitive data and its backup in the same manner as you treat the ordinary or less sensitive information. Therefore, you need to devise strategies and explore ways for the protection of your backup data.

d. **Communicating the processes to the concerning people:** After you have developed strategies to secure the backup data, these processes need to be communicated to the other levels in your organization so that people who are concerned with the security of information can handle the processes properly. The communication should be clear and proper in order to avoid any compromise with information security and hence with the organization's security.

e. **Executing and testing the process:** After the processes to secure data are developed and communicated, it is the responsibilities of the management to execute and test the processes so that any misgivings can be easily analyzed and removed.

Thus, apart from all the security measures established to secure data, you must secure your backup data for recovering from failures and any kind of casualty or disaster. Security of all kinds of data is crucial in today's fiercely competitive world.

Q22. What are intellectual property and Intellectual Property Rights? What different categories of intellectual properties have been defined in India? Explain the features of Indian Copyright Act.

Ans. Intellectual property refers to intangible property that has been created by individuals and corporates for their personal benefit or usage such as copyright, trade mark, patent, and digital data. It is created through human intelligence and mental efforts. It is therefore unethical to copy or steal the creativity and efforts of someone else. The technology that contributes to the creation and security of documents over the computer is the same that contributes in copying it easily. The dissemination of this copied document is also very quick and easy.

Intellectual property rights refer to the rights given to a person or an organization for their intellectual activity, i.e., creations of mind. This intellectual activity may be in the field of industry, science, literature, or any other artistic field. According to the Centre for Intellectual Property Rights, there are four major categories of Intellectual Property Rights in India, namely, Copyright, Patent, Trade Mark, and Design Protection.

Computer software come under the ambit of Copyright law and are protected by the Indian Copyright Act, 1957. The Indian Copyright Act was amended in 1994. These amendments came into effect from May 10, 1995. The main features of the Indian Copyright Act are as follows:

- The Act specifies clearly the rights of a copyright holder
- The Act deals with the rentals of software
- The Act clearly states the rights of a user to make backup copies

Since software copyright violation can be carried out very easily by simply copying the software and since it is difficult in most cases to distinguish between an original software and a duplicate software, it had become utmost necessary to implement the Copyright Act. Some of the key features of the Act are as follows:

- Copying and distributing of copyrighted software without proper authorization is illegal according to section 14 of the Act
- The violator of the Act is liable to be tried under civil as well as criminal law
- A violator may be subjected to civil and criminal action for injunction, actual damages (which includes the profits, if any, made by the violator), or statutory damages per infringement
- The Act provides for strict punishment and/or heavy fines for any violation of software copyright
- According to Section 63 B, jail term of minimum 7 days can be given for a software copyright violation, which can be extended up to 3 years

Q23. Discuss about patents, patentable inventions, and non-patentable inventions.

Ans. A Patent is a monopoly right granted by the State to an inventor for a limited period of time in exchange for the public disclosure of the invention. The monopoly rights mean the right to make, use, license, or sell an invention to the exclusion of others. Once the term of patent expires, the invention comes into the public domain. In India, all patents are granted for period of 20 years.

The system of granting patents serves many purposes. If the invention is commercially utilized, the patent ensures just reward to the inventor in terms of money and recognition, thus paying the inventor for investing his time and effort, knowledge and skills, and money and other resources. For the society, the commercial exploitation of an invention means newer and better products, higher productivity, and more efficient means of production. The main objective of granting patents is to accelerate the technological and industrial development.

According to the **Indian Patent Act**, a patentable invention is defined as follows:

"*A new product or process involving an inventive step and capable of industrial application*"

Thus, an invention must fulfill the following three requirements for being considered as a patentable invention:

- **The invention must be 'new'**: Something that is already present and known is not patentable. An invention is considered new if it does not form a part of the already available knowledge on the date of filing the application. If the invention is disclosed, in any way, before filing the application for patent, it is disqualified from being 'new'. For example, an English inventor was denied grant of a patent for inventing an improved design of a ball point pen because he had mistakenly published the details of his invention even before filing the application for patent.
- **The invention must involve an 'inventive step'**: 'Inventive step' means that the invention must not be obvious or follow directly from something which is already known. An example of an inventive step could be rolling of metals without affecting their original characteristics but adding on other characteristics like increasing toughness, etc.
- **The invention must have 'industrial application'**: To be patentable, the invention has to be capable of industrial application. Industry here refers to any practical and useful activity which is not related to creative and aesthetic activity. It may or may not be related to the use of machineries and manufacturing.

A patent that cannot be patented by an individual or an organization is termed as nonpatentable. There are a number of categories that are nonpatentable. Anything can be patented only if it is a fresh invention, and it causes no harm to the living beings in the world and follows the law.

The categories which cannot be patented under IPA are as follows:

- An invention, which is detrimental to public order, morality, environment, or health; for example, the invention of a new type of gambling machine.
- An invention related to atomic energy. In India, atomic energy is not a public domain. It is the sole responsibility of the Central Government. An invention which is against the laws of nature. A discovery of a scientific principle or the formulation of an abstract theory is not patentable on the grounds that it is not an invention.
- The discovery of a living thing or *non-living* substances or objects occurring in nature because it is not an invention.
- A substance obtained by a mere admixture of certain components or a process of producing such a mixture does not qualify as an inventive step and hence cannot be patented
- Arrangement or re-arrangement or duplication of known devices, where each functions independent of one another in a known way without changing the

end results also does not qualify as an inventive step and hence is non-patentable.

- Traditional knowledge is non-patentable because they are not new and form a part of the prior knowledge or state of the art. A mathematical or business method or a computer programme or algorithms are not patentable as they follow logically from a known premise.

The following items also do not qualify as inventions as defined by the Indian Patents Act and are therefore not patentable:

- A method related to agriculture or horticulture
- Any process related to the medicinal, surgical, curative, prophylactic, diagnostic, therapeutic, or other treatment of human beings and animals
- Plants and animals in whole or part, excluding micro-organisms
- Seeds and biological processes for the production of plants and animals

The following two categories belong to other forms of intellectual property and hence are not subject matters of patents:

- A literary, dramatic, musical, or artistic work, including cinematographic work and television productions. This is covered by Copyright Act.
- Layout designs of integrated circuits. These are covered separately by the SICLD Act.

There are certain substances which do not come under patenting, but the process of manufacturing those substances can be patented. Some examples are as follows:

- Substances which could be used as food or medicine or drug.
- Substances which are prepared or produced by chemical processes such as biochemical, biotechnological, and microbiological processes. However, if the substance itself is used as a medicine or drug, it can be patented.

Q24. Why do we require a policy for information security?

Ans. From the software professional's perspective, the overall objective of an information security policy is to protect the integrity, confidentiality, and availability of information. It is true from the security perspective; however, not the organization objective. It is known that information is an asset and the property of an organization. As an asset, the management of an organization is expected to ensure that the appropriate levels of controls are in place to protect this resource.

An information security policy should be part of any organization's overall asset security policy. This policy is not defined to meet the security needs or audit requirements; it is a business process that allows management with the processes required to perform the fiduciary responsibility. The management of an organization is charged with a trust to ensure that adequate controls are in place to safeguard the asset of an enterprise. The security policies, standards, and procedures define a security program.

The information security professionals of an organization are responsible to implement security policies that depict the business and mission requirements of an organization.

Q25. What are the ISO standards for information security? Discuss in brief.

Ans. It is known that security plays an important role in safeguarding the assets of an organization. As no single formula can guarantee 100% security, there is a requirement for a set of standards to ensure that the appropriate level of security is achieved, resources are utilized efficiently, and the best security practices are implemented. This section discusses the various standards and regulations available for information security.

The ISO, established in 1947, is a non-governmental international body that collaborates with the International Electrotechnical Commission (IEC) and the International Telecommunication Union (ITU). ISO has laid the following security standards:

- **ISO/IEC 27002:2005 (Code of practice for information security management)**: Refers to a code of practice for information security management which sets as a common basis and practical guideline for developing enterprise-level security standards and effective management practices.

  This standard specifies guidelines and best practices recommendations for the following ten security domains:

  - Security policy
  - Organization for information security
  - Asset management
  - Human resource security
  - Physical and environmental security
  - Communications and operations management
  - Access control
  - Information systems acquisition, development, and maintenance
  - Information security incident management
  - Business continuity management and compliance

- **ISO/IEC 27001:2005 (information security management system – requirements)**: Specifies the requirements for establishing, implementing, operating, monitoring, reviewing, maintaining, and improving a documented

Information Security Management System (ISMS) within an organization. This standard allows an organization to select the adequate and proportionate security control to secure information assets. This standard is applicable for all types of organizations, including business enterprises, government agencies, etc.

This standard defines a cyclic model known as "Plan-Do-Check-Act" (PDCA) model with the objective of establishing, implementing, monitoring, and improving the effectiveness of an enterprise's ISMS. The phases of the PDCA cycle are as follows:

- The Plan phase to establish the ISMS
- The Do phase to implement and operate the ISMS
- The Check phase to monitor and review the ISMS
- The Act phase to maintain and improve the ISMS

- **ISO/IEC 15408 (evaluation criteria for IT security)**: Consists of three parts: ISO/IEC 15408-1:2005 (introduction and general model), ISO/IEC 15408-2:2005 (security functional requirements), and ISO/IEC 15408-3:2005 (security assurance requirements). This standard helps an organization in evaluating, validating, and certifying the security assurance of a technology product against various factors such as security functional requirements specified in the standard.

- **ISO/IEC 1335 (IT Security Management)**: Consists of a series of guidelines for technical security control measures such as:
  - The ISO/IEC 13335-1:2004 standard defines the concepts and models for information and communication technology security management
  - The ISO/IEC TR 13335-3:1998 standard defines the techniques for the management of IT security
  - The ISO/IEC TR 13335-4:2000 standard covers the selection of safeguards
  - The ISO/IEC TR 13335-5:2001 covers management guidance on network security

Index

A

B

C

D

M

N

O

P

R

S